Raising Your Kids Right

The Rutgers Series in Childhood Studies

The Rutgers Series in Childhood Studies is dedicated to increasing our understanding of children and childhoods, past and present, throughout the world. Children's voices and experiences are central. Authors come from a variety of fields, including anthropology, criminal justice, history, literature, psychology, religion, and sociology. The books in this series are intended for students, scholars, practitioners, and those who formulate policies that affect children's everyday lives and futures.

Edited by Myra Bluebond-Langner, Distinguished Professor of Anthropology, Rutgers University, Camden, and founding director of the Rutgers University Center for Children and Childhood Studies

Advisory Board

Joan Jacobs Brumberg, Cornell University
Perri Klass, New York University
Jill Korbin, Case Western Reserve University
Bambi Schiefflin, New York University
Enid Schildkraut, American Museum of Natural History and
    Museum for African Art

Raising Your Kids Right

Children's Literature and American Political Conservatism

MICHELLE ANN ABATE

RUTGERS UNIVERSITY PRESS
NEW BRUNSWICK, NEW JERSEY, AND LONDON

LIBRARY OF CONGRESS CATALOGING-IN-PUBLICATION DATA

Abate, Michelle Ann, 1975–
    Raising your kids right : children's literature and American political conservatism
    / Michelle Ann Abate.
       p.   cm. — (The Rutgers series in childhood studies)
    Includes bibliographical references and index.
    Includes bibliographical references and index.
    ISBN 978–0–8135–4798–5 (alk. paper)
    1. Children's literature, American—History and criticism. 2. Politics and
    literature—United States—History—20th century. 3. Politics and literature—
    United States—History—21st century. 4. Conservatism and literature—United
    States—History—20th century. 5. Conservatism and literature—United
    States—History—21st century. 6. Right and left (Political science) in literature.
    7. Conservatism—United States. I. Title.
PS228.P6A23 2010
810.9'3581—dc22

                                               2009044966

A British Cataloging-in-Publication record for this book is available
from the British Library.

Copyright © 2010 by Michelle Ann Abate

Visit our Web site: http://rutgerspress.rutgers.edu

Manufactured in the United States of America

CONTENTS

Illustrations appear between pages 92 and 93

ACKNOWLEDGMENTS

Abraham Lincoln asserted, "Public sentiment is everything. With public sentiment nothing can fail; without it nothing can succeed. He who molds public sentiment goes deeper than he who enacts statutes or decisions possible or impossible to execute" (128).

This book examines a group of narratives that embody this idea. In everything from their characters and plots to their themes and illustrations these texts demonstrate a clear intent to influence the sentiment of the American public in general and the nation's children in particular. Hence, it seems only fitting to begin my examination of these books by thanking the many colleagues, friends, and family members who have helped to shape my sentiments about them.

First, I owe a very special debt to Philip Nel, who initially urged me to write a book based on my interest in conservative children's literature. Without his early encouragement, this project may never have come into being.

I would also like to express my affection and appreciation to my partner, Rachel MacKnight, who loves and supports me, no matter what books I'm reading or what project I'm undertaking.

I am very grateful to Hollins University, which supported my work on this project through various research grants and travel funds. I am especially indebted to Hollins University Librarian Joan Ruelle and her superb staff: Beth Larkee, Luke Vilelle, Maryke Barber, Renee McBride, and Katy Baum. A researcher could not ask for a more knowledgeable, helpful, or convivial group of librarians.

I would like to extend my gratitude to several colleagues who provided valuable feedback: Rhonda Brock-Servais, for her careful and insightful reading of a draft version of the manuscript; Pauline Kaldas, for her fantastic editorial suggestions on chapters 3 and 6; Greg Aplet for his prompt and generous assistance tracking down some specific information related to chapter 2; Ian Wojcik-Andrews for his many useful suggestions about an article version of chapter 6; and, finally, to the Children's Literature Association (ChLA), which supported this project with a faculty research grant, and CLA members, who formed the audience for conference paper versions of much of this material and offered many compelling comments.

I am also grateful to my editor at Rutgers University Press, Leslie Mitchner, for her support and encouragement during this process, along with the two anonymous outside readers who provided many insightful suggestions.

A version of chapter 3 initially appeared in the journal *International Research in Children's Literature* (vol. 2, no. 1, July 2009), published by Edinburgh University Press (www.euppublishing.com), as the article "The Politics of Prophecy: The U.S. Culture Wars and the Battle Over Public Education in the Left Behind Series for Kids." Likewise, some sections of chapter 6 were previously printed in *The Lion and the Unicorn* (vol. 33, no. 1, January 2009), from Johns Hopkins University Press. I would like to thank the publishers of these journals for their kind permission to reprint this material.

Finally, I'd like to dedicate this book to my mother-in-law, Peg MacKnight, who has a passion for politics in all of its forms and whose passion—as these pages attest—is highly contagious.

Raising Your Kids Right

INTRODUCTION

"In Adam's Fall, We Sinned All"

The Conservative Tradition
in U.S. Children's Literature, Culture, and Politics

In May 2008, the University of Colorado at Boulder made headlines when it announced its intention to hire a professor of Conservative Studies. The news came via the university's launch of a one-year capital campaign to raise the nine million dollars necessary to endow the position. According to Chancellor G. P. "Bud" Peterson, the hire was designed to promote "intellectual diversity" on campus, and, in so doing, it reflected the longstanding belief advanced by both past figures, like William F. Buckley Jr., and present ones, including David Horowitz, that academia is a hotbed of liberalism (qtd in Wilson "U of Colorado," par 3).[1] As Stephanie Simon wrote in the *Wall Street Journal*, the University of Colorado at Boulder's new endowed chair would be the nation's first "Professor of Conservative Thought and Policy" (par 3).

While the specific academic position envisioned by the University of Colorado may have been unique, the sentiment fueling it was not. Throughout the 1990s and into the first decade of the new millennium, American popular, intellectual, and material culture witnessed a rise not only in the conservative movement but also in rightist politics that was nothing short of meteoric. George H. Nash observed, "Signs abounded that the early twenty-first century was the best of times for American conservatives" (575–576). While these elements emanated from an array of sites and sources, arguably one of the most powerful indicators occurred in the realm of talk radio with the astounding success of Rush Limbaugh. His daily three-hour broadcast debuted in 1988 and quickly became a wildly popular nationally syndicated radio talk program. *The Rush Limbaugh Show* was broadcast on more than six hundred stations around the nation and reached an average of twenty million listeners per week (Bowman, par 9). By the early 1990s, Limbaugh's popularity, along with his cultural influence, was difficult to overestimate. In an oft-mentioned anecdote, Ronald Reagan sent the radio host an unsolicited note calling him "the Number One voice for conservatism in our Country" (Bowman, par 4). In addition, when the Republicans gained control of Congress in 1994, many first-term representatives dubbed Limbaugh the "Majority Maker" for the way in which he had helped to unite the GOP as well as the voting public in their favor (Carlson, par 4).[2]

The success of *The Rush Limbaugh Show* paved the way for AM stations to become a seedbed of talk programming in general and shows that featured conservative viewpoints in particular. In the years since Limbaugh's inaugural syndication, a parade of programs with similar ideological focus have debuted, many of them to great acclaim. From Michael Savage, Dr. Laura Schlessinger, and Mark Levin to Sean Hannity, Laura Ingraham, and Michael Medved, these figures have made AM radio, according to Alec Foege, the political as well as physical "right of the dial." Moreover, their success helped launch a growing cadre of conservative political television programs that adopted a similar news commentary and viewer call-in format. Most notable among these was *The O'Reilly Factor*. Hosted by Bill O'Reilly, the program first aired in 1996 and quickly became the most watched cable news show in the United States (see Crupi).

The power and prevalence of conservative issues in American visual media is rivaled perhaps only by their presence in the publishing industry. Although books addressing social topics or political subjects from a rightist perspective have always been a fixture in the U.S. publishing industry, such conservative publications experienced a rapid expansion in the late 1990s. The impeachment hearings about President Bill Clinton arguably set off the first wave of new conservative tomes. In books such as William Bennett's best-seller *The Death of Outrage: Bill Clinton and the Assault on American Ideals* (1999) and David Schipper's exposé *Sellout: The Inside Story of President Clinton's Impeachment* (2000), conservatives expressed their ire over the president's extramarital affair with a White House intern and his subsequent denials about it.

The 2000 election of Republican George W. Bush along with the terrorist attacks of September 11, 2001, increased both the publication rate and the ferocious tone of such books. The former event ushered in the inauguration of a born-again Christian commander-in-chief who supported faith-based initiatives and opposed same-sex marriage, while the latter event greatly amplified traditionally conservative rhetoric about national defense, patriotism, and religious faith. In the atmosphere created by these occurrences, as Christopher Dreher noted in 2005, "the influx of new titles forced even huge chain stores to stash books on, below, and around tables meant to hold all of their new nonfiction" (F8). The size and scope of this phenomenon can perhaps be best exemplified by the literary output of one figure: Ann Coulter. From 2002 to 2007, Coulter released five books, each with increasingly inflammatory topics and titles: *Slander: Liberal Lies about the American Right* (2002), *Treason: Liberal Treachery from the Cold War to the War on Terrorism* (2003), *How to Talk to a Liberal (If You Must)* (2004), *Godless: The Church of Liberalism* (2006), and *If Democrats Had Any*

Brains, They'd Be Republicans (2007).[3] Conservative works of nonfiction were not only among the most numerous titles in stores throughout the nation, but they were also among the most popular. All of Coulter's books, for example, made the *New York Times* best-seller list.

Adding to this atmosphere, many other conservative-themed books that were not as overtly political in nature enjoyed tremendous success during the first decade of the new millennium. While titles like Tim Russert's memoir *Big Russ and Me* (2004) and Mitch Albom's novel *The Five People You Meet in Heaven* (2003) did not contain the same acerbic tone as in Coulter's narratives, they can be placed on the spectrum of conservative social thought. Indeed, the synopsis provided on the jacket for Russert's book revealed that *Big Russ and Me* addressed traditionally conservative subjects such as "the indelible bond that links him to his father," "the lessons learned from his old-fashioned Catholic upbringing," and "the importance of hard work, the grace of daily obligations, and patriotism."[4] When viewed in tandem with their more overtly political counterparts, conservative-themed texts embodied, in the words of one commentator, "one of the fastest-growing parts of the nonfiction book trade" (Wyatt, par 1). Indeed, given the sheer number of books possessing conservative themes or right-leaning political viewpoints, along with their astounding commercial success, many major U.S. publishing houses launched divisions that were exclusively dedicated to these subjects. By 2005, Simon & Schuster, Random House, and Penguin Group USA all had such specialty imprints.[5] Especially when considered in conjunction with the rise of talk radio and the rhetoric about protecting traditional family values, George H. Nash aptly observed that in the early years of the twenty-first century "a veritable conservative counterculture was flourishing" (575–576).

Raising Your Kids Right adds another important but as-yet overlooked facet to the history of the conservative movement and the expansion of the politics of the right in the United States. The chapters that follow examine the growing genre of conservative-themed narratives for young readers that have been released since the early 1990s. My examination begins with William Bennett's best-selling collection *The Book of Virtues* (1993), which appeared just after the inauguration of President Bill Clinton and which enjoyed a critical and commercial success that effectively launched the genre. It ends with the 2008 presidential election and the campaign-fueled release of a flurry of right-leaning books for young readers, such as Meghan McCain's *My Dad, John McCain* and Lynne Cheney's *We the People: The Story of Our Constitution*.

My introduction provides an overview of the conservative movement in the United States since the end of World War II and the increasing national visibility, social power, and cultural influence of the politics of the right as the twentieth century progressed. During this process, I discuss everything from the defeat of Barry Goldwater and the rise of the New Right to the galvanizing power of Ronald Reagan and the transformative role of the Christian Right. I trace the origins, chart the trajectory, and discuss the transformations to children's books with messages, themes, and subject matter emanating from the right side of the political spectrum. In each of the following six chapters, I spotlight a different conservative-themed book for young readers; through this vehicle I demonstrate how the political perspectives and social viewpoints embodied by this movement began their migration from the world of adult affairs of state to the realm of literature for young readers. Although children's literature has often espoused didactic lessons, offered conservative morals, and even contained political themes, the new crop of books for young readers that began appearing in the early 1990s did so in a new and far more overt way. In texts ranging from patriotic-themed picture books by Lynne Cheney and advice guides by Bill O'Reilly to a pro-logging rebuttal of Dr. Seuss's *The Lorax* and a series of evangelical Christian young adult novels that dramatize the end of the world and the return of Jesus Christ, these works collectively embody the full range of factions that encompass the American political Right, the broad spectrum of subjects that comprise the U.S. culture wars, and the wide array of genres that constitute contemporary children's literature.

Some narratives featured in the chapters that follow contain cultural messages or embed narrative themes that are so far to the right of the sociopolitical spectrum that they can be characterized not simply as conservative but as right-wing. Accordingly, I consider the ways in which the conservative social movement and the political right-wing in the United States remain distinct societal forces at the same time that they have experienced social, cultural, political, and ideological crossover and even cross-pollination. Indeed, events such as the selection of firebrand conservative politician Pat Buchanan to deliver the opening speech at the Republican National Convention in 1992 and George W. Bush's executive order—sometimes called the "Global Gag Rule"—issued the second day after assuming office in 2001 that denied federal funds "to foreign nongovernmental organizations that finance efforts to provide women with legal abortions" (Pellegrom, par 1) embody powerful examples of the increasing imbrication of the conservative social movement with rightist facets of American politics as the twentieth century ended and the new millennium began.

Akin to the state of the conservative movement and right-leaning viewpoints in American social and political life, the narratives I feature embody neither a fringe literary movement nor a peripheral publishing phenomenon; they form a powerfully influential part of contemporary literature for children and a highly visible aspect of the nation's millennial popular culture. The authors are well-known figures: a then-current second lady, a former political appointee of the Reagan and Bush administrations, one of the most highly paid cable news commentators, and a prominent behind-the-scenes player in the Christian Right. In addition, the texts are widely available in national bookstores, including Barnes & Noble, Borders, and Amazon.com. Finally, they have become among the most commercially successful books. *The O'Reilly Factor for Kids*, for example, was named the best-selling nonfiction book for young readers of 2005 at the annual awards ceremony sponsored by the Book Standard and Nielsen Bookscan (see *"The O'Reilly Factor for Kids*: Winner," pars 1–2). In addition, Jerry B. Jenkins and Tim LaHaye's evangelical-based Left Behind series for kids now includes an astounding forty titles, and the novels had collectively sold more than eleven million copies by late 2009. Finally, William Bennett's *The Book of Virtues* appeared on the *New York Times* best-seller list for more than one hundred weeks ("PBS Becomes," par 24) and inspired nearly a dozen spin-off and sequel texts.

In spite of the massive media attention that conservative viewpoints and right-leaning political ideas have received since the 1990s—on national talk radio, in the realm of adult nonfiction, and on cable news programs—comparatively little scholarly work has been done on their presence in books for young readers. No mention of this growing crop of conservative-themed children's literature appears in such seminal texts of American political history as the revised and updated edition of George H. Nash's classic *The Conservative Intellectual Movement in America, Since 1945* (2006). Similarly, a consideration of these narratives is missing from Michael J. Thompson's essay collection *Confronting the New Conservatism: The Rise of the Right in America* (2007). Finally, an examination of conservative-themed children's books is also absent from texts aimed at nonacademic audiences. Thomas Frank's *New York Times* best-seller *What's the Matter with Kansas?* (2005) examines—as it subtitle indicates—"How Conservatives Won the Heart of America," but the volume never explores the role that the best-selling children's narratives by Bennett, Cheney, and O'Reilly may have played in this process.

My selected volumes have been likewise overlooked by critics working in the fields of children's literature and American popular culture. Scholars seeking information on Jerry B. Jenkins and Tim LaHaye's wildly popular Left Behind series for young readers will find no books, essays, or articles listed in databases for the academic disciplines of English, religious studies, or education.[6] Likewise, those looking for analyses about the literary content, demographic readership, or critical reception of *The O'Reilly Factor for Kids* will leave the library empty-handed. Finally, parents, teachers, or scholars interested in Cheney's picture books or Bennett's *The Book of Virtues* fare only slightly better; by 2008 one critical article had been published about each author.[7]

Raising Your Kids Right offers a long overdue corrective to this neglect. I seek to move the growing crop of conservative-themed narratives for children from the edge of mainstream intellectual inquiry and political consciousness to its forefront. I dispel lingering societal attitudes that narratives for young readers are unworthy of serious critical study and lack sociopolitical commentary, or even efficacy. Indeed, my discussion demonstrates that these books embody an important intellectual, material, and cultural component to the rise of the New Right, the power of millennial social conservatism, and the growth of the right-wing branch of the GOP. Bringing together such diverse and seemingly disparate fields of inquiry as cultural studies, literary criticism, political science, popular culture, childhood studies, brand marketing, and the study of the cult of celebrity in the United States, I spotlight a series of texts that offer information, ideology, and even instructions for how to raise kids right, not just figuratively but also politically.

"And When You're Out in the Woods, Walk Properly and Don't Stray from the Path": Conservative Themes in Literature for U.S. Children

Historian Gail Schmunk Murray has written, "On the whole, children's literature is a conservative medium" (xvi). She continues: "Clergy, teachers, parents, and writers have all used it to shape morals, control information, model proper behavior, delineate gender roles, and reinforce class, race, and ethnic separation" (xvi). Children's literature has a long history of didactic education, socialization, and acculturation among boys and girls. Not surprisingly, many lessons that both fiction and nonfiction texts offer young readers are conservative in nature: urging children to use good manners, obey their parents, and follow the rules. Even a cursory examination of the corpus of narratives that have either been written in the United States or are popular among American readers demonstrate the powerful conservative thread that runs through them. Jack Zipes and Bruno Bettelheim, for instance, have discussed the messages about filial loyalty, parental obedience, and affirmations of the status quo that permeate many fairy tales. In the Grimm Brothers' version of Little Red Riding Hood—known as "Little Red Cap"—the title character's mother gives her the following exhortation when she sends her into the woods on the well-known errand: "You'd better start now before it gets too hot, and when you're out in the woods, walk properly and don't stray from the path. Otherwise, you'll fall and break the glass, and then there'll be nothing for Grandmother. And when you enter her room, don't forget to say good morning, and don't go peeping into all the corners of the room" (14). The young girl, of course, does not obey this advice; she wanders off the path to pick flowers, and a terrible fate befalls her. After Little Red Cap is rescued from the belly of the wolf by a passing woodsman, she has learned her lesson about the importance of parental obedience. "Little Red Cap thought to herself: 'Never again will you stray from the path and go into the woods, when your mother has forbidden it'" (Grimm 16).

Analogous messages about obedience also permeate the text that is commonly considered the first work written explicitly for children in the United States: *The New England Primer* (1688). In passages like "A is for Adam: In Adam's

Fall, We Sinned All" and "R is for Rachel: Rachel Doth Mourn, For Her Firstborn," the text introduced boys and girls to the rudiments of literacy—teaching them the ABCs—while it simultaneously conveyed strong messages about faith, family, and civic duty.

Other children's books focus on reaffirming the gender status quo and maintaining patriarchal power. This message occupies one of the central themes in both Louisa May Alcott's *Little Women* (1868) and Carol Ryrie Brink's *Caddie Woodlawn* (1935)—two of the most perennially popular and critically acclaimed girls' books in the United States. Although each narrative initially endorses physically free, socially unfettered, and even culturally unrestricted childhoods for their tomboyish main characters, they ultimately endorse the need for these behaviors to be sloughed off and for their young female figures to conform to more conventional—and restricting—gender roles for women. This sentiment appears as early as the opening pages of Alcott's text, when Meg rebukes her topsy-turvy sister in a comment that proves prescient: "You're old enough to leave off boyish tricks and behave better, Josephine. It didn't matter so much when you were a little girl; but now you are so tall, and turn up your hair, you should remember that you are a young lady" (3). As this passage prefigures, by the end of the narrative, Jo has acquiesced to life as a proper "little woman." She has sloughed off her boyish behavior, given up her ambitions to be a famous professional author, and gotten married—an outcome that Alcott herself protested. In a letter to her uncle Samuel Joseph May, she complained about the pressure to conform to a traditional marriage plot: "publishers are very *perverse* & wont let authors have their own way so my little women must grow up & be married off in a very stupid style" (Alcott, *Selected,* 121–122; italics in original). Alcott's decision to have her tomboyish character marry the paternalistic Professor Bhaer instead of chum Laurie Lawrence—as not only her editor but many of young readers desired—was her tacit protest against this convention: "I wanted to disappoint the young gossips who vowed that Laurie and Jo *should* marry" (see Alcott, *Selected,* 120; italics in original).

Caddie Woodlawn follows a similar pattern of taming. In the closing pages of Carol Ryrie Brink's novel, Caddie's father urges his daughter to abandon the tomboyish ways that he had formerly advocated: "Do you think you would like to be growing up into that woman now? How about it, Caddie, have we run with the colts long enough?" (Brink 245). Although this exhortation initially causes the young girl to cry, she quickly embraces her new role. The very next day, Caddie forgoes joining her brothers for a romp in the barn and instead remains in the house to partake in a more feminine domestic task: she learns to quilt (249).

Meanwhile, some girls' books, such as Laura Ingalls Wilder's Little House series (1935–1943), take this phenomenon one step further by yoking conservative messages about women's proper gender role with conservative commentary about contemporaneous sociopolitical events. In the sixth novel of the Little House sequence, *The Long Winter* (1940), Laura, the tomboyish main character, undergoes a similar process of taming as Jo March and Caddie Woodlawn. As a series of harsh blizzards leave the Ingalls family without adequate food, heat, or shelter for nearly seven months, Laura is confined to the house and domestic duties. During this time, she is transformed from being independent, adventurous, and confident to being quiet, obedient, and almost utterly dependent on men. As Ann Romines has written about this transformation, "Laura's growing awareness of her own limits and duties as a woman brings new weight and sobriety to the Little House series" (36). Anita Clair Fellman, in her book *Little House, Long Shadow*, links these conservative messages about women's gender roles to a larger project: namely, a conservative backlash to the New Deal. Written and released against a backdrop of the hardscrabble conditions of the Great Depression, Wilder's books advocate not only for uncomplaining acceptance of often difficult economic circumstances but also for personal thrift, familial self-sufficiency, and individual resilience as the appropriate response to them. As Fellman details, Laura Ingalls Wilder opposed the New Deal legislation and—akin to the conservative fiscal viewpoint expressed in contemporary books like Jim Powell's *FDR's Folly: How Roosevelt and His New Deal Prolonged the Great Depression* (2004)—did not believe that large government subsidies were the proper solution to the nation's economic problems.

Other books for young readers reinforce racial, ethnic, and cultural hierarchies. Edgar Rice Burroughs's classic boys' book *Tarzan of the Apes* (1912 serial, 1914 book), for instance, clearly positions the young Lord Greystoke—the white, aristocratic central character—as innately superior to all other races. In an even more problematic detail, the black apes that form the orphaned boy's adoptive family can be read as thinly disguised surrogates for various racial and ethnic minority groups. As Marianna Torgovnick has documented, the hulking, volatile, and highly emotional apes begin calling Tarzan by the colonialist title "Big Bwana" in later novels; meanwhile, he refers to them as "my children" (*Gone* 57).

Comparable messages about maintaining the societal status quo and resisting impulses toward cultural change permeate many well-known picture books, including an array of titles from the popular Little Golden Books series. While the title character in *Tootle the Train* (1945) enjoys his brief romp off the tracks, the message of the book is that little trains—and, by extension, little children—must heed the all-important rule to "Stay on the Rails No Matter What" (Crampton). *Scuffy the Tugboat* (1946) endorses a similar ethos. The small bathtub toy who has always longed for "bigger things" is initially exhilarated when the young boy takes him outside and places him in a small stream. However, as the brook flows into the river and then the river leads to the mouth of the large ocean, his initial feelings of freedom, adventure, and exhilaration are replaced by fear, anxiety, and a sense of being overwhelmed. In the end of the story, Scuffy is relieved to be rescued by the boy's father and returned to the confines of the family bathtub (Crampton).

Such messages are not merely limited to more historical narratives for young readers. Even the more contemporary and seemingly more iconoclastic genre of young adult (commonly abbreviated as "YA") books or "problem novels" can be viewed in this way. As Roberta Seelinger Trites has written, YA narratives, which are commonly seen as challenging the status quo, routinely support it in some form or to some degree:

> Since institutions such as school, religion, church, identity politics, and family are invested in socializing adolescents, the depiction of these institutions in adolescent literature is logically implicated in the establishment of narrative authority and in the ideological manipulation of the reader. Cultural representations of death and sex also rely on the adolescent's need to feel empowered and the culture's simultaneous need to repress the adolescent. (142)

To illustrate this claim, she points to many classic YA texts, including Robert Cormier's *The Chocolate War* (1974), M. E. Kerr's *Is That You, Miss Blue?* (1975), and Scott O'Dell's *Island of the Blue Dolphins* (1960).

This longstanding conservative tradition in children's literature prompted Jacqueline Rose to make a case for the innately traditionalist themes, messages, and subject matters present in books for young readers. "A set of barriers is constructed which assign the limits to how far children's literature is allowed to go in upsetting a specific register of representation—one which . . . is historically delimited and formally constrained" (139). Even Kimberley Reynolds, in her 2007 book about the radical potential of narratives for boys and girls, concedes that such elements exist alongside a strong conservative tradition where "children's literature provides a curious and paradoxical cultural space: a space that is simultaneously highly regulated and overlooked, orthodox and radical, didactic and subversive" (3). These comments suggest that the acculturating impulse and radical potential exist as "both/and" rather than "either/or" in children's and adolescent literature.

While books for young readers have always been, to greater or lesser degrees, conservative in nature, some titles that began appearing during the latter half of the twentieth century greatly amplified these traits. These books were fueled not only by the long-standing conservative tradition in U.S. literature and culture but also by the emergence of an entire sociopolitical movement based on this viewpoint. Within this new framework, conservatism embodied a mode of thought and way of being that was not simply located to the right of center; rather, conservatism emerged as a series of actions, ideas, and entities that people increasingly classified as right-wing.

"Yelling Stop at a Time When No One Is Inclined to Do So": The Conservative Movement and Rightist Politics in United States since World War II

In the same way that conservative-themed books for young readers have always existed in the United States, so too have like-minded sociopolitical movements. As Seymour Martin Lipset and Earl Raab have written, from the Tories during the Revolutionary War and the Know-Nothing Party of the nineteenth century to the isolationists during the *fin-de-siècle* and the Americanization movement in the 1920s, such groups and the individuals who comprised them sought to put the common definition of conservative—"Characterized by a tendency to preserve or keep intact or unchanged" (*OED* 765)—into practice. The specific aims of these movements differ, but the desire to resist societal transformation and maintain the social, political, economic, and cultural status quo exemplifies them all.

For some of these groups—such as the Ku Klux Klan in the 1960s, Posse Comitatus during the 1980s, or the Branch Davidians in the 1990s—this desire to support the status quo becomes so strong, the goal so reactionary, and the tactics to achieve it so extreme, that they can be classified as not simply right-leaning and conservative but, more accurately, as "right-wing." This concept originated during the era of the French Revolution as shorthand for an individual's political viewpoint. William Murray has written that members of parliament who sat to the right side of the session room generally supported both the existing monarchy and the notion of aristocratic privilege (3). But, according to the *Oxford English Dictionary*, right-wing means "that section of a political party, assembly, or other body most tending to hold conservative or reactionary views" (937). In a detail that brings both the etymology and ideology of these concepts full-circle, many individuals on the right in the United States simply refer to themselves by the blanket—and less culturally loaded—term "conservative" (see Diamond 5).

Of course, delineating the relationship between the conservative social movement and political right-wing in the United States is more complicated. The history of conservatism since World War II reveals either a powerful paradox or, at least, an ideological conundrum wherein right-wing groups adopt the classification of merely "conservative." Diamond contends that the label "'conservatism' implies a reticence toward change, and that sentiment does not capture what many self-described 'conservatives' are all about. Participants in the Christian Right, for instance, sought change, not the status quo; they wanted to alter legislation to reflect their religious values throughout society" (6). Given that "conservative" is not an entirely accurate way to describe such organizations and their members, some journalists, historians, and political scientists employ the more broad term "rightist," which the *Oxford English Dictionary* defines as "a member or adherent of 'the right' in politics" or, simply, "of, pertaining to, or characteristic of 'the right' in politics; tending to conservatism" (935) For the same reason, I, too, often deploy this term—along with the classification "right-leaning"—in the pages that follow. Again Diamond argues that these descriptors "include a range of political activists who, nevertheless, bear a coherent set of policy references" (6). Indeed, Chip Berlet has written that the causes, constituents, and viewpoints held by the conservative social movement and political right-wing are often interconnected: "Recruitment across boundaries and coalitions projects [is] common" (Berlet 89). Especially during the historical period spotlighted in this project, social conservatism became increasingly aligned with the political right in the United States and—at certain times and amidst certain circumstances—also with the right-wing.

In spite of the long history and strong presence of conservative sentiment and rightist politics in the United States, the present-day movement and its accompanying political faction is commonly seen as originating during the 1950s. The modern conservative movement coalesced around three main issues: anticommunism, libertarianism, and traditionalism. By far, the most powerful force among these was anticommunism, which included opposition to existing communist nations—primarily China and the U.S.S.R.—as well as preventing the spread of this political ideology, via domestic efforts like the John Birch Societies and international ones such as the China Lobby. This firm anticommunist stance went hand-in-hand with an equal belief in the need for a well-funded military and strong national defense. Indeed, throughout the cold war, the United States engaged in numerous acts of armed intervention in the name of fighting communism, such as the wars fought in South Korea during the 1950s and Vietnam during the 1960s.

Closely related to the conservatives' commitment to anticommunism was their equally adamant belief in what is commonly classified under the umbrella term of libertarianism. As George H. Nash has written, men and women who subscribe to this ideology believe in "resisting the threat of the ever-expanding State to liberty, private enterprise, and individualism" (xx). Concerned that the United States is rapidly drifting toward socialism and that the size and strength of government is infringing on individual freedoms, they advocate for a drastic reduction in federalism—including an end to government subsidies, public assistance, and social welfare programs—along with a strict adherence to laissez-faire capitalism. For libertarians, "individuals should conduct economic transactions unregulated, as they please. The state should not intervene to *distribute* wealth among social classes but, rather, should allow whatever distribution pattern that emerges through natural market forces" (Diamond 8; italics in original).

The third and final tenet of postwar American conservatism was something known by the broad notion of "traditionalism" or, sometimes, "antimodernism." As these terms imply, this impulse opposed progressive social changes and promoted the status quo. Traditionalists fought to preserve conventional gender and sexual roles, long-standing and often religious-based notions of morality, and existing hierarchies of race, ethnicity, and class. Sara Diamond has noted that this facet of conservatism has often led to a paradoxical attitude about the role of government and its power to influence one's personal life. "In the realm of culture and morality, *traditionalists* back the state as enforcer of a religious moral order, through laws regulating sexual practices, reproduction, childhood education, and mass media content" (Diamond 9; italics in original). At the same time, she notes that traditionalists "oppose state initiatives to *distribute* civil rights and liberties among traditionally subordinate groups" (Diamond 9; italics in original). As a result, if a state law or piece of federal legislation seeks to maintain the status quo, traditionalists support it. But, if society has made progressive liberal changes—such as in the realm of black civil rights during the 1950s and 1960s, women's rights in the 1970s, and lesbian, gay, bisexual, transsexual, and queer (LGBTQ) rights during the 1990s—then they strive to overturn the status quo.

While the individual prongs of anticommunism, libertarianism, and traditionalism were important to the emergence of the conservative movement in postwar America, the union or—more commonly—the "fusion" of these elements was responsible for its rise to power. As Jerome Himmelstein has discussed, early leaders of the movement quickly realized that they would be able to exert more cultural influence as a unified front working for a common cause than as independent factions pursuing individual agendas. As a result, both during the postwar period and into the new millennium, the relative success or comparative failure of the conservative movement has centered on its ability to get its various constituents to set aside their ideological differences and unite behind a shared cause.

Whereas the conservative movement today permeates nearly every facet of American social, political, and cultural life, it initially began as an intellectual movement with the publication of Russell Kirk's *The Conservative Mind: From Burke to Eliot* (1953). As its title implies, Kirk's book discussed an array of past conservative thinkers, including John C. Calhoun, John Quincy Adams, and Irving Babbitt; in so doing, it established an important historical lineage as well as ideological pedigree for the fledgling movement (Nash 290).

In 1955, conservatism received another boost when William F. Buckley Jr. founded the *National Review*, which gave the movement its first public platform through which to disseminate ideas and debate issues. As the founding editor asserted in his oft-quoted "Publisher's Statement" that appeared in the first issue, the new publication "stands athwart history, yelling Stop at a time when no one is inclined to do so" (Buckley "Publisher's" 5). The *National Review* was equally revolutionary for the way that it brought disparate factions of the conservative movement together. Buckley called this effort "symbiosis" instead of fusionism, but—in the words of Nash—his "success in welding a coalition was substantial. New conservatives, libertarians, and anti-Communists were represented on the masthead and readily gained access to the pages of the magazine" (224).

Encouraged by these developments, the conservative movement grew steadily throughout the following decade. In 1960, Barry Goldwater published what would become the second seminal text of the fledgling group, *The Conscience of a Conservative*. The book sold 700,000 copies by mid-1961, making conservatism a household word and earning Goldwater the nickname "Mr. Conservative" (see Hixson). In 1964, as a testament to how much the conservative movement had grown and also how much it had infiltrated mainstream politics, the Republican party named Goldwater as its presidential nominee. Although Goldwater lost the election to Democrat Lyndon Johnson in a landslide—receiving a mere 52 electoral votes to the incumbent president's 486—Jerome Himmelstein contends that even this "defeat had a positive impact" (69). "His campaign gave conservatives a commanding voice in the Republican party that they would never wholly relinquish. It stimulated further conservative activism and initiated a new generation of conservative activists" (Himmselstein 69). Indeed, out of the "Draft Goldwater" movement, the New Right, as it is commonly known, was born.

The rise of the conservative movement and expansion of rightist politics during the 1950s and 1960s primarily fused the goals of defeating communism, advocating for libertarianism, and maintaining traditionalism. But another faction both directly and indirectly fueled this expansive movement: what historians refer to as the "racist Right." The 1954 Supreme Court decision mandating desegregation of public schools ignited a racial backlash. In locations around the United States, but especially in regions throughout the South, whites dubbed the *Brown v. Board of Education* ruling "Black Monday." Although the unanimous Court asserted that the desegregation of public schools was to take place with all "deliberate speed," little had changed two years later. Realizing that outside intervention was necessary to compel action in many locales, President Dwight Eisenhower exercised his constitutional right to enforce the Supreme Court ruling. On September 5, 1957, he mobilized members of the Arkansas National Guard to escort nine black students into a formerly all-white school in Little Rock. "Governor Faubus responded by closing all Little Rock high schools for an entire school year. For his stand, he was reelected for another four terms" (Diamond 83).

The passage of the Civil Rights Act ten years later only exacerbated these sentiments. The historic 1964 bill outlawed discrimination based on race in employment, education, and public space, and it sparked national upheaval. The situation reached its political apogee in 1968 when Alabama Governor George Wallace, famous for his promise of "segregation now, segregation tomorrow, segregation forever!" (qtd in Hixson 119), made a bid for president. Although Wallace was running as an independent, his prosegregationist stance "secured almost 10,000,000 votes, or about 13.5 percent of the total voting electorate. He captured five states with forty-five electoral votes" (Lipset and Raab 378). Moreover, in a statistic that reveals the powerful connection between the rise of the conservative movement, the transformation of the Republican party, and the role of the racist Right, four of the five states that Wallace won were also those that Goldwater had won in 1964 (see Lipset and Raab 378).[8] As polls by both the Gallup and Harris revealed, "within each occupational class, 1964 Goldwater voters were more likely to be favorable to Wallace than were Johnson backers" (Lipset and Raab 359).

To greater or lesser degrees, the racist Right played a recurring role in both the conservative movement and right-leaning politics in the United States. Diamond explains, "Over the next two and a half decades, the Republicans would link opposition to welfare, affirmative action, and street crime all to negative images of African Americans and their struggle for social equality" (91). George H. W. Bush, for instance, tapped into racist sentiments with his "Willie Horton" campaign spots. The television advertisements, which ran nationally, discussed how Horton, a black man who had been convicted of first-degree murder and was serving a life sentence, had received ten weekend furlough passes from the state of Massachusetts, where Bush's opponent, Democrat Michael Dukakis, was the current governor. During one furlough, the ad explained, Horton kidnapped a white couple, stabbing the man and repeatedly raping his girlfriend. Larry McCarthy, the creator of the campaign spot, said that the crime scenario, combined with the menacing photograph of Horton that it projected on screen, embodied "every suburban mother's greatest fear" (qtd in Tapper, par 11).

The role of the racist Right in the rise of the conservative movement and formation of the political right pales in comparison to that of another demographic entity: evangelical Christians. For generations, these men and women had almost completely removed themselves from politics, an arena they considered utterly corrupt and hopelessly amoral, but they underwent a radical reversal during the 1970s. "The political awakening of evangelicals responded to profound social changes, especially around issues of women's equality, reproductive choice, and homosexual civil rights" (Diamond 161). Given the massive changes in American culture and the ways in which many Americans seemed not simply biblically incongruent but morally depraved, many evangelicals felt that they could no longer afford to remain disengaged from political life; instead, restoring traditional biblical values to American society required their involvement. Chip Berlet describes the effect of this evangelical activism on social issues like gay rights, abortion, and school prayer as "an apocalyptic frame that raise[d] the stakes of political struggle to a cosmological level" (81). To members of the Christian Right, the need "to restore America to its proper status as a Christian nation built on 'family values' and to defend the idealized Christian family against the sinful feminist, homosexual, secular humanist, and socialist subversives" was nothing less than an epic showdown between good and evil (Berlet 80).

Using communication methods ranging from nationally syndicated televangelist programs and radio preachers to the sermons delivered at individual churches and the use of something known as "direct mailings"—information pamphlets sent directly to people's homes—evangelicals educated their members about the harmful changes taking place in American culture and urged them to take action. In this way, "An emergent Christian Right forged a symbiotic relationship with the nominally secular conservative movement, whose leaders were then working to become a major faction of the Republican Party" (Diamond 161). By the end of the 1970s, the evangelical movement had emerged on the scene as a bona fide force in American politics. Televangelist Jerry Falwell formed the political lobbying group the Moral Majority in 1979. "Within a year of its formation, the Moral Majority claimed 400,000 members and $1.5 million in contributions; in 1980 Falwell claimed to have registered three million new voters" (Diamond 174). William Hixson found that for countless evangelicals, "support for the Moral Majority was a 'politicized extension of their religious beliefs'" (261).

The massive changes taking place in American society during the 1960s and throughout the 1970s were not only bringing evangelical Christians into the conservative movement and the Republican party; but these shifts were also attracting a new faction that became known as neoconservatives. Irving Kristol, who is often described as "the godfather of neoconservatism" (Aronowitz 58), defined the movement as "a 'persuasion' or a 'mode of thought' inspired by 'disillusionment with contemporary liberalism,' favorable toward capitalism and traditional institutions, but also toward a 'conservative welfare state' that 'takes a degree of responsibility for helping to shape the preferences that the people exercise in the free market'" (Diamond 178). Jacob Heilbrunn has documented that many neoconservatives had formerly considered themselves liberals and some had even been active in the Democratic party; they came to the New Right out of their dislike for the New Left. Indeed, as Sidney Blumenthal has written, "At every juncture in their journey, neoconservatives had been propelled by a feeling of disillusionment" (*Rise* 145). Neoconservatives hailed from numerous facets of society, but many were drawn from the ranks of conservative Jews and Roman Catholics. Conservative members of these faiths frequently held views on issues like abortion and homosexuality that opposed the Democratic party's more permissive policies. To be sure, Irving Kristol himself had once remarked: "A neoconservative is a liberal mugged by reality" (qtd in Blumenthal

Rise 145). During the 1970s neocons continued the intellectual tradition of the conservative movement that had begun in the 1950s: "During their early phase of development, the neoconservatives wielded little influence with political elites. Instead, neoconservatives operated primarily in the realm of ideology, through conferences, books, magazines, and newspaper columns, in efforts to influence political opinion" (Diamond 179).

These various facets of the conservative social movement and the New Right faction of the Republican party came together in the event that is commonly regarded as its crowning achievement: the 1980 election of Ronald Reagan, which recalled the origins of the New Right; Reagan actually got his start in politics during the Barry Goldwater campaign. At the National Republican Convention in 1964, in fact, many believed that Reagan upstaged the nominee when he delivered his now-famous "A Time for Choosing" speech with its oft-quoted closing line about the nation having a "rendezvous with destiny" (Reagan "Time" par 34). When Reagan occupied the Oval Office years later, his agenda was, in many ways, a classic portrait of the fusionist aims of the New Right. In a historic speech before the British Parliament, Reagan vowed to "leave Marxism-Leninism on the ash heap of history" (Reagan "Address," par 49) while he strongly supported anticommunism. In addition, he held many libertarian beliefs as evidenced by his adherence to supply-side economics, promise for an across-the-board tax cut, and a political mantra to "get government off your backs." Finally, Reagan was an adamant traditionalist, and his presidential campaign was greatly assisted by the work of evangelical Christians. "Pollster Henry Harris estimated that white evangelical voters accounted for two thirds of Reagan's 10-point margin over Jimmy Carter" (Diamond 233). Reagan won such strong support from Christian voters by advocating for an array of value-based issues, including a promise to introduce legislation to reinstate voluntary prayer in public school, support for a constitutional amendment banning abortion, and a vow to roll back or, at least, halt measures for gay rights. Taken collectively, the social vision and political mission of his administration was dubbed nothing less than the "Reagan Revolution."

Neoconservatives, although not as publicly visible, also played an important role in Reagan's election. Individuals working at conservative think tanks like the Heritage Foundation and American Enterprise Institute wrote articles and op-ed pieces that helped sway public opinion and shape Reagan's popular perception. After his election, many neoconservatives, including notably Jeane Kirkpatrick and William Bennett, were appointed to high-profile cabinet positions.

Through this successful fusionist approach, Reagan won the presidency in 1980 by a landslide; he captured an astounding 489 electoral votes compared to the mere 49 earned by his opponent, Jimmy Carter. His reelection in 1984 was even more lopsided. The incumbent president won an astounding 49 of the 50 states and earned a whopping 525 electoral votes, the most of any candidate in U.S. history. Through this sociopolitical achievement, Reagan both broadened the nature of conservatism by incorporating new ideas and individuals and unified the movement by energizing its core. George Nash described the phenomenon:

> By the end of President Reagan's second term, the American Right encompassed five distinct impulses: libertarianism, traditionalism, anti-Communism, neoconservatism, and the Religious Right. And just as William F. Buckley Jr. had done for conservatives a half generation before, so Ronald Reagan in the Eighties did the same: he performed an emblematic and ecumenical function. Much of Reagan's success as a spokesman for conservatism derived from his embodiment of all these impulses simultaneously. (559)

The 1990s witnessed a renaissance for not simply the right-leaning conservative movement and Republican party but also its more right-wing facets. Arguably the first step in this process occurred in 1992 when conservative politician, broadcaster, and commentator Patrick Buchanan challenged incumbent Republican president, George H. W. Bush, in the primaries. The former Nixon speechwriter and White House communications director under Reagan did quite well in the polls: Buchanan won 38 percent of the vote in the New Hampshire primary and earned "a quarter to a third of Republican votes" in primaries throughout the nation (Diamond 1). Buchanan ultimately lost the nomination, but in powerful recognition of the way in which evangelical Christians had moved from the periphery of the GOP to its forefront, he delivered the opening speech at the Republican National Convention in Houston. His address represented the culmination of the postwar conservative intellectual movement, the powerful influence of evangelical Christians, and the ongoing debates over changing morals. As Buchanan thundered near the end of the speech, "There is a religious war going on in our country for the soul of America. It is a cultural war, as critical to the kind of nation we will one day be as was the Cold War itself" (par 37).

He would not be wrong. The fall of the Berlin Wall and collapse of the Soviet Union ended the unifying force of anticommunism. But conservatives refocused their attention on domestic issues, especially those related to values, diversity, and morality. The 1990s saw a sharp rise in what became collectively known, following Buchanan's speech, as the "culture wars." Heated and often bitter debates erupted over efforts to make the canon of Western literature, history, and philosophy more diverse by including the voices of women, the working class, and racial and ethnic minority groups. In addition, many expressed outrage over the use of taxpayer funds via the National Endowment for the Arts to support what they felt was "objectionable" art, including the homoerotic photographs of Robert Mapplethorpe and the sexually explicit performance pieces by Karen Finley. Moreover, controversy over the legalization of abortion reached a fever pitch. Throughout the decade, instances of clinic barricades and bombings, the harassment, threats, and even assaults against clinic workers as well as clients, and—with the rapid expansion of the activist group Operation Rescue in the wake of the "Summer of Mercy" event in 1991—even the assassination of abortion doctors appeared with increasing frequency in headlines throughout the nation. Finally, antigovernmental libertarianism rose to new extremes as exemplified by the deadly clash between federal agents and members of the Branch Davidian compound in Waco, Texas, on April 19, 1993, and Timothy McVeigh's bombing of the Alfred P. Murrah Building in Oklahoma City on Waco's second anniversary. The racist Right also remained active. The 1990s witnessed the rise of white supremacist groups like the neo-Nazis, skinheads, and the Aryan Nation. Far from occupying the lunatic fringe, these groups and the figures that comprised them made headway into mainstream culture. David Duke, a former Grand Wizard of the Ku Klux Klan and a self-acknowledged advocate for "white rights,"[9] was elected to the Louisiana state legislature in 1989. In 1991, he made a bid for governor, and, although he was defeated, he won 55 percent of the white vote and 39 percent of the balloting overall (Bridges 236–237).

Conservatives suffered one of their first major political defeats in more than a decade when they lost the White House to Democrat Bill Clinton in 1992, but they recovered quickly. During the midterm elections two years later, the GOP not only regained control of both houses of Congress—an event that had not happened in forty years—but they did so in a commanding victory: Republicans won eight new seats in the Senate and control of fifty-four additional seats in the House (see Judd 125). Evangelical voters played a major role in this outcome. "Nationwide exit polls indicated that evangelical Christians comprised about 30 percent of those who voted in 1994" (Diamond 2). Equally important to the 1994 Republican success was the leadership savvy of soon-to-be Speaker of the House Newt Gingrich and his promotion of the RNC's "Contract with America." The document, which outlined the policies that the Republicans would enact if they obtained control, included such hallmarks of conservatism as a vow to return to "fiscal responsibility" for government spending, an act calling for the "restoration" of national security, and a policy mandating "personal responsibility" with regard to teen pregnancy, illegitimacy, and eligibility for welfare benefits (Republican National Committee). In a detail that was as substantive as it was symbolic, the "Contract for America" incorporated language that was taken directly from Reagan's 1985 State of the Union Address.

This fusionist atmosphere carried into the first decade of the new millennium. Given strong support among evangelicals and the appeal of "compassionate conservatism," George W. Bush won the election in 2000. The phrase and accompanying concept had first been coined during the late 1970s in a speech by Doug Wead at the annual Washington Charity Dinner, but Bush employed the term both ahistorically and very successfully, as a way to make the conservative movement more attractive to moderate voters. Indeed, with a campaign platform that included stances against illegal immigration, antipathy toward same-sex marriage, opposition to abortion, and support for faith-based initiatives, he cast himself as Reagan's figurative heir.

The attacks of September 11, 2001, rejuvenated political purpose and unified the conservative movement and rightist politics while the new initiatives fighting terrorism filled the void left by earlier legislation to combat communism. The racist Right was also empowered as anti-Islamic sentiments and questions concerning religious difference moved from the margin to the mainstream. Meanwhile, debates over values, which continued to rage, made the 2004 presidential campaign one of the most divisive in national history. The polarization of American culture—along political, social, class, regional, and economic lines—was perhaps never more pronounced; individuals in so-called "Blue" or largely Democratic states and those in "Red" or strongly Republican states were sharply divided over not only foreign policy concerning the war on terror but also domestic issues, especially questions regarding same-sex marriage. Although Bush won reelection by a slim margin—receiving just under 2.5 percent more of the popular vote than his opponent (2004 Election Results)—conservatives perhaps never exerted more cultural influence in the United States. Indeed, as George H. Nash has written, with the movement celebrating milestones like the fiftieth anniversary of the founding of the *National Review* and the publication of the nearly one-thousand-page tome *American Conservatism: An Encyclopedia*, the *New York Times* "took notice on its front page" (575).

As Bush's second term progressed, the political power of conservatism steadily declined and, ultimately, completely unraveled. Commentators attributed this drop in public standing to growing frustration with the war in Iraq and its growing expense. The explosion at the al-Askari Mosque in the city of Samarra on February 22, 2006, marked the beginning of what became the deadliest year in the U.S. military effort since the invasion three years earlier. A rapid uptick in the number as well as lethality of suicide bombings—targeted both at coalition forces and at the nation's civilian population amid growing strife between Sunni and Shi'a religious sects—caused Iraq to inch ever closer to civil war. According to statistics gathered by the U.S. government, "Total attacks in October 2006 averaged 180 per day, up from 70 per day in January 2006. Daily attacks against Iraqi security forces in October were more than double the level in January. Attacks against civilians in October were four times higher than in January. Some 3,000 Iraqi civilians are killed every month" (Baker and Hamilton 3). By the end of 2006, the Iraq Study Group—a bipartisan commission cochaired by former Secretary of State James A. Baker and former Democratic Congressman

Lee H. Hamilton—began the executive summary of their report with the blunt pronouncement: "The situation in Iraq is grave and deteriorating" (Baker and Hamilton xiii).

Throughout this time when the American military situation in Iraq was spiraling steadily downward, the budget for these operations was rapidly escalating. Amy Belasco, in a Congressional Research Service report, "The Cost of Iraq, Afghanistan, and Other Global War on Terror Operations Since 9/11," placed the average monthly obligations for Operation Iraqi Freedom at $7.2 billion (table 4, page 17). Meanwhile, Anthony Cordesman, in his analysis for the Center for Strategic and International Studies, asserted that when these on-the-ground costs were combined with related expenses, such as military recruitment and retention as well as veteran's care and benefits, the total cost was closer to $9.8 billion per month (5–6), a figure that was nearly double the amount—of $5 billion/month—spent during 2003 (see Moniz, par 2). By February 2008, Senator Amy Klobuchar testified in a hearing before the congressional Joint Economic Committee that costs in Iraq had spiked even further, to the staggering amounts of "$1.2 million every 4 minutes, adding up to $430 million every day, $12 billion every month" (United States *War at Any Cost?* 15). Joseph E. Stiglitz, in a prepared statement entered into the record at the same hearing, pointed out that this figure meant that every three months in Iraq the United States was now spending what the Bush Administration had initially forecast as the estimated cost for the entire war effort (United States *War at Any Cost?* 125).

Deteriorating conditions regarding foreign policy led to growing public disaffection for the president, his administration, and even his entire political party. These frustrations were expressed most plainly during the midterm elections in November 2006, when the Democrats regained control of Congress and obtained a new majority with 233 seats in the House and 51 in the Senate ("Democrats Retake"). President Bush called the outcome of the midterm elections, in what became an oft-referenced remark, "a thumpin' for Republicans" (qtd in Duffy and Tumulty, par 2). Meanwhile, political analyst Sidney Blumenthal went one step further by predicting "Vietnam ended a Democratic era as definitely as Iraq is closing a Republican one" (*Strange* 7).

While the conservative movement may have encountered a political setback in 2006, it remained strong on the social front. John Micklethwait and Adrian Woodbridge astutely remarked, "The Right clearly has ideological momentum on its side in much the same way that the Left had momentum in the 1960s" (380). Echoing this observation, for the bulk of Bush's second term, rightist figures and their ideas dominated the American social, cultural, and intellectual landscape. Books like Ann Coulter's *Godless: The Church of Liberalism* (2006) reached the top spot on the *New York Times* best-seller list, while cultural phenomena such as the new musical genre of Christian rock—via songs like Lifehouse's "You and Me" (2005) and "First Time" (2007)—enjoyed mass popularity, and talk radio host Rush Limbaugh received a record-setting renewal deal: in 2008, he signed a new nine-year contract worth $400 million, which translated into a salary of $38 million per year, plus a $100 million signing bonus (Garrity, par 2).

Such paradoxes within the nation's sociopolitical climate during this period prompted Michael Thompson to argue that despite President Bush's claim to practice "compassionate conservatism," a more accurate label was "new conservatism" ("Introduction" 1). Akin to previous incarnations of this social movement and mode of thought, this most contemporary form operates via three interconnected principles that vastly differed from those of previous historical eras. Instead of pivoting around the issues of libertarianism, traditionalism, and anticommunism/antiterrorism Thompson explained:

> The new conservative landscape I am describing can be defined through three different but interlocking dimensions of modern American social life and political culture: first, a redefinition and reappropriation of liberalism with a more radical emphasis on individualism; second, a resurgent capitalism that has brought back a new and resilient form of economic hierarchy and that has rearranged previous forms of economic life; and third, the narrowing and "provincialism" of everyday life—structured partially by the suburbanization of American culture—which feeds the other two dimensions and narrows the sphere of social interaction largely to the realm of work and family at the expense of broader forms of civil society. (Thompson "America's" 12)

Thompson delineated the way in which the new conservatism did not simply reconfigure the movement's long-standing ideals but actually contradicted them. For example, rather than espousing a libertarian view of small government and greater individual freedoms, the new conservatism asserted "a renewed respect for institutional authority in politics" ("America" 9). Indeed, as Elizabeth Drew among others has documented, Bush engaged in an unprecedented expansion of executive branch powers throughout his two terms as president (Drew, par 1). Moreover, he used this increase in power to greatly expand—not contract—the size, scope, and reach of the federal government, especially in the realms of public surveillance and prisoner detention.

The 2008 presidential election unseated the right from power and thus offers the historical endpoint for this project. Nonetheless, by this point, social conservatism and its accompanying political agenda no longer existed on the fringe of society; they were permanently woven into the fabric of the nation. Thompson defined "the new conservatism" as "not the purview of a minority; it has become hegemonic in the public discourse, has displaced a waning postwar liberalism as a public philosophy, and has succeeded in attaining political and ideological power in many branches of government and within many of the organs of the public sphere" ("Introduction" 2). Given the way in which conservative views and rightist political ideas had penetrated nearly every facet of American life, Thompson concluded his assessment of the United States at the dawn of the 2008 presidential election season: "A new culture has been constructed with new predispositions, and it is at the level of culture *as well as* at the level of political and economic institutions that any fruitful analysis of the present situation must proceed" ("Introduction" 2; italics in original)—a maxim that *Raising Your Kids Right* both heeds and extends.

Raising Kids Right: The Political Soap Box Comes to the Print Sand Box

The chapters that follow examine the convergence of the conservative social movement and rightist political viewpoints within the realm of children's literature. In so doing, they draw on numerous facets from the history of these phenomena during the late twentieth century and first decade of the new millennium. The opening chapter on William Bennett's *The Book of Virtues* (1993), for instance, examines the return to power of the New Right in the early 1990s and the role that neoconservatives like Bennett, a lifelong Democrat prior to becoming a political appointee of Ronald Reagan, played in this event. Bennett's book, published only one year after Buchanan's infamous "culture wars" speech at the Republican National Convention, took up a position on the front lines of battle. Echoing the antiprogressive and even antimodernist strain of conservatism, *The Book of Virtues* reflected a desire to roll back the transformations to American family life and morality during the 1990s that were precipitated by events like the successes of second-wave feminism, the advent of multiculturalism, and the rise of the LGBTQ rights movement.

Chapter 2, on the pro-logging picture book *Truax* (1995), demonstrates the important function that grassroots efforts—exemplified in the actions of concerned mother and longtime employee of the wood products industry, author Terri Birkett—played in expanding conservative viewpoints during the 1990s. At the same time, this chapter also points to the increasing influx of corporate money, influence, and involvement in the politics of the right and, as a result, the emergence of one of the newest planks of its platform: opposition to environmentalism.

Chapter 3, on the Left Behind books for kids, examines the powerful place of evangelicals in the rise of the conservative movement and the construction of the right-wing faction of the Republican party. I demonstrate that, although authors Jerry B. Jenkins and Timothy LaHaye claim to be writing religious novels aimed at saving young adult souls, their books can more accurately be viewed as political narratives engaged in a battle over values. Detailing the prominent behind-the-scenes role that LaHaye has played in the Christian Right, this chapter reveals how the Left Behind series for kids is an extended argument for the general place of Christianity in American public education and evangelical faith more specifically.

Chapter 4 spotlights the picture books by former Second Lady Lynne Cheney. Paying special attention to *America: A Patriotic Primer* (2002)—her first of what are now five narratives—I discuss how the attacks of September 11, 2001, gave the conservative movement a new unifying force or common crusade. Given that Cheney wrote *America: A Patriotic Primer*, like all of her other picture books, as an official project for the American Enterprise Institute, the chapter also explores the important role that conservative think tanks play in the construction and dissemination of rightist viewpoints. Indeed, Cheney, who was the former chair of the National Endowment for the Humanities, is not simply fighting the war on terror with her patriotic-themed picture books; she is also continuing her previous fight over the canon wars.

Chapter 5, on *The O'Reilly Factor for Kids* (2004) by the popular political pundit and cable news commentator Bill O'Reilly, signals both the high-water mark for conservative-themed books for young readers and their important transformation. In his 2004 text, O'Reilly brings the popular and rapidly growing genre of advice literature to young readers while he simultaneously replicates its many flaws. From its main title and basic premise to its overall format and specific chapter discussions, *The O'Reilly Factor for Kids* puts the self in self-help. His book may be cowritten with Charles Flowers and shelved as a nonfiction advice text for young people, but it is really little more than an extension of the O'Reilly product, brand, and especially persona—a way to extend his media franchise into a new market and broaden his audience to a new demographic.

Chapter 6 examines this genre at perhaps its most overtly political and directly partisan, via Katharine DeBrecht's picture book *Help! Mom! There Are Liberals under My Bed!* (2005). Especially when viewed in the company of its sequels—*Help! Mom! Hollywood's in My Hamper!* (2006) and *Help! Mom! The 9th Circuit Nabbed the Nativity!* (2006)—DeBrecht's work illustrates the perceived erosion of so-called traditional family values and the escalating stakes of the culture wars. Echoing this sense of political urgency and social anxiety, DeBrecht moved the ugly slugfest known as contemporary partisan politics to fictional storybooks for young readers. Moreover, given the thread of anti-Semitism that runs throughout the books, the *Help! Mom!* series also illustrates the ongoing role of the racist Right in the construction of conservative viewpoints.

Finally, my conclusion examines the current state of conservative thought and the future of rightist books for young readers. Focusing on the 2008 presidential election, I discuss the steady decline in conservative political power and social influence as the presidency of George W. Bush drew to a close, but then its seeming rejuvenation in the wake of the naming of Alaska Governor Sarah Palin as the Republican vice presidential nominee. The closing sections of the concluding chapter consider whether the election of President Barack Obama—along with a Democrat-controlled Congress—signals the death knell for conservative-themed books for young readers or whether, given that the genre began soon after the inauguration of Democratic Bill Clinton, these political events will only reinvigorate them.

During the course of these discussions, this book uncovers important but long overlooked coordinates on the map of the conservative movement and rightist politics in the United States. Sara Diamond asserted the importance of attempts during the 1990s to ban sexually explicit art, reinstate prayer in public school, and curtail abortion rights: "Each of these news events was part of a much bigger story. Each was a landmark along the road to political power" (2). The narratives by Bennett, Birkett, Cheney, LaHaye/Jenkins, DeBrecht, and O'Reilly form another facet to this phenomenon. More than simply embodying an aspect of millennial print, material, and popular culture, they are agents of social change and indices of political power. As Antonio Gramsci would characterize it, these texts form part of the myriad practices by which the hegemonic or "ruling class" gains the support of its citizenry "by a combination of force and consent" (156).

Accordingly, my book fulfills a dual purpose; it both explores the sociopolitical ideology underpinning these books for young readers and tracks their cultural influence. Indeed, my discussion reveals that although the narratives by Cheney, Bennett, and O'Reilly may not have received mainstream critical attention, they are certainly seeking to influence the mainstream. As the ideological division between Red States and Blue States has become increasingly more polarized, and the views held by the political left and the political right have become exponentially more entrenched, these authors have turned their attention to a potentially more impressionable audience. In so doing, they lend added agency to a youth demographic that has historically been seen as lacking in power, while they simultaneously participate in a growing phenomenon in the United States by which "children and childhood have become pawns in an ideological war" (Murray 212).

Of course, the books by Bennett, Cheney, O'Reilly, and others do not mark the first or only time that advocates for a particular political ideology have written children's books designed to educate or even indoctrinate young people. Because children are often seen as "the nation's most open-minded citizens" and because children's literature has the potential to reach this impressionable audience "on a massive scale, because of the ready market provided by school libraries" (Mickenberg 9), numerous social and political groups have used it to disseminate their ideas. The Ku Klux Klan, both during its initial emergence in Reconstruction and amid its various revivals during twentieth century, penned assorted works of fiction and especially nonfiction for young readers that offered a pro-white, pro-southern, and pro-Confederate view of history. One such example is *Catechism for Children*, released by the United Daughters of the Confederacy in 1904. Likewise, various denominations of American Christians and especially Protestant sects have done the same. From Elizabeth Cheap's *My Station and Its Duties* (1810) during the early years of the American Sunday School Movement through Sheila Butt's *Does God Love Michael's Two Daddies?* (2006)—which emerged as a product of the evangelical revival in the new millennium—these books reflected a specific spiritual worldview. Nor is this phenomenon simply limited to more conservative facets of society. Julia Mickenberg, in her book *Learning from the Left* (2006), for instance, discusses the various narratives for children that were written by political radicals, cultural revolutionaries, and social progressives from the 1910s through the 1970s. In "ABC for Martin" (1935), for example, author M. Boland offers juvenile readers the following proletarian spin on the alphabet book: "A stands for Armaments—war-mongerers' pride; B is for Bolshie, the thorn in their side" (20).

What differentiates the phenomenon that I am tracing is how, in contrast to these generally marginalized and largely niche narratives, the current crop of conservative-themed books for young readers has staked a claim in the mainstream. As the following chapters detail, these texts have not only been written by many well-known figures, but they have also sold hundreds of thousands of copies, topped national best-seller lists, and even been adopted in public schools as a focal point for curricula. Hence, they mark one of the few times in U.S. history when what would formerly have been considered a specialized minority faction has become firmly implanted in mass culture.

One final note about methodology: although the six writers profiled in the chapters that follow embody prominent voices in the growing new subgenre of rightist books for young readers, they—and the narratives that they have written—are not the only ones who comprise it. To this list, I could add William F. Buckley Jr.'s *Treasury of Children's Classics*, James Finn Garner's satirically titled *Politically Correct Bedtime Stories* (1994), and John H. Wilson's *Hot House Flowers*. Initially published in 2003, *Treasury of Children's Classics* reprints stories, poems, and tales that were published in the renowned children's periodical *St. Nicholas Magazine*, which was founded by Mary Mapes Dodge in 1874 and remained in circulation in the United States until 1941. Buckley's criteria for choosing which of the many tales that appeared in *St. Nicholas* to republish in his collection were both simple and straightforward, especially for those who know Buckley's name and his reputation as a leading conservative critic, thinker, and writer: "There are no children's tales in this collection that would have stimulated base appetites" (xv). In the following paragraph of the book's introduction, Buckley elaborates that all the selections in his book are "wholesome," a "much rejected" term in the modern era (xv). Lest the politics fueling Buckley's text remain unclear, *Treasury of Children's Classics* is not simply sponsored by the *National Review*, but the name of the conservative magazine actually appears above its title.[10]

Politically Correct Bedtime Stories: Modern Tales for Our Life and Times (1994) possesses an equally clear ideological agenda. James Finn Garner's book presents itself as reimagining classic children's stories through the post-modern and largely leftist lenses of diversity, inclusion, and multiculturalism. But—as Lynne Vallone has written—his collection can more accurately be seen as engaging in a rightist project: "Garner's book is a cutesy attempt to ridicule . . . those who value the 'significant beliefs in the environment, feminism, the rights of minorities, and a multicultural academy'" (Vallone, par 7). In Garner's retelling of "The Three Little Pigs," for example, the eponymous characters are not satisfied with simply repelling the solitary lurking wolf; they annex a nearby wolf condominium by staging an armed raid complete with machine guns and rocket launchers. Once the three pigs have forcibly overtaken the settlement, they establish a model socialist state that includes, as Garner notes, "free education, universal health care, and affordable housing for everyone" (12). As Vallone has aptly observed, the coda to Garner's story can be seen as "attack[ing] both Latin American revolutionaries (the Sandinistas so vilified by the Reagan Administration) as well as anyone who believes in 'free education, universal health care, and affordable housing for everyone'" (par 8). To be sure, Garner refers to the brigade of swine insurrectionists as *porcinistas* (12).

Hot House Flowers arises from even stronger rightist impulses. Published in 2006, the picture book tells the story about Red Rose, Yellow Rose, and Orchid, who enjoy a happy, healthy, and prosperous life in a greenhouse until a jealous dandelion deliberately releases her seeds through a vent in the roof. Her offspring take root in the lush environment and quickly begin overtaking the limited resources of water, light, and food. The native plants, however, are unable to discuss the negative impact that the recent arrivals are having on their home, partly because the new seedlings speak a different language from them and partly because they are afraid of being seen as "intolerant." Just when the central trio is nearly dead from lack of food, water, and light, they are saved when the hothouse master returns. He chides Yellow Rose, Red Rose, and Orchid for behaving so irrationally and then promptly weeds out all of the dandelions. The next spring, when the mother dandelion again releases her seeds into the vent that leads into the hothouse, the native plants "used their roots and stems to push the Dandelion seeds to the floor, where they could not grow. And seeing the fate of her seeds, the Dandelion stopped trying to send more into the hot house." The book concludes with the following single sentence: "And the flowers of the hot house lived in peace." *Hot House Flowers* is commonly—and correctly—read as a thinly disguised allegory about illegal immigration. Moreover, its author, John H. Wilson, is an active judge who currently serves in the criminal court of Brooklyn. In an article that appeared in New York's *Daily News*,

Wilson offered the following commentary about his picture book: "It's intended to describe defense of home and defense of country, and the reasons for that defense" (Lisberg, par 3).

In *Raising Your Kids Right* I demonstrate that the books by Wilson, Garner, and Buckley are not isolated, unusual, or exceptional. They are part of a growing new subgenre of texts for young readers in the United States and, by extension, an important new facet of the nation's conservative social movement and rightist political faction. These texts reveal a blueprint of the political debates and social battles waging at the end of the twentieth century and first decade of the new millennium. At the same time, they illuminate a portrait of the ever-evolving nature of children's literature, shifting conceptions about the construction of childhood in the United States, and changing beliefs about the purpose or intent of books for young readers.

IN WHAT HAS BECOME AN OFT-REFERENCED REMARK, historian Robert Hine wrote: "What society wants its children to know reveals what that society wants itself to be" (238). Although such knowledge can be evidenced in everything from public school curricula to the questions on standardized testing, books written for children embody another powerful locus of information. Laura Apol has argued, "As a form of education and socialization, the literature written and published for children reveals a great deal about what adults wish children to know, to preserve, and to put into practice" (90). She notes that Anne Scott MacLeod, a critic of children's literature who has written about the development of childhood in the United States, echoes this observation: "When I read books written for children, I look for authors' views, certainly, but I also try to discover what the culture is saying about itself, about the present and the future, and about the nature and purposes of childhood" (vii). After all, "adults write the books that children read; they edit them, publish them, buy them, promote them, read them to children, and teach them. They have a stake in the representations that are found in those books and in the ideological messages they (overtly or covertly) contain" (Apol 90). For these reasons, Apol concludes: "children's literature provides a unique window into the pervasive values and deeply-held beliefs of a culture" (Apol 90). The chapters that follow present another, as-yet untold, chapter in this ongoing narrative of discovery.

1

"Give Me Some
of That Old-Time Reading"

William Bennett's *The Book of Virtues* and the Rise of Right-Leaning Literature for Young Readers

"All of a sudden the Ten Commandments weren't posted on the wall,
but Johnny was coming home with a handful of condoms."
—William Bennett, testifying at the congressional hearing "Parents,
Schools and Values," December 1995

Arguably, no single American political figure has been more responsible for bringing the foundational conservative issue of values into the national public debate than William J. Bennett. Joshua Green offers his assessment: "For more than 20 years, as a writer, speaker, government official, and political operative, Bennett has been a commanding general in the culture wars" (par 1). A lifelong Democrat before becoming a political appointee of the Reagan administration, Bennett has been one of the most prominent voices for neoconservatism during the past three decades. Selected as chairman of the National Endowment for the Humanities in 1981, he used the position—as he himself later remarked—as a "bully pulpit" (Bennett *De-Valuing* 69) to champion traditional approaches to the study of history, philosophy, and literature. Bennett believed that the left-leaning professoriate was adopting scholarly viewpoints and research methodologies that were not simply politically motivated, but factually invalid, professionally irresponsible, and, thus, morally reprehensible. In a much publicized report released in 1984 and appropriately titled *To Reclaim a Legacy*, he argued that these efforts "had dislodged the canon of great books that traditionally had been at the center of the American curriculum in favor of a fashionable mix of media studies and minority writing" (Carton and Graff 265). As a result, through his work at the NEH, Bennett sought to end what he viewed as a distorted and inaccurate view of American history, literature, and philosophy. While at the organization Bennett commented about one particular battle that aptly characterized his entire NEH career: "What I was trying to do . . . was to put a halt to taxpayers' subsidizing of left-wing, anti-American propaganda" (*De-Valuing* 19).

Later, as the secretary of education from 1985 to 1988, Bennett turned this same sense of moral outrage toward the nation's public school system. Throughout his time in office, Bennett campaigned relentlessly on issues ranging from the institution of competency testing, the implementation of performance-based pay, and the benefits of ending teacher tenure to the creation of national curriculum standards, the failure of college education programs to prepare future teachers properly, and the need for parental choice through school vouchers. As before, Bennett frequently framed these issues in terms of values. He pointed to the moral responsibility that we have as a society to educate our children; moreover, he frequently cited Thomas Jefferson's view that the public education should facilitate not simply intellectual growth but also personal and public virtue.[1] Consequently, in numerous articles, reports, and speeches, the secretary of education advocated incorporating morality education—which he often termed "the teaching of character"—into the national public school curriculum.

Finally, as the first director of the Office of National Drug Control (NDC) under George H. W. Bush, Bennett regularly viewed his work through the lens of morality. Adopting what both supporters and detractors categorized as a "get tough" approach, he shunned medico-scientific views of drug addiction as a debilitating disease from which individuals suffered. Instead, he insisted that men and women take responsibility for their actions, and—failing that—he called on the nation's judicial system to hold them accountable: by sentencing drug offenders to long prison terms instead of to rehabilitation programs. Bennett's strident advocacy for personal responsibility and self-control—coupled with his staunch support for jail time and fewer drug treatment programs—earned him the not-so-affectionate nickname (still associated with that office) of "drug czar."

Since leaving public office, William Bennett has remained actively involved with issues surrounding values. In 1991, Bennett accepted a position at the Heritage Foundation, a conservative think tank in Washington, D.C. His first project was to compose a book-length version of his report *The Index of Leading Cultural Indicators*, which provided statistical analysis about American "behavior, habits, beliefs, and mores—matters that in our time often travel under the banner of 'values'" (Bennett *Index* 7). In addition, in 1993, he cofounded, with former Secretary of Housing and Urban Development Jack Kemp and former U.N. Ambassador Jeane J. Kirkpatrick, a political lobbying group called Empower America. According to its mission statement, the organization is "devoted to ensuring that government actions foster growth, economic well-being, freedom, and individual responsibility" (Empower America).[2] The year 1998 was especially busy for Bennett, as the sex scandal involving President Clinton and Monica

Lewinsky occupied much of his attention. In articles, op-ed pieces, and speeches, Bennett cast the event not simply as one concerned with legality—given Clinton's sworn testimony that he had not had sexual relations with the White House intern—but one that pivoted around national values, acceptable standards of personal behavior, and notions of virtue and vice.[3] The former chairman of the NEH was so morally incensed by whole incident that he wrote *The Death of Outrage: Bill Clinton and the Assault on American Ideals* (1998). The book, which was a *New York Times* best-seller, "decried, among other things, the public's failure to take Clinton's sins more seriously" (Green, par 2).

When Bennett is not engaged in a particular political cause or social crusade, he remains intimately involved in a conservative mission to promote values, standards, and morality. In 1992, he published *The De-Valuing of America: The Fight for Our Culture and Our Children*. The book is part memoir of his time in various political posts and part polemic about what he sees as the problems facing the nation's children. From failing schools and rising divorce rates to racial strife and drug abuse, these problems, in Bennett's view, can all be linked to questions of values and morals. Indeed, the former drug czar flatly asserts in the preface to *The De-Valuing* that "it is, finally, a book about that which is profoundly good and right and decent about this nation on the one hand, and about some of what has gone very wrong on the other" (11). The subject of all of Bennett's subsequent books pivot around analogous themes: *Body Count: Moral Poverty . . . and How to Win America's War Against Crime and Drugs* (1996), *The Broken Hearth: Reversing the Moral Collapse of the American Family* (2001), and *Why We Fight: Moral Clarity and the War on Terrorism* (2003).

Bennett continues to remain in the public eye. Since 2004, he has conducted a weekday radio program, called "Morning in America," named after one of the most popular television campaign ads for Ronald Reagan. The show is broadcast on 115 radio stations around the nation and has an estimated audience of 1.25 million listeners ("Media Matters Exposes"). In addition, Bennett has been a longtime contributor to the conservative *National Review* and the *National Review Online* where he frequently writes on issues related to personal conduct, national character, and individual values. Finally, as a devout Roman Catholic, Bennett has taken a public stance on a wide range of what he sees as moral questions, including same-sex marriage, abortion, euthanasia, sex education, and adoption by gay or lesbian couples. For example, with his wife, Elayne, Bennett has been heavily involved with the Best Friends Foundation, a nonprofit group that teaches adolescents about abstinence.

For his work on these other efforts, Bennett has been dubbed everything from the "self-appointed guardian" of American traditional values (D'Entremont, par 6) and a "conservative cult-hero" (Wagner, par 1) to the "morality czar" (Fink with Guest 21) and "national scold" (Rogers, par 4). Far from shying away from these monikers—both positive and negative—Bennett embraces them. He frequently refers to himself in articles and interviews as the "virtuemeister" (Duin A2). Indeed, Bennett's strong moral positions made him a contender for the Republican presidential nomination in 1996, but he declined to run ("Update—Campaign '96").

Given William Bennett's longstanding personal interest and active public involvement with questions of values, it came as no surprise when, in 1993, he published *The Book of Virtues: A Treasury of Great Moral Stories.* The eight-hundred-plus page volume contains more than five hundred works by poets, novelists, philosophers, folklorists, political figures, and historians that are designed, as Bennett asserts in the opening sentence of the introduction, to "aid in the time-honored task of the moral education of the young" (11). The selections are grouped thematically according to ten specific virtues that Bennett seeks to impart to the nation's children: Self-Discipline, Compassion, Responsibility, Friendship, Work, Courage, Perseverance, Honesty, Loyalty, and Faith.

The Book of Virtues not only strives to instill such traditional moral qualities in its young readers, but, echoing Bennett's conservative efforts while chairman of the NEH, the book also aims to impress youth by drawing on traditional reading selections taken from the canon of Western civilization, classical Greco-Roman philosophy, and so-called "Great Books" of American and British literature. In so doing, *The Book of Virtues* embodies more than simply a conservative tome; in keeping with the antiprogressive impulses of this sociopolitical movement, it has become a retreat to the past. William B. Hixson has remarked that the conservative movement in the United States can perhaps be best understood as "promoting Victorian values in late twentieth-century world" (xvii). Echoing this observation, Bennett creates what can be seen as a backward-looking text in *The Book of Virtues*, a work that is shaped by the wistful romanticization and even nostalgic idealism of a "kinder, gentler" time before the upheavals of the civil rights movement, the rise of postmodernist thought, and the numerous transformations to American family life through the advances made by second-wave feminism, the advent of multiculturalism, and the growth of the LGBTQ movement. Indeed, as historians Seymour Martin Lipset and Earl Raab have observed, "In almost every generation, 'old American' groups which saw themselves 'displaced,' relatively demoted in status or power by processes rooted in social change, have sought to reverse these processes through the activities of moralistic movements or political action groups" (xvii).

The Book of Virtues arises from such impulses. Through both its form and its content, the collection responds directly to the massive transformations that had taken place in American life by the 1990s. Whereas books for children published during the final decade of twentieth century increasingly pivoted around contemporary issues, such as multiculturalism and the subjective nature of truth and beauty, *The Book of Virtues* conveys more traditionalist messages about the presence of definitive truths and the existence of common culture.

Written and released during the final decade of the twentieth century that was characterized by massive social flux and radical cultural upheaval, these traits helped catapult *The Book of Virtues* to best-seller status. In an arguably even more important detail, they also caused Bennett's book to launch a whole new subgenre of conservative literature for American children.

This chapter finds the literary content and commercial popularity of *The Book of Virtues* to be products of its successful blend of the politics of the Republican Right, growing fears about the state of American society on the eve of the new millennium, and Bennett's neoconservative social vision. Published only one year after Pat Buchannan delivered his infamous "culture wars" speech at the Republican National Convention, *The Book of Virtues* assumed a position on the front line of this battle.

Brave New World: The Eve of the Millennium and the Transformations to American Life and Values

The final decade of the twentieth century was one of the most dynamic times in American history. The 1990s witnessed an array of social, political, cultural, and technological transformations. For both the inhabitants in the nation's large cities and the residents of its small rural towns, the final decade before the dawn of the new millennium was a time when American life—along with its social values and standards of morality—shifted dramatically.

While the realms of science and technology played major roles in the transformations of the 1990s—with the proliferation of the personal computer, the emergence of cellular phones, and the debut and then rapid expansion of the Internet—the areas that most affected national morals and values occurred in the realms of American social, political, and cultural life. As I have written elsewhere, "During the 1990s, the fight for homosexual rights made unprecedented strides in the United States" (Abate 228). Through the work of advocacy groups like ACT-UP (AIDS Coalition To Unleash Power), GLAAD (Gay and Lesbian Alliance Against Defamation), the Lesbian Avengers, and Queer Nation, gays and lesbians attained both a cultural visibility and a political voice never seen before in American history. "Many state governments along with private companies amended their policies of nondiscrimination to include sexual orientation, while an array of major cities passed legislation that recognized domestic partnerships between cohabitating unmarried couples, whether heterosexual or homosexual. In addition, the field of gay and lesbian studies emerged as a new academic discipline" (Abate 229).

The growing national interest in multiculturalism and an increased concern for the perspective of racial, gender, and ethnic minority groups had a similarly transformative impact. Numerous Black studies, Latino/a studies, and American

Indian studies programs appeared on campuses around the nation throughout the 1990s. These programs frequently questioned established historical accounts and cultural canons: "They asked, about curricula, textbooks and research: 'where are the blacks?' 'where are the women?'" (94). In the wake of these inquiries, "The canon, which had largely been a given, became over a decade and more a question" (Lauter 94). From the elementary through the doctoral levels, classroom curricula moved away from the former pantheon of what came to be known derisively as "dead white males" to include the voices of racial, ethnic, gender, sexual, and socioeconomic minorities.

These modifications also had an impact outside academia because they altered public perceptions about the celebratory nature of certain historical happenings, the veracity of various cultural events, and the seemingly sacrosanct status of present as well as past public figures. Emblematic among these was the five hundredth anniversary, in 1992, of the arrival of Christopher Columbus in North America. While some saw the event as a commendable one that memorialized individual courage, personal perseverance, and cultural vision, others viewed it as a lamentable one that set into motion horrendous acts of genocide, enslavement, and cultural destruction for the indigenous peoples of the Americas.

The seemingly innocuous realm of American popular culture was also a site of powerful changes in American life, values, and morality during the 1990s. Raves—large, often all-night, dance parties that featured electronic music, laser lights, and fog machines—became exceedingly popular among young people. So, too, did the hallucinogenic drug known as "Ecstasy" or simply "X," a common feature at raves that brought drug use back not simply to the mainstream but to the middle class. In addition, the influence of grunge rock, coupled with heightened concern for the natural environment, sparked a new unisex clothing style during the 1990s. "Carpenter (or workmen's) jeans, flannel shirts, and 'all-terrain' shoes became fashionable for both men and women" (Abate 223). Moreover, formerly taboo activities like tattooing and body piercing moved into the mainstream. Echoing the era's increasing interest in multiculturalism, designs that were patterned—however loosely—after the cultural practices of tribal peoples in Africa, the Pacific Rim, and the Americas were especially popular (Torgovnick 172–208). These changes fueled beliefs, first presented in books like *Gender Trouble* (1991) by queer theorist Judith Butler, about the artificial, malleable, and ultimately performative nature of masculinity and femininity.

In the realm of entertainment, the relatively new musical genres of hip-hop and gangsta rap, with their aggressive, in-your-face style and raw, unapologetic portrait of black urban street life, attained massive popularity, sweeping not simply the nation but the globe. Those who were not listening to rap songs like Ice-T's controversial 1992 hit "Cop Killer" may have had their radios tuned to shock jocks like Howard Stern. His phenomenally successful nationally syndicated program, which frequently focused on sexual humor, scatology, and race relations, made him not only the highest-paid radio host in the United States but also one the most frequently and heavily fined (see Ahrens). On the small screen, tabloid talk shows, most notably *The Jerry Springer Show*, which debuted in 1991, with their spotlight on sensationalist subjects like bestiality, incest, and adultery—along with the melees that routinely broke out among guests—were ratings winners and inaugurated a new tell-all, no-holds-barred broadcasting style. Meanwhile, *Beavis and Butt-Head* (1993–1997), an animated series that aired on MTV, featured the two eponymous teenage characters who spent the bulk of their time eating junk food, trying to "score with chicks," and making sarcastic comments about everything from music videos to their mothers being "sluts." Finally, films like Quentin Tarantino's *Reservoir Dogs* (1992)—which Rob Edelman has described as a "brilliant but unrelentingly violent saga of some crude, foul-mouthed criminals who come together to pull off a robbery" (1244)—and his follow-up *Pulp Fiction* (1994)—which combined a clever nonlinear chronology, an array of eclectic personalities from the criminal underworld, and numerous witty pop culture references—helped to redefine the American cinematic landscape while they reinvigorated it.

In American popular culture it was significant that the 1990s saw a renewed interest in the fashions, fads, and styles of the 1960s and 1970s in the United States, evidenced by everything from the revival of lava lamps and re-release of the Volkswagen Beetle to the ubiquitous nature of "flared" (i.e., bell-bottomed) jeans and the popularity of the television comedy *That '70s Show* (1998–2006). For, the nation was once again in the midst of a profound change. Many social movements that shaped the 1990s—feminism, gay and lesbian rights, and civil rights for racial and ethnic minority groups—were also prominent during the period of the Vietnam War and were responsible for much of the era's well-known societal upheaval.

The 1980s, with the election of Republican Ronald Reagan and his conservative vision, saw a halt to and even backlash against the social rebellions of 1960s and 1970s; the 1990s, however, revived them. Indeed, the final decade of the twentieth century seemed to pick up where the Vietnam era left off. The election in November 1992 of baby boomer Bill Clinton, who had come of age during the 1960s and admitted to trying marijuana when he was in college, only confirmed these fears. The fact that the new Democratic president "didn't inhale," as he infamously asserted, mattered little. Almost overnight, everything in American life, culture, and politics seemed to have changed. Furthermore, events such as increased acceptance of homosexuality, the popularity of shocking radio celebrities, and the ascendency of tabloid television programming revealed that national morality had changed along with it.

"Once Upon a Better Time": Bringing the Past Back to the Present with *The Book of Virtues*

William Bennett was acutely aware of the numerous changes to American life and culture during the 1990s. To the conservative Republican who had first entered public life under the Reagan administration, the various social, cultural, and political transformations to morality were not simply unsettling but shocking. In what has become an oft-quoted comment, for instance, he characterized the new tabloid talk genre in general and *The Ricki Lake Show* in particular as "cheap, demeaning, and immoral" and likened the program to "the moral equivalent of watching a train wreck" (qtd in Philo 78). Bennett likewise railed against the growing acceptance of gays and lesbians. On the ABC television show *This Week* in November 1997, he declared that given the proliferation of HIV/AIDS among gay men, homosexuality "takes 30 years off your life" (qtd Olson, par 1). Although his statistics were not accurate,[4] he reiterated them in an editorial that appeared in the November 24, 1997, issue of the *Weekly Standard*. Finally, Bennett decried the increasingly popular new genre of hip-hop music. In 1995, Bennett led a protest—with C. Delores Tucker—over the lack of regulation in the music industry and the glorification of sex and violence in gangsta rap. Targeting the media mogul Time Warner—the parent company for Ice T's recording of "Cop Killer"—Bennett and his cohort launched an advertising campaign highlighting the numerous indecent messages that they argued permeated this popular genre of music and protesting its exceedingly easy access to the nation's children (Ramstad). The former NEH chairman framed these artists and the companies who distributed their albums as engaging in nothing less than an assault on decency, taste, and values (Ramstad).

In Bennett's *The Index of Leading Cultural Indicators*, which was first published in 1994 and then revised and re-released in 1999, he provided data and statistics to support these views. With an often histrionic tone, in the opening pages of the book he claimed that the United States was experiencing nothing less than a "unilateral moral disarmament" (Bennett *Index* 8). Bennett reported that from 1960 to 1993 "there was a 500 percent increase in violent crime; more than a 400 percent increase in illegitimate births; a tripling of the percentage of children living in single-parent homes . . . a doubling in the divorce rate; and a drop of seventy-five points in the SAT scores of high school students" (Bennett *Index* 8). On the basis of these and other similar statistics, the former drug czar concluded: "Over the past three decades we have experienced substantial social regression" (*Index* 8). Unless changes occurred, he worried that the United States would be defeated, not by external threats like communism, but by internal ones "in the realm of behavior, habits, beliefs, and mores—matters that in our time often travel under the banner of 'values'" (*Index* 7). In remarks that typified those that he made throughout the decade, the former secretary of education asserted in a 1994 speech: "This country needs to shift its values. We need a kind of moral . . . revival" (qtd in Coyle A17).

The Book of Virtues was intended to inspire this kind of rejuvenation or, at least, instill virtues that the author believed were eroding at an alarming rate in the final decade of the twentieth century.[5] Bennett announced this intention directly on the opening page of the introduction: "This book, then, is a 'how to' book for moral literacy. If we want our children to possess the traits of character we most admire, we need to teach them what those traits are and why they deserve both admiration and allegiance" (11). Interestingly, Bennett insisted that his collection was not a primer on current hot-button ethical issues: "The reader scanning this book may notice that it does not discuss issues like nuclear war, abortion, creationism, or euthanasia. This may come as a disappointment to some" (12). Such comments notwithstanding, his text is clearly a product of the transformations to American life and morality that have taken place during the 1990s. Near the middle of his prefatory comments Bennett remarks: "Moorings and anchors come in handy in life, moral anchors and moorings have never been more necessary" (12). Lest this comment go unnoticed or be unclear, he reiterates it on the following page. Bennett reminds readers that The Book of Virtues will not address abortion, homosexuality, or euthanasia, but he clarifies his purpose: "I would add, a person who is morally literate will be immeasurably better equipped than a morally illiterate person to reach a reasoned and ethically defensible position on these tough issues" (13).

In keeping with Bennett's longtime interest in halting the radical transformations to American life that occurred during the 1960s and were being revived again in the 1990s, his book likewise seeks to roll back recent social, cultural, and political developments. The Book of Virtues has the dual purpose of not simply offering children lessons in old-time morality but doing so via a slate of old-time, historical readings—before the advent of multiculturalism and the transformations to the canon of Western literature, history, and philosophy; the book strives to "help anchor our children in their culture, its history and traditions" (12).

Ironically though, in teaching children about so-called classic texts and timeless morals, Bennett draws on stories, tales, and authors that offer a reductive, problematic, and even misleading view of morality. Bennett may long to return to the seemingly simpler eras of the late nineteenth and early twentieth centuries, but the child readers of his anthology cannot avoid living amid the complexities, ambiguities, and quandaries that permeate the eve of a new millennium. As a result, Bennett's book becomes not so much a "how-to" guide for moral living, but—in keeping with the antimodernist tendency of conservatism—a text about "how-not-to" face many pressing social problems and contentious cultural challenges of the late-twentieth century. For Bennett, who has long made a case that the purpose of studying the humanities is the opportunity to grapple with difficult questions like "What is justice? What should be loved? What deserves to be defended?" (Bennett *To Reclaim* 16), this stance seems contradictory, at best. Indeed, to the next generation of children who are going to inherit a morally complicated world, the simplistic lessons in *The Book of Virtues* are even less relevant, applicable, and useful. Providing a largely homogeneous view of culture and a series of moral maxims that are as neat and tidy as they are impractical and unrealistic, the lessons offered in *The Book of Virtues* are not simply unhelpful; they may even be harmful, painting a portrait of the world that does more harm than good.

THE CONSERVATIVE MESSAGE EMBODIED in Bennett's *The Book of Virtues* is evident before readers even open the book. The cover image that Bennett selected for his text is not simply traditional, but retrograde. Drawn by contemporary illustrator Mark Summers, it presents two little children—a boy and a girl—sitting in front of a large book. Their backs are turned to the viewer, and the duo appears to be sitting on the floor. Both children are white, seemingly middle-class, and are dressed in clothing that is as cute as it is unmistakably gender-appropriate. The little girl, who is on the left of the illustration, is wearing a polka-dot green dress with white trim at the neck and sleeves, and matching knee-socks with tan leather shoes. Her bobbed red hair is tied up with a ribbon, and her white bloomers peek out the bottom of her dress. Meanwhile, the little boy on the right side of the image has an equally traditional appearance. He is wearing a brick-colored plaid shirt with a wide sailor-type collar and tan knickers. Black patent leather shoes with what appear to be spats and brick-colored socks complete the outfit. Both figures have an exceedingly stiff posture, and it is significant that, although they are both reading from the same book, they are doing so neither collaboratively nor cooperatively; instead, with their backs angled away from one another, each child examines a different side of the page.

As these details indicate, both figures embody a traditional, stereotypical, and even idyllic representation of children. Indeed, the boy and girl seem more in keeping with images of childhood from the early twentieth century than from the final decade before the new millennium. The style in which the figures are drawn—hyper-realistic engravings on scratchboard—is likewise more reminiscent of the images found in print media from the 1930s or 1940s than the illustrated narratives for children populating the 1990s. Even the book that the two figures are reading in the cover image is a historical throwback. With its large format and oversized first letter on each page, the text more closely resembles an illuminated manuscript from the medieval era than a children's book from the eve of the new millennium. When these details are combined with both the

morality-driven title of *The Book of Virtues* and its colossal length—exceeding
eight hundred pages—the volume reveals how it has taken its cue not from the
time in which it is published, but from a bygone era.

Opening *The Book of Virtues* and examining its selections confirms these
initial impressions. Bennett does not include a comprehensive table of contents,
but the way in which his book draws on poems, stories, speeches, and fables
largely from canonical historical sources quickly becomes clear; "its contents
have been defined in part by my attempt to present some material, most
of which is drawn from the corpus of Western Civilization, that American
schoolchildren, once upon a time, knew by heart" (15). Bennett, aware of the
largely traditional range and in some ways even archaic style of many selections included in his book, comments in the introduction, "I know that some
of these stories will strike some contemporary sensibilities as too simple, too
corny, too old-fashioned" (13). However, in a remark that is difficult not to read
in light of the influence of multiculturalism and debates over the changing
nature of the canon during the 1990s, he notes: "But they will not seem so to a
child, especially if he or she has never seen them before. And I believe that if
adults take this book and read it in a quiet place, alone, *away from distorting
standards*, they will find themselves enjoying some of this old, simple, 'corny'
stuff" (13; my emphasis). Later, Bennett reiterates these sentiments with
regard to questions of morality rather than simply aesthetics: "This book
reminds the reader of a time—not long ago—when the verities were the moral
verities. It is thus a kind of antidote to some of the distortions of the age in
which we all live" (14).

This description is more than accurate. *The Book of Virtues* is comprised
almost entirely of so-called classic texts illustrating the ten qualities that
Bennett identifies as "fundamental traits of character" which the "vast majority
of Americans share" (12).[6] Moreover, the specific lessons about individual
morality and daily conduct that these sections spotlight are equally conservative. The opening section on Self-Discipline, for instance, contains messages
concerning table manners, controlling one's temper, and cleanliness. Likewise,
a later segment on Responsibility offers exhortations about the duty to obey
one's parents, perform one's chores, and be resourceful.

To convey these lessons, Bennett offers what one reviewer aptly character-
ized as a "who's who of Western literature" (Cullum 601). He includes poems
and stories by writers such as Longfellow, Aesop, Tennyson, Hawthorne,
Shakespeare, Dickinson, Kipling, Tolstoy, Fitzgerald, Whittier, Blake, Faulkner,
Chaucer, the Brontë sisters, Twain, Pope, Stevenson, Emerson, Dickens, Goethe,
Frost, Defoe, and Yeats. He incorporates philosophical treatises from Aristotle,
Bacon, and Plato. He reprints speeches, letters, and accounts from historical and
political figures, including Jefferson, Washington, Madison, Lincoln, Tocqueville,
Revere, Churchill, and Roosevelt. He reprints fairy and folk tales, such as Jack

and the Beanstalk, Hansel and Gretel, and William Tell. He retells well-known Greco-Roman myths, like the story of Hercules, Odysseus, and Androcles and the Lion, along with writings by classical figures including Cicero and Archimedes. Finally, he features passages drawn from both the Old and the New Testaments of the Bible, including the gospels of Matthew, Luke, and John, as well as the books of Daniel, Job, Samuel, and Ruth.

Most passages are merely excerpts of the original and thus do not exceed four or five pages; many are much shorter. Finally, they are arranged by increasing level of difficulty, with the simplest verses and tales appearing first and the most challenging and complex ones at the end. Bennett did not mean for his book to be read cover-to-cover: "It is, rather, a book for browsing, for marking favorite passages, for memorizing pieces here and there" (Bennett 15). Above all, though, it is meant as "a long-term companion for the child, to be put away only when one's intellect has surpassed the likes of William Faulkner and C. S. Lewis" (Collum 601). To ensure that children glean the correct moral message from the material, Bennett offers prefatory comments about not only each virtue but also each selection. Most remarks are short, such as this solitary clause that serves as the prologue to Laura E. Richard's poem "To the Little Girl Who Wiggles": "In which we learn to sit still" (32).

In spite of the seemingly large number of different writers and texts that appear in *The Book of Virtues*, the range, variety, and diversity of voices that are represented is limited. In the introduction Bennett insists that his book "is for everybody—all children, of all political and religious backgrounds, and it speaks to them on a more fundamental level than race, sex, and gender. It addresses them as human beings—as moral agents" (13). However, the text is comprised overwhelmingly of historical selections from white, middle-class Europeans. In short, the choices are almost exclusively from the canon of so-called "classic" works of Western civilization that was coming under increasing attack or at least scrutiny during the 1990s in light of new interest in multiculturalism. Indeed, few of the narratives were written or released after the 1970s, and the most recent selection is taken from a January 1982 article in the *Washington Post* ("Instant Hero," 505–507). Similarly, the first selection by an African American appears on page 253, with an excerpt from Frederick Douglass's "The Conscience of the Nation Must Be Roused." All told, in a volume that contains more than five hundred selections from almost as many different individuals, it includes only six that are either written by African Americans or can be connected to African American literature, history, and culture: Martin Luther King's "Letter from a Birmingham Jail" (258–262), a selection from Booker T. Washington's "Up from Slavery" (404–408), an account of Rosa Parks's momentous refusal to move to the back of the bus on December 1, 1955 (489–492), a brief biography of Harriet Tubman (501–504), the plantation spiritual "Go Down, Moses" (560–562), and King's speech "I Have a Dream" (572–576).

A similar modus operandi applies to passages concerning Native American literature, culture, and tradition. Bennett's huge volume contains only fifteen pages about the indigenous peoples of North America: "The Story of Scarface," a Blackfoot Indian tale, by Amy Cruse (546–552); "The Indian Cinderella," described generically as a "North American Indian tale," by Cyrus Macmillan (612–614); "The Boy Who Went to the Sky," a Cherokee story by Carolyn Sherwin Bailey (634–635); and "Thunder Falls," a narrative from the Kickapoo Indians, by Allan Macfarlan (686–671). Even more problematic, not one of these tales is written by men and women who—as far as I could discern after examining both past and present biographies—are members of the specific tribe from which the story is taken or of any American Indian tribe.[7] Finally, their retellings are not even contemporary. In the case of "The Story of Scarface" and "Thunder Falls," for instance, they are culled from books written during the 1920s. Scholars and historians of American Indian folklore agree that there is no single definitive version of tales like Scarface; instead, these tales exist in multiple forms that belie their root in an oral tradition (see Schenck 495). Bennett's reliance on versions told by white American and Canadian writers from the early twentieth century rather than those presented by indigenous storytellers from the late twentieth century is questionable; thus, while *The Book of Virtues* includes facets from American Indian history, it acknowledges only white-authored versions of this history.

Meanwhile, the voices of Asian Americans and Latino/a Americans are virtually nonexistent—exclusions that place these men and women not only outside the canon of "great" writers, thinkers, and storytellers but also outside the realm of being sources of virtue or morality. Selections by individuals from non-Western cultures are likewise just as scarce—omissions that firmly link traits like honesty, compassion, courage, loyalty, and friendship with Europe and the United States.[8] In his introduction Bennett claims, echoing numerous similar comments that he made while chair of the NEH and secretary of education, to "welcome our children to a common world" (12), but the unifying trait of the world that he envisions appears to be whiteness.

Bennett's offerings of many well-known Western fables, canonical stories from British and American literature, and classic tales from the annals of Greco-Roman mythology are themselves often equally problematic. The fairy tale "The Frog Prince" by the Grimm Brothers forms a poignant example. As Donald Haase has written, the version of the tale that appears in *The Book of Virtues*—either Bennett's own adaptation or one taken from an unidentified source—"diverges significantly . . . at that point where the Grimms' tale makes its unique, but problematic, turn—the transformation episode" (Haase 22). Haase explains: "In the Grimms' German text, of course, the angry princess finally rebels against the father's authority when the frog insists he be taken to bed. Grimm writes: 'This made the princess extremely angry, and after she picked him up, she threw him against the wall with all her might. 'Now you can have your rest, you nasty frog!' However, when he fell to the ground, he was no longer a frog but a prince. . . .'" (22). Bennett's text, however, modifies this scene drastically. In the version that appears in *The Book of Virtues*, the princess reacts in a radically different way to the frog's insistence that he be taken to bed: "He looked so sad, she suddenly felt ashamed. 'Father is right,' she thought. 'I must keep my promises.' She lifted him and gently dropped him onto a pillow" (626). Haase concedes that "many variants and American adaptations of this tale do replace the violent, disobedient act with a kiss or other alternative," yet he also notes that "such a princess as the one Bennett depicts—ashamed and a voluntary witness to her father's story—is certainly a rarity" (22).

More than simply a point of contention for specialists in German fairy tales, this alteration's larger implication undercuts Bennett's stated intention in *The Book of Virtues*: to offer lessons in traditional morality via traditional texts. The tacit change to "The Frog Prince," according to Haase, exposes "the contradiction between the cultural importance attributed to Grimms' stories because of their traditional authority and the ease with which they are ignored and substantively altered by those who revere them for that very authority" (22). In so doing, Bennett may invoke the "the classical name of Grimm," but he ironically "ignore[s] history and rewrite[s] tradition, inscribing [his] own values and meanings onto the very texts [he] purports to value for their traditional, unchanging truths" (Haase 22).[9]

These alterations are not limited to comparatively "light" literary fare like fairy tales; they also apply to "weightier" works of literature, such as the story of Ulysses. In the section dedicated to the virtue of Courage, Bennett excerpts a portion of the epic about the adventurer's encounter with Cyclops. The episode is far more complex than "simply a tale of virtue rewarded and vice punished," as Bennett's explanatory headnote suggests (Schulman, par 21). Miriam Schulman reminds us, "Ulysses must call on his courage [in this episode] because he has failed in some other moral dimension. Remember, before Polyphemus began making dinner out of Ulysses' men, the men had stolen into his cave and planned to carry off his cheese, and were, in fact, feasting on his food when he came home" (par 21). Bennett omits these contextual details, however, and he thereby erroneously casts the story as one of straightforward noble courage in the face of seemingly unwarranted discord. Schulman explains, "Children—especially in conversation with their parents—can learn from [the original] tale something about how wrongs proliferate as well as how cleverness can be a form of courage" (par 21)—a lesson that is lost in Bennett's version.[10]

In other passages, Bennett revises not simply the original text but also its moral message. In the introduction, the author expresses his belief that stories must present clear and unequivocal lessons to be instructive to young people: "Children must have at their disposal a stock of examples illustrating what we see to be right and wrong, good and bad examples illustrating that, in many instances, what is morally right and wrong can indeed be known and promoted" (12). Although most of the stories present good behavior that is rightly rewarded, he also includes tales where bad behavior is swiftly and soundly punished. On the surface, Bennett's schema seems like a fail-safe method for imparting moral lessons. But, as Miriam Schulman has aptly pointed out, "There's only one problem with this approach: it only works in poetry" (par 14). . . . " Because children, like the rest of us, live in an ethically complex world, they need stories where the moral landscape more closely reflects the ambiguities of their own lives" (par 17). Unfortunately, *The Book of Virtues* does not reflect this reality. Akin to its interest in going back to a time when there was a concrete and unquestioned Western canon, the book also attempts to offer concrete and unquestioned moral certainties, which were arguably never really that certain in the past and are surely no longer steadfast amid the complications, complexities, and upheavals of the postmodern world. Bennett's collection "prefers an easy unity of feeling to the hard puzzles of moral reflection" (Nissbaum 38). In many ways, Bennett's desire for explicit, clear-cut morals helps to account for his heavy reliance on sentimental poems from the nineteenth and early twentieth centuries. For example, there is little ambiguity in the message from these lines by Edgar Guest:

> It matters not what goal you seek
> Its secret here reposes
> You've got to dig from week to week
> To get Results and Roses (389)

If some moral lessons in *The Book of Virtues* are too reductive or simplistic, then others, ironically, seem lacking in virtue. Hilaire Belloc's poems "Rebecca, Who Slammed the Door for Fun and Perished Miserably" (26–27), "Jim, Who Ran Away from his Nurse, and was Eaten by a Lion" (33), and "Matilda, Who Told Lies, and Was Burned to Death" (607–608) form a collective case in point. A reader who is familiar with contemporary children's literature might be tempted to say that these verses are reminiscent of popular author Edward Gorey, who is known for his darkly gothic humor in lines such as "A is for Amy who Fell Down the Stairs" from *The Gashlycrumb Tinies;* however, because Belloc's poems were written during the nineteenth century, they are devoid of Gorey's twentieth-century sense of play and irony. As a result, they send both a clear and a macabre message to children: misbehave and punishment will be as swift as it is certain.

The rules in life are not always that simple or uncomplicated. Given the frequency with which boys and girls utter the phrase "That's not fair," they are acutely aware that sometimes good behavior does not get rewarded while bad behavior may go unnoticed or remain unpunished. Similarly, many young people have realized that hard work does not always result in success and that success comes to some without hard work. Because of differing levels of personal aptitude or social access, an individual may diligently "dig from week to week" and still not "get Results and Roses." Meanwhile, another person who possesses more innate ability or simply better social, cultural, or familial opportunities may achieve the proverbial beautiful garden with little or no effort.

This myopia recurs in numerous scenes and situations. The message conveyed by the passage "The Chest of Broken Glass" (202–204) grossly over-simplifies family dynamics. The selection suggests that "if adults do not take care of their aged parents, they can have no reasons for their neglect except sheer selfishness, because the realities of caring for elders and the chronically ill do not intrude in this magical world" (Porter 896). Meanwhile, stories that represent the working poor are arguably the most two-dimensional: "A hard-working family man who falls ill can expect to be cared for by elves, thus eliminating the need for health insurance" (Porter 896). Consequently, Bennett's book repeatedly sends the message: "We need not worry too much about the poor, because they themselves admit that they are happy just as they are. Alternatively, the experience of poverty is prettified beyond recognition ('No one imagined what sweet visions she had had, or how glorious she had gone with her grandmother to enter upon the joys of a new year'—this, said of the death of a child from exposure)" (Porter 896). In these and other instances, Bennett not only greatly underestimates the intellectual capacity of his readers, but he also does them a disservice. Schulman points out the folly of disallowing complicated situations: "Grappling with morally problematic issues like this has provided grist for generations of ethical thinkers" (par 24). By either omitting morally complex stories or including only bowdlerized versions that abolish these ambiguities, Bennett denies his readers a chance to participate in this tradition, an ironic twist given the author's oft-stated "conviction that rigorous thinking is the right way for a human being to respond to the mysteries of life" (qtd in Nussbaum 38).[11]

The historical era in which many of the pieces reprinted in *The Book of Virtues* were originally written leads to other problems besides simply the "corniness" that Bennett mentions in his introduction. Appearing before the advent of the modern-day feminist and civil rights movements, some contain language that may seem sexist and even racist to contemporary readers. The refrain of Sam Walter Foss's "The House by the Side of the Road," for instance, discusses the importance of being "a friend to man" (305). Meanwhile, P. T. Barnum's "Truth in Advertising" (655–667) discusses how one British manu-facturer found a way to cleverly market its goods: by having agents write "Buy Warren's Blacking, 30 Strand, London" in large letters on the side of one of the pyramids in Ghiza, Egypt. Although Bennett prefaces this passage with the parenthetical aside "Barnum's environmental and cultural sensitivities apparently had not caught up with his concern for the truth," the story is presented positively as an amusing anecdote about a daring and eminently successful marketing stunt.

Moreover, other selections, such as Theodore Roosevelt's "In Praise of the Strenuous Life" (416–418), have a problematic gender and racial vision. As T. J. Jackson Lears has written, the twenty-fifth president's advocacy for active physicality emerged out of a concern that middle- and upper-class white boys had become too weak, effeminate, and even "overly civilized." As a result, he encouraged them to embrace their primal instincts toward physicality. Through rough-and-tumble athletics like football, wrestling, and boxing, Roosevelt believed "a delicate, indoor race" would receive "a saving touch of honest, old-fashioned barbarism" (qtd in Lears 108). Although Bennett praises Roosevelt's commitment to "rigorous physical exercise," he overlooks the way in which his cult of the strenuous life was a product of the era's concern over the perceived deterioration of white male racial stock. "In Praise of the Strenuous Life" was, at its core, an outline for a eugenic practice that was designed to bolster the white male race during a time of fears about racial weakness and possibly even future white race suicide.[12]

Consistency of tone and continuity of message are other features with which *The Book of Virtues* often struggle. For instance, although Bennett identifies Compassion as a virtue—and includes a lengthy section with passages devoted to compassion toward people and animals—the lessons offered by selections in other segments contradict this message. In the section on Work, for instance, Bennett retells Aesop's fable about the ant and the grasshopper. One cold day in winter, a poor hungry grasshopper arrives at the anthill and begs the ants to give her a few grains of corn, "'For,' she said, 'I'm simply starving'" (355). When the ants ask her what she was doing all summer that she wasn't able to collect a store of food, the grasshopper confesses, "I was so busy singing that I hadn't the time" (355). Upon hearing this reason, the ants not only refuse to help, but also offer the following judgmental sneer: "'If you spent the summer singing,' replied the ants, 'you can't do better than spend the winter dancing.' And they chuckled and went on with their work" (355).

Other selections encourage children to be unquestioningly obedient or, at least, not to challenge parental—and especially patriarchal—authority. The poem "Table Rules for Little Folks" offers a rather authoritarian view of appropriate dinnertime deportment. Together with offering boys and girls guidance in polite behavior at mealtime—"I must not scold, nor whine, nor pout, / Nor move my chair nor plate about"—the anonymous work also conveys a more severe message about the place of the child within the family and, by extension, society as a whole: "I must not speak a useless word, / For children should be seen, not heard" (42). In this way, although Bennett frequently asserts that his book is intended to improve and even empower children, he paradoxically defines the appropriate status of young people as one of obedience and subservience.

Perhaps the most disturbing message in *The Book of Virtues* about the power relationship between parents and children comes from a letter by F. Scott Fitzgerald. Writing to his daughter Frances, the Jazz Age author of *The Great Gatsby* informs her: "if you call me 'Pappy' again I am going to take the White Cat and beat his bottom *hard, six times for every time you are impertinent*. Do you react to that?" (Bennett 225; italics in original). This threat of violence and use of the family pet as a proxy for it is disturbing. Bennett prefaces Fitzgerald's letter with the comment, "In this letter we see the molding of character: a father gently but explicitly telling his daughter what her duties are" (225).

The Many Books of Virtue: Popular Success, Collection Sequels, Picture Book Spin-Offs

In a detail that says much about Bennett's views regarding the state of the nation's morality in the 1990s when the book was written and released, *Virtues* was intended for an adult as well as a child audience. Bennett indicates the dual focus or—as critics of children's literature would characterize it—cross-written nature of his collection on the opening page of the introduction: "The purpose of this book is to show parents, teachers, students, and children what the virtues look like, what they are in practice, how to recognize them, and how they work" (11). Many of the headnotes that discuss the virtue featured in that section are addressed to adults. An early paragraph in his discussion of Friendship, for example, states flatly: "Every parent knows how crucial the choice of friends is for every child" (269). Likewise, many selections contained in the book itself offer moral guidance for mothers and fathers as well as for their children. The very first selection in the section dedicated to the virtue of Responsibility, for instance, is directed at parents. In prefatory comments about "Over the Meadow" by Olive A. Wadsworth, Bennett makes the intended audience clear: "This poem shows us parents' first responsibility: the nurture of the young" (187). A later passage, C. S. Lewis's "Men Without Chests," reiterates this message with regard to instruction in morality. Bennett argues that the excerpt highlights "the responsibility of adults in educating the young" (263). In a comment intended to openly chide parents while simultaneously offering a tacit commentary on the radical transformations to American life and morality occurring during the 1990s, Bennett notes how in "Men Without Chests" Lewis "makes the case that if we fail to pass along specific standards of right and wrong, of what is worthwhile and worthless, admirable or ignoble, then we must share blame for the consequent failings of character" (263). As these features indicate, children present not the only segment of the population in need of instruction on virtues; in Bennett's view, amidst the current cultural climate, so are adults.

By all estimations, the nation overwhelmingly agreed. In November 1993 when *The Book of Virtues* was first released, Bennett was not the only one who was concerned about the radical transformations to American life and morality. A poll conducted in April 1994 by *U.S. News and World Report* revealed that 84 percent of individuals surveyed believed that "our government would be better if policies were more directed by moral values" (Barone 50). Public figures on both the left and the right side of the political aisle echoed such sentiments. Conservative columnist Cal Thomas said the current era was engaged in "a civil war for the soul of the nation" (A9). Meanwhile, the more left-leaning *Washington Post*, also lamenting the demise of longstanding morals, commented in an article about the rise of cheating, drug use, and violence among the nation's children: "Somewhere, somehow . . . the traditional value system got disconnected for a disturbing number of America's next generation" (Oldenburg D5).

Given this climate, *The Book of Virtues* found a receptive critical and commercial audience. The book received overwhelmingly favorable reviews by right-leaning and mainstream print venues alike. In a comment that was reprinted as a back-cover blurb, the *Washington Post* said of Bennett's collection: "Parents and teachers can, indeed should, use this book." Likewise, Larry King touted it as "a very readable and very important book." *The Book of Virtues* also enjoyed strong commercial sales. Despite its hefty length, high price tag (selling for almost $30) and the fact that it contained—as Bennett often publicly joked—"no photos and no sex" (qtd in Duin A2), the collection appeared on the *New York Times* best-seller list for more than one hundred weeks and sold more than two million copies by October 1995—less than two years after its release ("PBS Becomes," par 24). As Stephen Goode has written, these statistics "underscored the interest among literate Americans for old-fashioned moral tales" (6).

While many individuals who purchased copies of *The Book of Virtues* were parents and grandparents, an equally large number were teachers and school librarians. Almost immediately after Bennett released his text, it began to be used in elementary classrooms for character education. In 1995, classroom use of *The Book of Virtues* had become so pervasive that Thomas Morley, the former school district superintendent of the Sugar-Salem and Cassia County school system in Idaho, wrote *Discipline Through Virtue*. Morley designed this companion guide, which received financial backing from Lockheed Idaho Martin Technologies, to help teachers quickly and easily find selections in Bennett's book that addressed a specific problem behavior, from bullying and cleanliness to drug use and interrupting when someone else is talking. One principal said of Morley's companion text and, by extension, Bennett's original book: "It should be on every teacher's desk across the United States" ("Schools Give" A7).

The success of *The Book of Virtues* inspired Bennett to launch a series of sequel and spin-off texts.[13] In 1995, Bennett published *The Moral Compass: Stories for a Life's Journey*, a follow-up tome to his 1993 original. The new book embodied, as Bennett explains in its introduction, a "second collection of moral stories" that he "agreed to do . . . only at the urging of readers who loved the material they found in *The Book of Virtues*" (13). *The Moral Compass* was also more than eight hundred pages in length, and it likewise made the *New York Times* best-seller list by selling more than 550,000 copies in its first year of release (Duin A2).

The public appetite for morality-themed literature, however, was still not satiated. Also in 1995, Bennett released *The Children's Books of Virtues*. Based on his 1993 original book, this shortened version featured only about thirty different passages to represent Bennett's ten virtues and also contained color illustrations by Michael Hague. The text was followed by an array of similarly-themed spin-offs: *The Book of Virtues for Young People* (1997), *The Children's Book of Heroes* (1997), *The Children's Book of America* (1998), *The Children's Book of Faith* (2000), *The Children's Treasury of Virtues* (2000), *The Children's Book of Home and Family* (2002), and *The Book of Virtues for Girls and Boys* (2008). The five books in the middle of this list were illustrated by Hague, but all of them adopted the same format: passages from poetry, stories, speeches, and history illustrate certain personal qualities or character traits. Several of these texts appeared on various best-sellers lists, including the *New York Times*, *USA Today*, and *Publisher's Weekly*. In addition, many were released on audio CD.

Given Bennett's former disdain for television, it is ironic that he adapted his best-selling book into a cartoon series. The program was privately funded and aired on PBS from 1996 through 1999.[14] *Adventures from the Book of Virtues* featured central human characters Zach Nichols and Annie Redfeather, an American Indian, along with their animal friends—Aristotle the woodchuck, Plato the buffalo, and Socrates the bobcat. Each segment retold various stories, poems, and historical tales that illustrate the virtue that forms the theme for the show, such as the story of William Tell for courage and Rudyard Kipling's poem "If" for perseverance. A well-known and sometimes surprising collection of celebrities voiced many passages. Episodes that aired during the program's first season, for example, offered the voices of Kathy Najimy, Paula Poundstone, George Segal, Elijah Wood, Tim Curry, Pam Dawber, and Mark Hamill (Moore 5E). Meanwhile, later years showcased the voices of Ed Asner, Kathy Bates, Shelley Duvall, Malcolm Jamal-Warner, and Mark Harmon (Moore 5E). *Adventures from the Book of Virtues* originally aired in the United States and Great Britain, but reruns are now broadcast in more than sixty-five countries around the world ("Biography"). In early 2008, three episodes—*Adventures in Honesty*, *Adventures in Courage*, and *Adventures in Faith*—were released on DVD by Warner Home Video.

Echoing the commercial trajectory of many other successful contemporary children's books and television shows, Bennett's texts inspired various toy tie-ins and merchandising spin-offs. As one marketing magazine reported, *Book of Virtues*–themed "story books, coloring books, posters, magnets, activity kits, learning toys and a series of home videos related to the PBS series" appeared on store shelves in time for Christmas 1996 ("PBS Becomes," par 9). Over time, this list increased. In 1997, the conservative toy manufacturer Family Co. released plush doll versions of the five central characters from the *Adventures from the Book of Virtues* series on PBS. As journalist Rosland Briggs noted, "Each comes with a booklet of stories and a certificate of achievement so children can place stickers by each value that they achieve" (13). Likewise, Patch Products offered a Virtues Bingo game based on the cartoon show that promoted the cultivation of desirable personality traits like honesty and responsibility. Finally, restaurant chains like Wendy's and Chick-Fil-A featured an array of *Virtues*-themed toys as promotional give-aways in their kids' meals. Starting in 1998 and extending through 2000, they included everything from playing cards, wristbands, and mini-books to posters, puzzles, and window clings (see Boyles 43–46). The sheer number of these merchandising tie-ins prompted journalist Joshua Green to remark that *The Book of Virtues* has "spawned an entire cottage industry" (par 3).

In an equally important implication, the popularity of Bennett's book also inaugurated an entirely new subgenre of conservative-themed children's books. Although *The Book of Virtues* was not the first text for young readers that had a traditionalist viewpoint or Republican political flavor, it was, by far, the most famous. Bennett's book demonstrated that right-leaning texts for children were not simply socially needed but also had the potential for commercial success. Moreover, with its emphasis on issues like conservative moral values, conventional views of the nuclear family, and Judeo-Christian religious beliefs, *The Book of Virtues* became an emblematic prelude to much conservative-themed children's literature and served as the benchmark for future texts. In this regard, the otherwise backward-looking collection embodied a forward-looking one— foretelling the release and predicting the subject matter of many subsequent narratives.

"One Man's Virtue Is Another Man's Vice": William Bennett's Moral Rules—and Moral Relativism

A plurality of Americans may have agreed during the 1990s that the nation needed to return to many of the morals presented in *The Book of Virtues*, but few could agree on which values or whose morals to adopt. Throughout the decade, bitter debates arose over the various ways of viewing, defining, and interpreting these terms. When an individual called for a need to revive "family values," for example, did they mean only a traditional nuclear family, or did their conception of family include single parents, blended families, and same-sex couples? Likewise, when citizens talked about young people becoming unmoored from the anchor provided by faith, did they mean only those provided by Judeo-Christianity, or did they also include religious precepts embodied by Hinduism, Islam, and Native American spiritual traditions?

Given the differing answers to these questions and the passion with which individuals often held their specific beliefs, Michelle Mahoney noted the dilemma in a 1995 *Denver Post* article: "Nothing ignites the tinderbox of public debate in America these days like the 'V-word.' Values. American values. Family values" (par 1). Meanwhile, fellow commentator Rochelle L. Stanfield was even more blunt in her remarks about the subject dominating the sociopolitical climate: "It's values, stupid. But, which values? Whose values?" (1235).

Although William Bennett has long claimed to believe in timeless moral absolutes—or "verities," as he calls them in his introduction to *The Book of Virtues*—his own actions demonstrate their subjective, contested, and even individualistic nature. Both before the release of his 1993 book for children and in the years since its publication, readers have questioned his specific values as well as the way in which they sometimes seem more suitable for that moment than for all time. The first of these incidents occurred only weeks after Bennett became director of the Office of National Drug Control Policy. While appearing as a guest on *Larry King Live* on June 15, 1989, a caller frustrated by the growing epidemic of crack cocaine use suggested that we "behead the damn drug dealers," as laws in some Middle Eastern countries allow (qtd in Hawkins). Bennett amazingly agreed and told King: "What the caller suggests is morally plausible," but "it's legally difficult" (qtd in Hawkins). Bennett later backtracked to say that he would simply support capital punishment for habitual drug offenders. Nonetheless, such remarks stand in stark contrast to his assertions only a few years later in *The Book of Virtue* about the importance of cultivating traits like compassion.

In the years since the release of *The Book of Virtues*, several events cast increasing doubt on Bennett's commitment to moral absolutes and his own possession of allegedly timeless virtues. During the 2000 presidential election, for example, political commentators accused Bennett of being inconsistent in applying standards of morality. Although he vociferously attacked the Democratic nominee Al Gore for being a "habitual liar" in an op-ed piece in the *Wall Street Journal* ("Lifetime" A26), he overlooked George W. Bush's numerous indiscretions. These included—as political blogger Rebecca Knight usefully summarized—"possible drug use, a drunk driving record kept hidden until a few days prior to the 2000 election, being deceptive when questioned, avoiding Vietnam, and possible perjury in a funeral home scandal" (par 25). When critics pointed out both the political partisanship and personal hypocrisy inherent in not chastising the Republican nominee for his own failures of responsibility and transparency, Bennett responded that these issues would only be a problem if Bush had lied about them (Bennett "Answer" A14).

The most damaging event for Bennett, however, occurred in May 2003, when news broke that he was a longtime high-stakes gambler who frequented casinos in Las Vegas, Atlantic City, and other locales. Journalist Joshua Green reported in a *Washington Monthly* article: "A review of one 18-month stretch of gambling showed him visiting casinos, often for two or three days at a time (and enjoying a line of credit of at least $200,000 at several of them)" (par 6). The article revealed how Bennett "prefers the high limit room where he's less likely to be seen and where he can play the $500-a-pull slots" (par 6). Green's discussion of Bennett's gambling habits closes with what is perhaps the most eye-opening detail: "The documents show that in one two-month period, Bennett wired more than $1.4 million to cover losses" (par 6).

Although gambling, of course, is not illegal, many saw it as being out of step with Bennett's position as a spokesperson for morality and his advocacy for traits like self-restraint. Indeed, he advised children in *The Book of Virtues*: "We should know that too much of anything, even a good thing, may prove to be our undoing . . . [W]e need . . . to set boundaries on our appetites" (22).[15] With various sources reporting that the policy-maker-turned-children's-author had lost in excess of eight million dollars gambling over the years, his many homiletic messages about responsibility and self-control seemed hypocritical at best and disingenuous at worst.[16]

Two years later, in September 2005, Bennett again found himself on morally questionable ground that undermined his position as a guardian of virtue, let alone universal moral absolutes. During a discussion with a caller on his *Morning in America* radio program, he remarked: "I do know that it's true that if you wanted to reduce crime, you could . . . abort every black baby in this country, and your crime rate would go down" (*Morning*). Although Bennett conceded that doing so "would be an impossible, ridiculous, and morally reprehensible thing to do," he nonetheless reiterated "but your crime rate would go down" (*Morning*).

CONTEMPORARY PHILOSOPHER LORRAINE CODE wrote in an essay that was published around the same time as *The Book of Virtues*: "Objectivity requires taking subjectivity into account" (206). This seemingly paradoxical statement stresses the importance of considering the particularity of one's own subject position when attempting to make an impartial decision. Rather than trying to ignore our beliefs, background, and attitudes, Code urges individuals to be mindful of them because they can produce biases and generate blind spots.

William Bennett is quick to take his own personal situation or political position into account when determining his moral decisions, but he is far less willing to concede the particularity of others. Commentator Jean Porter remarked, "We all may agree that it is good to be compassionate, but it does not follow that we agree on what it means to be compassionate here and now. One person's courage is another person's rashness, and one person's prudence is another person's small-minded caution" (896). Given the subjectivity inherent in any seemingly objective value position, Porter asserted: "Once we attempt to translate general virtues into a set of specific ideas about how people should conduct their lives, it is inevitable that a good deal of controversy and, yes, political content will be introduced" (896). In the introduction to *The Book of Virtues*, Bennett claims "the task of teaching moral literacy and forming character is not political in the usual meaning of the term" (13), but he knows better. And so do many of his readers, be they children or adults.

Historians Seymour Martin Lipset and Earl Raab noted: "Politics is the working of a pluralistic society. It is the constant process of negotiation through which conflicting interests come to live with each other" (12). For all of Bennett's affirmations about his strong patriotism, firm commitment to democracy, and unyielding defense of national values, he does not seek to foster political pluralism and encourage cultural heterogeneity. Given the content of *The Book of Virtues* along with his longstanding advocacy for a "common culture," he strives to institute, and, if necessary, even to enforce white, middle-class homogeneity. William Bennett is commonly known—and will likely be remembered—as a neoconservative, but he can perhaps more accurately be described as an adherent to what Joseph Gusfield and William B. Hixson have termed "status politics." A sentiment commonly found among right-leaning movements, a status group, in the words of Hixson, "consists of individuals who share 'a common culture in the form of standards of behavior' and who seek to control the distribution of prestige" (101). He continues: "what those engaged in 'status politics' seek therefore is the use of governmental power (often merely the symbols of legitimacy) to sanctify their subculture and to stigmatize others" (Hixson 101). From Bennett's political appointment as chair of the National Endowment of the Humanities back in the 1980s to his new career as an author of books for young people on the eve of the new millennium, he has worked to protect the societal status and affirm the hegemonic power of the traditional social, cultural, and political order.

In the end, the astounding commercial success of *The Book of Virtues* demonstrated the tremendous impact that the efforts of a concerned individual could have on furthering the conservative movement and advancing the Republican political agenda. This single book spearheaded by an individual did an astounding job of raising public awareness about the perceived decline in both moral standards and the literary canon, while it undoubtedly inspired others to join the crusade to combat such problems.

As the 1990s progressed, the seemingly small efforts of individual people became increasingly important to both the conservative movement and politics of the American right. Chapter 2 continues this theme while modifying it, as I examine the impact not of a high-profile figure like William Bennett but of an ordinary citizen: concerned mother Terri Birkett.

2

"I Speak for the National Oak Flooring Manufacturers Association"

Truax, the Anti-Green Movement, and the Corporate Production of Children's Literature

"How far will we go? How much will we pay?–
To keep a few minnows from dying away?"

—Terri Birkett, *Truax*

In 1971, Dr. Seuss published the book that biographers Judith and Neil Morgan indicate was not only his self-acknowledged favorite (211), but also his most overtly political: *The Lorax*. After penning narratives for young readers that addressed serious social issues like racial discrimination in *The Sneetches* (1961), tyranny in *Yertle the Turtle* (1958), and civil rights in *Horton Hears a Who!* (1954), Theodore Seuss Geisel's later "message" book concerned the topic of environmental destruction. In what has become a well-known plotline, *The Lorax* tells the story of an entrepreneur—the Once-ler—who cuts down Truffula trees to manufacture a bizarre-looking item called a Thneed from the plant's brightly colored tufts. Throughout, he ignores the conservationist pleas of the title character. The result is nothing short of environmental holocaust: the Once-ler's clear-cut logging tactics denude the landscape, while his Thneed factory pollutes the air, contaminates the water, and compels the local wildlife to leave in search of more habitable terrain.

Ruth MacDonald has called *The Lorax* Dr. Seuss's "most thinly-veiled . . . allegory" (148). The book is commonly read as a cautionary tale about the irresponsible plundering of natural resources by greedy corporations, the attendant need for environmental protections, and the excessive materialism and unnecessary consumption that typifies late twentieth-century American capitalism. As Ian Marshall has pointed out, the entrepreneurial Once-ler is represented in the illustrations by Seuss only as a pair of green hands—an apt symbol for avarice—while his name points to the ephemeral faddishness of his product, which is presumably used once and then tossed aside (8). Moreover, Lisa Lebduska observed that the word "Thneed" itself is a type of portmanteau for "the need," and thereby the term constitutes a further comment on the seemingly insatiable appetite of our consumer-driven modern society (174).

Published in the year following the first Earth Day celebration and within months of the founding of the environmental activist group Greenpeace, *The Lorax,* one of the first environmentalist children's books, has since become among the most well known. Jennifer Zicht has written that the narrative is both "one of the most poignant and sobering pieces of environmental literature" written for elementary-aged children and often "their first introduction to environmental education" (27). Even years after encountering Seuss's Lorax and Once-ler, young people remember the story and, more important, its moral. As a result, during the three decades since the author-illustrator released the text, *The Lorax* has become synonymous with conservation efforts while its title character's tagline "I speak for the trees" has become an oft-used catchphrase for environmental stewardship. A 2004 National Public Radio segment called the book's title character "a symbol for environmentalists" ("Talk of the Nation" 10 February 2004). The mustachioed figure has been adopted as the official mascot of American Forests, the nation's oldest nonprofit conservation group (Nel *Icon* 174). In addition, the Lorax's name and likeness have been used to encourage young people to partake in conservation efforts. In 1997, for example, American Forests launched its "Be a Lorax Helper" campaign, which urged kids to make "contributions that would pay for trees to be planted in 'the Dr. Seuss Lorax Forest'—actually the Francis Marion National Forest, located just north of Charleston, South Carolina" (Nel *Icon* 174). For these reasons, by the time that a bronze statue of the Lorax made its debut in Springfield, Massachusetts, to commemorate what would have been the author-illustrator's hundredth birthday, the connection between this character and the environmental movement was well known even to those who had never read the text.

Given the Lorax's interest in promoting conservation, cautioning about the hazards of frivolous consumerism, and encouraging children to be environmental stewards, one can hardly imagine him being cast as anything other than a positive character, a role model for children. However, for many corporations in general and individuals involved in the logging industry in particular, he is far less admirable; for these entities, the Lorax is often seen as a mustachioed menace. Formalized objections to Seuss's picture book first emerged in 1989 in Laytonville, California, when residents Judith and Bill Bailey attempted to get *The Lorax* removed from the required reading list at the public school where their son was in the second grade. The couple—who made their livelihood selling wholesale logging equipment—argued that *The Lorax* "criminalized the foresting industry" and sent a message to young children "to make sure another tree is never cut!" (qtd in Lebduska 170). To advocate for their position, the Baileys—along with several other families in the small logging town—took out advertisements in the local newspaper attacking *The Lorax* and calling for the book to be banned. One full-page ad read: 'Teachers [. . .] mock the timber industry, and some of our kids now are being brainwashed. [. . .] We've got to stop this crap right now!' (qtd in Nel *Icon* 175).

Seuss, a longtime resident of California, weighed in on the debate. In various articles and interviews, the then eighty-five-year-old author-illustrator argued that the message of his narrative was being misinterpreted or, at least, misunderstood: "*The Lorax* doesn't say lumbering is immoral. . . . I live in a house made of wood and write books printed on paper. It's a book about going easy on what we've got. It's antipollution and antigreed" (qtd in Morgan and Morgan 278). Lest any doubts remained, Seuss asserted that his 1971 picture book concerned "the waste of natural resources in the world in general, [and was] not a direct attack against specific industries in the USA" (qtd in Moje and Shyu 675).

The Laytonville School Board agreed, and the efforts by Judith and Bill Bailey to get *The Lorax* banned failed. However, the incident in California did not mark the end of such criticisms. In the early 1990s, Terri Birkett, a concerned mother, active school board member, and employee of the Stuart Flooring Company in southwestern Virginia, revived the controversy. Upon visiting a 4-H camp where her sons were enrolled, she was appalled to discover that the facility's counselors were using *The Lorax* "to preach a liberal environmental message to children" ("Enter, Truax" par 5). Although Birkett conceded, "I don't think Dr. Seuss really meant it to be an all-encompassing statement on losing forests as much as encouraging kids to be in favor of planting trees and things like that," she was nonetheless alarmed by the way in which the picture book "was used by people who had an environmental slant to scare kids that we were losing our trees" ("Enter, Truax" par 5). When this phenomenon was combined with the classic status of *The Lorax*, she concluded: "I felt like the children were being given information that was one-sided" (qtd in Moran A1).

Birkett resolved to take action. Learning, perhaps, from the previous failed effort to have *The Lorax* banned in California, or realizing instead that attempting to take a beloved picture book away from small children is not the best public-relations strategy, she opted for a different approach: Birkett decided to compose a rebuttal. Written with the same sing-songy style as Seuss's narrative and containing illustrations—drawn by first-time children's book artist Orrin Lundgren—that include Truffula-looking trees, Birkett called her book *Truax*. As its title implied, the text sought to correct what she felt were the misleading, harmful, and even damaging myths about the timber industry that have been disseminated by books like *The Lorax*. In Birkett's narrative, a kindly logger—the allegorically dubbed Truax—calmly explains to a hysterical and tantrum-throwing environmentalist who bears the equally symbolic name

"Guardbark" the importance of cutting timber, the many benefits provided by new growth forests, and the numerous essential items made by the wood products industry. By the end of the narrative, the Guardbark's fears have been so thoroughly assuaged that he has become an enthusiastic supporter of the logging industry.

Dr. Seuss's *The Lorax* was released by Random House, a publishing company that had no obvious stake in promoting its message of environmental conservation. If anything, in fact, as a for-profit company that sold books printed on paper made from felled trees, it was a participant in both the deforestation and the seemingly endless consumption criticized in *The Lorax*.[1] By contrast, *Truax* was printed by an organization that had a direct and unmistakable interest in disseminating its message: Birkett's book was released in 1995 by the National Oak Flooring Manufacturers Association (NOFMA).[2]

In this chapter I examine *Truax* as emblematic of two seemingly contrasting strains that had emerged within the conservative movement by the 1990s. The first is the bottom-up influence that grassroots efforts by individuals, like concerned mother and first-time author Birkett, had in advancing the movement's social, cultural, and political agenda. As Sara Diamond has noted, the 1990s witnessed a surge in the number of ordinary right-leaning men and women "who ran for elected office for the first time in their lives, [and] who took charge of local school boards" (2). With varying degrees of success, these individuals effected numerous societal changes, from banning what they saw as objectionable books from public libraries and fighting the influx of multicultural materials into the local school curricula to advocating for the removal of what they felt was obscene art from community spaces and instituting the teaching of creationism in their districts. *Truax* was part of an analogous personal effort.

At the same time, Birkett's pro-logging picture book arises from a second and seemingly contradictory impetus: the top-down influence that the growing involvement of big business—and especially their massive influx of funds—had on the agenda of the conservative movement and political right. While corporations like Amway, Coors, and ExxonMobil began channeling funds into conservative causes during the 1970s, their participation reached epic proportions by the 1990s. No longer were these businesses simply shaping the issues or influencing the argument; in many instances, their millions in monetary donations were allowing them to dictate the agenda. Nowhere, perhaps, was the power of this corporate sponsorship more evident than in what became known as the anti-green movement. While leftists were pushing radical new solutions to environmental problems like global warming, pollution, and deforestation—solutions which posed huge costs to corporations—opposition to such efforts emerged as a firm plank in the right's sociopolitical platform.

In the pages that follow, I discuss how *Truax* embodies a vivid example of the growing conservative backlash against environmental messages directed at the nation's young people, while it simultaneously points to the increasing corporate sponsorship of children's literature. Whereas books for young readers have a long history of being printed and promoted by large publishing companies, they are now being conceived and composed by them. *Truax*, with its authorship by an active member of the wood products industry and its publication by the National Oak Flooring Manufacturers Association, offers kids a message about the environment that is, not coincidentally, as probusiness as it is anti-green. In so doing, the book blurs the line separating commerce from creativity, scientific information from slanted infomercial, and storybooks aimed at young readers from public relations campaigns directed at future consumers, prospective stock holders, and even potential environmental regulators.

A Convenient Truth: *Truax* and Environmental Education According to the Wood Products Industry

At least since the Age of Enlightenment, young people have been associated with nature. Society sees boys and girls as possessing the same untainted beauty, unsullied innocence, and uncorrupted demeanor as the environment (Lesnik-Oberstein 28). As a result, from the eighteenth century through the present day, the natural world is seen as "a space for children to play and be cosseted, it provides a safeguard against all too early integration in the adult world" (Lindenpütz 188).

Environmentally themed literature for young people often challenges this longstanding association. Instead of positioning nature as a refuge from the problems of the adult world, these books reveal how it is actually a repository of them. In light of challenges like pollution, overdevelopment, and endangered species, green space is no longer a realm about which anyone—child or adult—can be carefree (see Lesnik-Oberstein 210–212). Such messages not only contribute to the controversial status and often resistant readership of environmentally themed children's books, but they also impact the perennial association of young people with the outdoors by inviting a reexamination of the role, function, or position of the child in relation to the conflict between adult civilization and unadulterated nature. As a result, children's literature about the green movement implicitly or explicitly asks the question: should young people serve as intermediary between these two realms, or should they be exempt from shouldering such responsibilities and assuming such burdens? (Dagmar Lindenpütz 187–188). Either way, "the increasing seriousness of environmental problems . . . poses us with a pressing educational question: How should we educate our children so that they can best take up the environmental challenges ahead?" (Kahn and Weld 165).

In keeping with these traits, both Dr. Seuss's *The Lorax* and Terri Birkett's *Truax* reflect the close connection between children and nature, and these books also address the question of what messages we should send young people concerning environmental problems. The area in which they differ, however, is the answers that they provide. Whereas *The Lorax* urges children to take an active role in the environment by becoming engaged with issues like pollution and deforestation, the message of *Truax* is markedly different. Birkett's book tells young people not to worry about environmental problems, either because they are the product of an unfounded hysteria or—in the rare cases where they do actually exist—because big business has already solved them.

BIRKETT'S INTENTION OF NOT SIMPLY PARODYING *The Lorax* but also countering its message about environmental conservation and the hazards of clear-cut logging is apparent from the opening page of *Truax*. Whereas the Truffula tree-cutting Once-ler is the villain in Seuss's narrative and the environmentalist Lorax is its admirable character, these roles are reversed in *Truax*. On the opening page, Birkett establishes her title character as more than simply the text's narrator; she announces him as its kindly hero. Writing in the first person and using a rhythmic style that mimics that of *The Lorax*, *Truax* commences:

> A warm day in June, way out on Oak Knoll,
> With my saw and my axe hung up on a pole,
> I was fixing a wheel on my Board-Flipping Packer
> When I glimpsed what I thought was a Green-crested Quacker.[3]

The image that accompanies this stanza reinforces Truax as the figure with which child readers are meant to identify and even empathize. Whereas the Once-ler is presented by Seuss as a faceless pair of greedy green hands in *The Lorax*, Truax is depicted by illustrator Orrin Lundgren as a fully embodied and eminently unthreatening white person. With his red flannel shirt, yellow hard hat, and blue jeans complete with suspenders, he is the quintessential workman. In fact, even though Truax is human and not animal, he resembles the cute, kind, and completely innocuous creatures who populate Richard Scarry's *What Do People Do All Day?*

The flying "Green-crested Quacker" that Truax sees in this opening stanza is not a species of duck, but the book's villain, Guardbark. In the same way that Birkett's illustrator presents the logger in a pleasing way, he depicts his environmentalist counterpart as ugly, unusual, and even frightening. Guardbark has buck teeth, a bulbous face, and small horn-like trees growing out of his scalp. In addition, because for some unexplained reason he is squinting in the opening illustration, he appears to be missing one eye. When these traits are combined with his green bodysuit, vest constructed of bark, and inexplicable ability to fly, Guardbark resembles nothing less than the fearsome villain from a comic book.

In an even more problematic detail, Birkett's Guardbark also has brown skin. While his coloration is perhaps meant to resemble tree bark, it adds a racially charged overtone to the text. "In representing environmentalists as a short-tempered brown hippie and loggers as a patient white man, Birkett inadvertently invokes racist ideologies in support of her point—that is, when a good white person corrects a misinformed, ill-mannered brown person, we cannot escape the racial overtones, even though those overtones may not have been intentional" (Nel *Icon* 178).The racially charged implications of Birkett's brown-skinned Guardbark are exacerbated further by the factual inequalities between population demographics and exposure to pollution. In the words of one environmental commentator, "All humans may ultimately share the same fate on this planet, but we don't all breathe the same air; we aren't fishing from the same streams; and our children aren't playing in the same soil" (Truax 12). On the contrary, "Studies are showing that poor and disadvantaged communities, particularly people of color, are exposed to higher levels of environmental pollution than other sectors of society" (Truax 12). Moreover, they receive unequal protections offered by the largely white and affluent green movement.

Birkett's tall, lean Guardbark may look nothing like Seuss's short and plump Lorax, but Birkett makes it clear that she expects them to be read as twinned characters. While Guardbark is still "drifting along just riding the breeze," he shouts to the logger protagonist a variation on the Lorax's well-known tagline: "'Mister!,' he yelled with a whiskery wheeze, 'I am Guardbark, protector of trees.'" However, as Truax and, by extension, Birkett's readers quickly learn, this figure's primary method for being the "protector" of trees is to throw tantrums. The friendly and hospitable Truax greets Guardbark and welcomes him to the forest. "And not to be rude, I got off my knees," he tells readers. The Guardbark does not possess similarly good manners, or—as Truax relays—seemingly any manners at all: "But before I could shake or offer a seat, / The Guardbark stopped, / stiffened, / and stamped his two feet."

Thus begins Birkett's portrayal of environmental advocates as rude, pushy, and hysterical alarmists. The Guardbark's first words to the title character are brash, accusatory, and clearly meant to reflect the Lorax's beliefs about the profit-driven Once-ler:

'Sir!' he said loudly, 'you are grisly with greed.
Cutting Hagbarks is MEAN—a horribus deed.
Look what a mess your hacking has made.
You did all of THIS just to get your bills paid?'

The composed, confident Truax does not get defensive in the face of these allegations; instead, the logger tries to calmly explain his work while speaking with "a smile" and inviting his visitor to "Have a seat on that pile." The unreasonable Guardbark rejects such kindly offers. He shouts at Truax in a tone that is even more irate: "*I WON'T take a seat, or LISTEN, or LOOK*,' / the Guardbark raved on. He snarled and he shook" (italics in original). In a passage that calls equal attention to this character's demanding tone as to his intractable beliefs, Guardbark commands Truax: "You must stop this hacking and whacking and stacking. / You should NOT be here. I MUST send you packing." The illustration that accompanies these lines shows the Guardbark throwing what looks like a child's temper tantrum. He is jumping up and down on a pile of wood planks, sending the boards flying while waving his arms, shaking his fists, and scowling. By contrast, on the opposing page, Truax's facial expression and his body posture could not be less threatening: the kindly logger's eyes are opened wide, he has a warm smile on his face, his arms are extended open, and his palms are facing up.

This first encounter between Truax and Guardbark largely sets the tone for the remainder of Birkett's book. No matter what Truax says or does, Guardbark responds in a manner that is hysterical, unreasonable, and irrational. On one page alone, for example, the histrionic environmentalist is described as throwing "a fumulous fit," "losing [his] head," and being openly "angry." Meanwhile, the kindly Truax is always placid, patient, and—in every illustration except one—warmly smiling.

Truax is eventually able to convince Guardbark to stop yelling long enough to engage in a civil conversation about logging. At this point, the already less-than-subtle pro-timber message in Birkett's book becomes even more overt. When the logger formally introduces himself to Guardbark, he offers the following positive overview of his occupation, "I harvest trees for ballbats and houses and things such as these." As Donella Meadows has aptly commented about this passage, "No frivolous Thneeds, no junk mail or throwaway chopsticks or fall-apart wooden knick-knacks. Only good stuff gets made from these trees" (A4). In addition, Birkett uses the neutral verb "harvest" to describe Truax's process of cutting timber. This word choice misleadingly implies that logging does not involve chopping down entire trees but merely requires collecting their nonessential portions.

Birkett also offers a radically different view from the *Lorax* about the process by which wood products are made. Whereas the Once-ler's Thneed factory is an egregious polluter in Seuss's book—poisoning the sky with "smogulous smoke" and contaminating the water with "Schloppity-Schlopp"—not so with Truax's industrial process. Nowhere in the book does Birkett show his logging equipment, the Seussian-sounding "Board-Flipping Packer," emitting exhaust or producing any waste products. In fact, every illustration in *Truax* depicts the title character against the backdrop of bright, clear skies and unspoiled, even flawless woodlands.

A few pages later, *Truax* takes such public-relations one step further. In a statement that seems paradoxical, the logger asserts that he actually plants far more trees than he cuts:

> In fact, for every ONE tree that I need,
> I place FIVE food-stowing, tree-growing seeds!
> My friends do the same all over this land
> Six million a day—it's part of the plan.

Truax offers more specific data that indicate the environmental benefits of this tactic: "Thirty-some years ago (just this past May), we had HALF the trees that are growing today."

This information, however, is not reliable. Many logging companies do plant trees to replace the ones they have cut, but there is no universal silviculture replacement ratio. The number of seeds sown varies by region, by company, and by historical time period. The California Licensed Foresters Association, for example, asserts that they plant seven new trees for every one that they cut (par 1). In many other regions, however, this ratio is reversed. According to Patricia S. Muir, "In general, forests are being cut much faster than they are being replanted. Globally, the cut:replant ratio is about 10:1 (that is, 10 are cut for every 1 that is replanted)" (par 8).

In a single passage Truax does acknowledge that logging has contributed to the depletion of the nation's forests, but he casts it in a positive light, as a means to prevent fires: "Back in the 30s, with wildfires unchecked, / Millions of acres of forests were wrecked. / . . . / Now every year 49 million acres / Of trees are spared from this lawless tree taker." Although Truax prefaces these comments with another claim to veracity—commenting that Guardbark "looked rather gloomy there shaking his head, / I guessed he must not know the truth, so I said"—such statistics are not widely accepted as factual. While timber advocates like Birkett may claim that logging actually saves trees, environmental groups assert that this view is as oxymoronic as it sounds. William H. Meadows, president of the Wilderness Society—a nonprofit organization that advocates for environmental protection—has argued that logging even dense forests "will not protect homes and lives from wildfire" (qtd in Entous, par 12). A more effective solution is to strategically thin the lush undergrowth of ground-level plants and regularly clear the accumulation of dried leaf litter, dropped pine needles, and dead vegetation. Meadows asserts that "history and science clearly demonstrate that clearing fuels away from the immediate area around homes is the best protection" (qtd in Entous, par 12).

Perhaps because Birkett includes factually dubious or scientifically disputed information, she often appeals to her readers' emotions. The illustration that accompanies her lines about how logging helps to prevent forest fires depicts a cute, cartoonish-looking bird narrowly avoiding a large lightning strike while an equally adorable small furry creature on the forest floor frantically flees an advancing wall of tall flames. Completing this portrait of pathos, the woodland animal is carrying its small baby on its back.

Equally important as offering a more positive portrait of logging than *The Lorax*, *Truax* presents a vastly different message concerning the loss of animal habitat, the importance of maintaining ecodiversity, and the protection of endangered species. In Seuss's book, the forced displacement of the Brown Bar-ba-loots owing to the loss of food supply from the Once-ler's chopping of Truffula trees and the similar dislocation of the Swomee-Swans and Humming-Fish as a result of the pollution from his Thneed factory forms a central facet of the title character's argument for environmental conservation. Various pages decry how the Swomee-Swans "can't sing a note! / No one can sing who has smog in his throat" and how the Humming-Fish have been compelled to literally crawl out of the water and "walk on their fins and get woefully weary / in search of some water that isn't so smeary."

Truax, however, offers a radically different viewpoint and level of empathy. In a series of questions, ostensibly addressed to the Guardbark but really directed at the reader, Truax wonders about the correlation between lost animal species and logging:

> Would anyone mind if we lost, say, a tick
> That carried a germ that made Cuddlebears sick?
>
> Or what about something that's really quite nice,
> Like the Yellow-Striped Minnow that lives in Lake Zice?
> How far will we go? How much will we pay?—
> To keep a few minnows from dying away?

This passage is ironic, for Birkett claims to be offering a message that differs from the negative one in Seuss's *The Lorax,* but, her book ultimately still places industrial profit above environmental concern. Moreover, the Truax's disregard for the fate of the ticks and minnows is far more crass than the Once-ler's attitude. In Seuss's book, even the greedy industrialist is saddened by the loss of animal species: "I, the Once-ler felt sad / as I watched them all go."

By contrast, Birkett's argument "How far will we go? How much will we pay? / To keep a few minnows from dying away?" trivializes the endangered species crisis by ignoring the inherently interdependent nature of ecosystems and suggesting that only a couple of small and, ultimately, insignificant creatures are affected.

Even more significant, Birkett's point does not seem particularly persuasive to her intended child audience. The actions of young people—unlike those of adults and especially corporations—are usually not influenced by a cost-benefit analysis. They are, however, often powerfully shaped by a strong connection with animals; many boys and girls have a personal fascination and even strong psychological bond with creatures ranging from cuddly koala bears to ferocious lions. Children's literature has long reflected this link. Karin Lesnik-Oberstein has documented this connection: "It would not be an exaggeration to state that, on average, at least two-thirds of the books are in some form or another linked with nature and the environment, and—specifically and most importantly—with animals" (208). She notes, in works ranging from *Aesop's Fables, Charlotte's Web, Peter Rabbit, Black Beauty*, and *Watership Down* to *Curious George, Babar, Dr. Doolittle, Frog and Toad, The Wind in the Willows*, animals— whether actual or anthropomorphized—embody a common protagonist in, or at least narrative focal point for, books for young readers (Lesnik-Oberstein 208–210). For these reasons, Birkett's strategy of discounting the importance of any animal creature seems grossly out of sync with not simply a common facet of children's literature but also the history of children and childhood in the West.

Interestingly, Birkett does include the word "biodiversity" at various points in her text. Instead of using the term as an opportunity to teach her young readers a new vocabulary word and, by extension, a lesson in earth science, she belittles it: "BIODIVERSITY. Now there is a word. / A Science-y, Frogbirdy word I have heard." When her book finally does address the impact that the timber industry has on animal populations, it casts even clear-cut logging in a positive light. In a passage that is as memorable as much for its audacity as for its inaccuracy, Birkett's narrator-protagonist suggests that the devastation of their habitat actually benefits animals:

The newly-cut forest has sun on the ground
And BIODIVERSITY leaps and abounds.
All kinds of new species move in together,
From scales to warts, from fur to feathers.

As before, such claims simply are untrue. While some animals are able to persevere after trees have been felled, logging—in the words of Meadows again—"deeply disturbs rarer deep-forest species and natural population balances" (A4).

A few pages later, *Truax* makes what is perhaps its boldest and arguably most preposterous claim. In keeping with the absolutist standpoint often adopted by the conservative movement and political right, *Truax* takes the environmentalist argument to the extreme. The logger tries to imagine "just how it would be / If we could NEVER, EVER again cut a tree." He ruminates about this world where logging is forbidden:

Then what would happen after a bit of time passes
To the animals that live in the shrubs and the grasses?
With no opening up of the dark forest floor,
There'd be no new habitat for them anymore.

More than simply arguing that the timber industry *facilitates* biodiversity, Birkett's book takes this argument one step further and asserts that it actually *prevents* the extinction of certain animals.

"Things ARE NOT Quite as Bad as They Seemed": *Truax* and the Growing Genre of Anti-Environmental Literature for Young Readers

Because *Truax* was written and released more than two decades after *The Lorax*, it confronts more than simply the issues of deforestation, the plight of endangered species, and the irresponsible plundering of natural resources. The narrative also addresses environmental problems that have emerged in the years since Seuss's book was published: namely, global warming and the loss of old-growth timber. Near the middle of the book, Guardbark raises concerns about the importance of preserving virgin forest: "what about trees that are really, quite old. That are cooling our planet and shouldn't be sold?" Once again, Truax's response casts logging in a positive light. First, he justifies cutting old-growth timber by locating it within the natural life cycle of the forests themselves: "With wildfires and wind, insects and disease, / Nature, herself, renews stands of old trees." Logging, he suggests, is essentially no different.

To Birkett's credit, Guardbark is not persuaded by this answer. But, his disbelief does not stem from the false nature of Truax's analogy. Instead, Guardbark rejects the logger's explanation because of his own personal shortcomings. Birkett reiterates the environmentalist's complete intractability, a personality flaw that she assigned this figure early in the book: "Guardbark did not want to know / How the earth keeps on changing, so I spoke kind of slow." In addition, the character repudiates Truax's explanation because Guardbark, too childishly impatient responds to the logger in an outburst so hysterical that it appears in both caps and italics for emphasis: "*Nature is patient and willing to wait. / I want old trees NOW. / The wait's what I hate!*"

Although the Guardbark is clearly misguided, Truax nonetheless works to assuage his fears about the loss of old-growth forests. The narrator-protagonist points out, for example, that millions of acres of virgin timber are off-limits to loggers, protected by the nation's numerous public parks, wildlife habitats, and nature preserves:

We're teaching our people just how to conserve
And we've set aside land in National Preserves.

95 million Acres (to be quite precise)
Have been set aside JUST to look nice.
(Well,—critters and plants DO use this land.
It just isn't used by woman or man.)

Once again, not all of this information is accurate. Birkett asserts that forests belonging to the National Preserve "have been set aside JUST to look nice," but their function is far from merely aesthetic. Truax's assurance that this land "isn't used by woman or man" omits the many recreational camping grounds, public picnic areas, and miles of hiking trails found in these woodland regions. In addition, contrary to expectations, lands that are part of the National Wilderness Preservation System do permit certain types of commercial natural resource use, a detail that Birkett also conveniently overlooks. According to the U.S. National Park Service's own explanation, "National preserves are areas having characteristics associated with national parks, but *in which Congress has permitted continued public hunting, trapping, oil/gas exploration and extraction*" (National Park Service; my emphasis). Likewise, areas designated as part of the National Wilderness Preservation System do prohibit certain industrial activity, such as mining and road-building (National Park Service, par 4). Consequently, Birkett's declaration that protected land is not being used really means that it is not being used by the timber industry.

Of course, Birkett also does not mention how, under the auspices of the so-called "wise-use" argument, the timber industry routinely lobbies to overturn these environmental regulations so that they can begin logging in protected areas (see Beder 47–62). Hence, when Truax informs Guardbark and, by extension, his readers, "We're teaching our people just how to conserve / And we've set aside land in National Preserves" his comments are not entirely sincere. As Sharon Beder and David Helvarg, among others, have written, far from willingly and eagerly participating in conservation efforts, the timber industry has had environmental regulations imposed upon them and abides by these statutes only forcibly and—often—under protest.

Even if protected lands like the National Preserves did not exist, the Guardbark learns that he still has no reason to be alarmed about the loss of old-growth forest. As Truax explains, young trees are actually the ones that help generate oxygen, contain greenhouse gases, and control global warming by absorbing carbon dioxide:

But if we examine the scientists' rule:
We see that the planet's clean air and its cool
Depend on YOUNG trees in tree-growing school.
That's where they learn how to use C-O-2
To make lots of oxygen. Really, it's true!

Actually, it's not. Donella Meadows contends that this remark embodies one of the most "misleading mantras of the logging industry" (A4). An article by Mark E. Harmon, William K. Ferrell, and Jerry F. Franklin in a 1990 issue of the journal *Science*—and thus available when Birkett was writing *Truax*—demonstrates how "conversion of old-growth forests to young fast-growing forests will not decrease atmospheric carbon dioxide (CO_2), as has been recently suggested" (699). On the contrary, the authors argue that "on-site carbon storage is reduced considerably and does not approach old-growth storage capacity for at least 200 years" (Harmon, Ferrell, and Franklin 699). The published findings from numerous subsequent studies aver these claims.[4] Such inaccuracies in Birkett's book, however, are obfuscated once again by Truax's claims to veracity. On the page that precedes this information, the logger asserts: "I gave him the facts, the truth of the matter / This Guardbark did NOT want to hear idle chatter."

Perhaps the most significant difference between *Truax* and *The Lorax* emerges in their endings. Seuss's book concludes on a hopeful note. Before the Lorax flees the environmental wasteland that was once the Edenic Truffula forest, he offers the Once-ler and, by extension, the reader a sobering exhortation: "UNLESS someone like you / cares a whole lot / nothing is going to get better. / It's not." On the final page, the now reclusive Once-ler drops the last Truffula seed from his castle-like hideout into the hands of a young boy, the next generation. Revising his former assertion that material objects like Thneeds are what "everyone, EVERYONE, EVERYONE needs!," he now asserts "Truffula Trees are what everyone needs." The closing lines of *The Lorax* are directed as much to the young character who has been entrusted with the final seed as they are to the book's young audience:

Plant a new Truffula. Treat it with care.
Give it clean water. And feed it fresh air.
Grow a forest. Protect it from axes that hack.
Then the Lorax
and all of his friends
may come back.

The closing message of the *Truax* is radically different. Whereas Seuss encourages young readers to be aware and get involved, Birkett informs them that there is no reason for concern, let alone action. After listening to the Truax's various arguments that most environmental concerns are either false fears or are already being effectively handled by the timber industry, the Guardbark is persuaded. By the final page of the book, the previous sworn enemy of the timber industry has become its newest ally: "I am Guardbark, ward of the trees—/ And I like the way that you're managing these." It is significant that in this concluding passage the Guardbark, who formerly cast himself in the empowering position of being the "protector" of trees, now casts himself in the dependent role as the "ward" of the trees. In the view of Birkett, he has rightly come under the power of Truax. The Guardbark's parting words encapsulate the attitude of not only the timber industry but also the National Oak Flooring Manufacturer's Association about logging: namely, there is nothing to worry about. "'And perhaps best of all,' the Guardbark beamed. / 'I think things ARE NOT quite as bad as they seemed.'"

ALTHOUGH *TRUAX* MAY BE UNIQUE with regard to its parody of *The Lorax*, it is not alone when it comes to its message about environmentalism. In light of growing public awareness about issues like global warming, pollution, and deforestation during the past twenty years, educational materials for young people that rebut both mainstream perceptions and scientific theories concerning the environment have grown exponentially. Edward Helmore has written, "Anti-conservation groups, often supported by the Religious Right, have accused schools of teaching Satanism, of lying about the threat of global warming and ozone depletion, and of threatening their communities' economic foundations"; these entities "contend that environmental education is creating a generation of 'eco-cultists,' indoctrinated by 'emotionalism, myths and misinformation' from green activists, simply repeating the mantras of 'Save the World' or 'Green is Beautiful' without any understanding of the issues" (Helmore 24).

As a result, both isolated individuals and professional organizations have engaged in lobbying efforts to halt current forms of environmental education or, at least, to prevent new initiatives from being passed. Reflecting the simultaneous bottom-up and top-down nature of Terri Birkett's *Truax*, these actions have come from both ordinary citizens and from corporate-funded professional lobbying groups. Epitomized in many ways by the efforts of Judith and Bill Bailey in Laytonville, California, concerned parents have used letter-writing campaigns, public opinion, town hall meetings, direct mailings, and newspaper advertisements to disseminate their message on the local level. Meanwhile, Sharon Beder noted in *Global Spin: The Corporate Assault on Environmentalism* that big business plays a major role in advancing and especially funding the anti-green movement on a national scale. Whether challenging pro-green rulings in the courts, disseminating anti-environmental messages via the media, funding scientific research to counter existing data about problems like global warming, or lobbying for the abandonment or repeal of environmental legislation, multinational corporations spend hundreds of millions of dollars annually to defeat or discredit earth-friendly measures that will cost them many more millions to implement (see Beder 5–13). Indeed, as Russ Bellant has noted, "For corporations, the financial advantage of minimizing environmental regulation is obvious" (85).

Their efforts have yielded measurable success. In Arizona during the late 1990s, for instance, the state legislature "repealed its environmental education requirement after a legislator complained that elementary students dancing to wolf howls and whale songs amounted to 'eco-cultism'" (Allen "Truth" A1). In addition, in many public school districts throughout nation, "teachers are not to promote activism; no more planting trees, raising money to save whales, no letters protecting against polluting industries or rainforest destruction" (Helmore 24).

In instances where anti-green groups have not been able to prevent environmental education, they have worked to discredit it. In 1992, for example, Jonathan H. Adler published "Little Green Lies: The Environmental Miseducation of America's Children." The report sought to expose ten alleged myths perpetuated by environmentalists. These included the notions that "Recycling is always good," "Plastic is bad," and "There is too much garbage" (Adler 18, 19, 20). A subsequent point is devoted to dispelling the erroneous belief that "Acid Rain Is Destroying Our Forests" (Adler 21). On the contrary, Adler writes, "the nitrogen contained in acid rain actually helps much of the eastern forest by providing the necessary nutrient" (22). "Little Green Lies" was supported, both ideologically and monetarily, by the Heritage Foundation, a powerful conservative think-tank in Washington, D.C., that was founded in 1973 with money donated by Joseph Coors of the Coors Brewing Company. Russ Bellant has documented, since the 1970s, that "the Coors Company bankrolled organizations and individuals that wanted to destroy or minimize environmental protection legislation" (85). Indeed, the company has been so ideologically and monetarily committed to the anti-green movement that *Reader's Digest* once dubbed Joseph Coors "one of the nation's leading anti-environmentalists" (qtd in Bellant 84).

The most recent addition to the literature of the anti-green movement is *The Sky's Not Falling!: Why It's OK to Chill about Global Warming*. Released in 2007 by the ironically named Holly Fretwell, the book was written in response to the widespread classroom use of both Al Gore's 2006 Academy Award–winning documentary *An Inconvenient Truth* and Laurie David and Cambria Gordon's text *The Down-to-Earth Guide to Global Warming* (2007). *The Sky's Not Falling* takes a similar stance on the issue of temperature shift as "Little Green Lies" does about pollution and *Truax* does concerning deforestation: namely, the situation is not as bad as it seems, and children are being cruelly manipulated and unnecessarily frightened into thinking the worst. The back cover of *The Sky's Not Falling*, for example, lists one of the many child-voiced fears that it will dispel: "I'm scared that every time I ride in the car, I'm hurting polar bears and other animals." Accordingly, the opening chapter addresses the topic of "Chicken Little and Climate Change."

It's Not Easy Being Green: Insights and
Oversights in Ecology-Themed Children's Books

Although *Truax* clearly has its shortcomings, *The Lorax* is itself far from perfect. Dr. Seuss's classic ironically contains some of the same argumentative problems and even ideological oversights as Birkett's book, albeit on a different scale and alternative scope. Seuss himself acknowledged the overt and even biased political message of *The Lorax*. In a comment that reflects Birkett's motivation for writing *Truax*—and stands in contrast to the author-illustrator's more moderate remarks about *The Lorax* during the dispute in California—Seuss called his 1971 narrative "propaganda with a plot" (qtd in Moje and Shyu 675). Moreover, he frankly confessed that the inspiration for *The Lorax* "came out of my being angry" (qtd in Lebduska 170). Living in La Jolla, California, an artists' community that had witnessed a massive boom in development, Seuss was appalled by the way in which the region's formerly open landscape now "teemed with condominiums and look-alike houses" (qtd in Morgan and Morgan 209). Seeing events in his local town as sadly indicative of those around the nation, and finding books on conservation exceedingly "dull . . . full of statistics and preachy" (Morgan and Morgan 209), the author decided to tackle the issue in a direct and unapologetic way. Seuss acknowledged this intention soon after *The Lorax* was published: "I was out to attack what I think are evil things and let the chips fall where they might" (qtd in Lebduska 170).[5]

In so doing, Dr. Seuss also emotionally manipulates or at least prods his readers in ways that previewed Birkett's tactics. Seuss creates lovable creatures with cute-sounding names who live in a state that is nothing short of Edenic at the start of the text. When the Once-ler first arrives in the Truffula forest, for example, he observes of the region's flora and fauna:

> And, under the trees, I saw Brown Bar-ba-loots
> Frisking about in their Bar-ba-loot suits
> As they played in the shade and ate Truffula Fruits.
>
> From the rippulous pond
> came the comforting sound
> of the Humming-Fish humming
> while splashing around.

Later, these same creatures suffer from heart-tugging maladies, such as, in the case of the Bar-ba-loots, getting "crummies in their tummies." One would need to be not simply a greedy Once-ler, but, perhaps more accurately, a heartless Grinch not to be moved by their plight.

The illustrations that Seuss creates to accompany these passages only enhance their effect. Akin to Birkett's pleasant, unthreatening, and perpetually smiling Truax, Seuss's various creatures are visually appealing. Even when the Bar-ba-loots are faced with starvation, they do not become angry with the Once-ler. Instead, Seuss presents them sadly approaching the entrepreneur's factory office while pathetically holding their stomachs and looking faint from lack of food. The following page presents the Bar-ba-loots being compelled to finally leave the Truffula forest in search of a more hospitable habitat. A long line of meek-looking Bar-ba-loots stretches off into the distance; several peer back over their shoulder, morosely waving goodbye to the Lorax. One of the small creatures, presumably too weak to walk on his own, is being carried by the others. The Swomee-Swans are even more pitiable, with their plaintive eyes, drooped body posture, and sad facial expressions. In these and other passages, Seuss appeals at least as much to his reader's emotions as their intellects, perhaps even more so. Indeed, Philip Nel has commented that these types of images recur in all of Seuss's books and help to set the tone of his stories, "offering emotional cues" to child readers about what they should be feeling (*Icon* 67).[6]

The Lorax suffers from other, arguably more serious, problems. As Ian Marshall first pointed out and critics like Suzanne Ross have elaborated, Seuss's title character is not exactly a role model for how to conduct a successful negotiation or engage in productive environmental activism. In what has become an oft-mentioned detail about the Lorax, "The first words he speaks to the Once-ler are uttered in a voice that is 'sharp and bossy'—as cutting as an ax-blade. He speaks 'at the top of [his] lungs' and snaps at the Once-ler" (Marshall 89). While Ruth MacDonald has interpreted this tone as an indicator of "the stridency that Dr. Seuss permits the reader to use in opposing polluters" (153), it can also be read as a gross error with regard to rhetorical strategy. Rather than trying to rationally persuade or logically convince the Once-ler about the error of his ways, Lorax attacks and insults him. Seuss's character calls "the Once-ler 'crazy with greed' in their first encounter and sneeringly addresses him as 'you dirty old Once-ler man you' in their last meeting" (Marshall 89). His accusatory statements only increase as the story progresses. Many remarks that the Lorax makes are punctuated by exclamation marks. Meanwhile, his word choices and body language are equally aggressive. Akin to Birkett's tantrum-throwing Guardbark, Seuss's figure variously "shouted and puffed," "cried with a cruffulous croak," and peppers the Once-ler with a seemingly endless stream of "gripes." By the middle of the book, Seuss himself acknowledges about the Lorax, "His dander was up." Such an aggressive approach is a poor strategy for making individuals sympathetic to your cause and persuading them to take your side. As Bob Henderson, Merle Kennedy, and Chuck Chamberlin have pointed out, the Lorax's tactics can only lead to "frustration" and "futility" (140).

Even more disconcertingly, the Lorax's accusatory tone at times seems to exacerbate the situation, causing the Once-ler to become more entrenched in his attitude. Early on, for example, an exasperated Once-ler sharply tells the nagging Lorax, "Shut up, if you please." Before long, the two begin exchanging insults: "I laughed at the Lorax, 'You poor stupid guy!'" Finally, after pages of more badgering, the Once-ler becomes even more irate, exploding: "And then I got mad. / I got terribly mad. / I yelled at the Lorax, 'Now listen here, Dad!'" In the wake of this outburst, the Once-ler announces his plan of "figgering / on biggering / and BIGGERING / and BIGGERING" his Truffula-cutting and Thneed-making operations even more. Ian Marshall has argued that this decision "seems in large part an angry response to the Lorax's belligerent provocations" (89).

Even more tragically, the Lorax fails to see the one argument that might actually persuade the Once-ler: his tactic of clear-cutting Truffula trees is not a sustainable business plan. Although the ambitious entrepreneur is clearly uninterested in preserving the forest for its own sake, he might have been swayed to the idea of environmental conservation when presented from the angle of preserving future Thneed production (see Marshall 90). The Lorax, however, never presents his case from this perspective, and thus he overlooks an important area of common ground. As Henderson, Kennedy, and Chamberlin have pointed out, "neither the Lorax nor the Once-ler attempts to explain the basic principles governing his practices" (140). Had they done so, the seemingly oppositional environmental conservationist and industrial capitalist may have discovered that "each 'hold the same basic understandings of the world and that they differ only in their priorities'" (Henderson, Kennedy, and Chamberlin 140).

Viewed from this perspective, the Lorax is not the arch nemesis of the Once-ler, simply his mirror image. Both characters think of the environment as either their own personal property or a commodity that they can possess: the Once-ler with his view that the Truffula trees are his for the taking, and the Lorax with his tag line touting how he speaks "*for* the trees" and his repeated remarks regarding "*my* Truffula tuft" and "*my* poor Bar-ba-loots." Ruth MacDonald has written how "the possessive pronoun seems inappropriate for a spirit of nature whose message asserts the responsibility of all creatures for the welfare of others" (149). Meanwhile, Ian Marhsall takes this line of reasoning even further, by arguing, "No wonder the Once-ler feels no concern for the other living things in his environment; according to the Lorax, they are *his* property and responsibility" (89; italics in original). Such attitudes give rise to an "us versus them" stance or, at least, "insider/outsider" worldview. The Once-ler and the Lorax advocate for a position that is largely predicated on eliminating the other. In the words of Ross: "The Once-ler's is a community made up of his family and the consumers of the Thneeds he produces; it excludes the Truffula forest and its inhabitants, the Lorax among them. The community the Lorax argues for is exclusionary, too; the Once-ler is significantly absent" (101).

Perhaps most disappointing of all, the Lorax never realizes the error of his ways or the mistakes that he made in his failing efforts to save the Truffula forest. By contrast, the Once-ler eventually regrets his clear-cut logging of the Truffula trees and recognizes the environmental devastation that his Thneed factory has caused: "Now all that was left 'neath the bad-smelling sky," he laments, "was my big empty factory . . . / the Lorax . . . / and I." Seuss's title character, however, remains unchanged. In the words of Marshall, Seuss's ostensible hero is "strident and angry to the end, sounding his single note of rebuke as repetitively (and perhaps as ineffectually) as the overly conscientious fish in *The Cat in the Hat*" (90). For these reasons, while the Once-ler is commonly identified as the guilty party in the destruction of the Truffula forest, the Lorax is not entirely without blame. While the eponymous figure, of course, did not engage in the physical act of cutting down the trees, he is—as Ross has aptly phrased it—a "dismal failure" as an advocate for the environment (100).

This alternative way of viewing *The Lorax* may diminish some of its esteemed status, but it also adds an important new social message to the book. Coupled with the common theme of promoting environmental conservation, Seuss's 1971 text offers a cautionary tale about productive rhetorical strategies and effective activist approaches. Critics have long held that greedy corporations can benefit from the lessons of the profit-driven Once-ler, and—as Suzanne Ross has pointed out—environmentalists likewise "have something to learn from the Lorax's experiences" (99). The contemporary environmental movement will only succeed by adopting "a rhetoric favoring inclusion over exclusion, participation over competition, inducement over domination, identification over isolation. . . . Such a rhetoric would help the Lorax to fundamentally reconceive his 'speaking for' in order for his 'speaking at' ('yapping,' the Once-ler calls it) to become 'speaking with'" (Ross 103).

Truax, of course, does not heed this lesson either. The Guardbark may utter the closing assertion, "I'm glad that we chatted, conversed and confided. / I think now our views aren't quite so one-sided," but the book's presentation of the issues is anything but even-handed. With its celebratory views about logging, inaccurate scientific information, and flippant comments concerning the protection of endangered species, Birkett claims to offer a corrective to the problems of *The Lorax*, but her narrative simply inverts them. The title character's desire to talk with the Guardbark is admirable, but he fails to remember "that talking involves listening too" (Meadows A4).

LAURA APOL, IN A COMPELLING JOURNAL ARTICLE, explores the representation of the environment in two books for young readers that were published exactly one century apart: Myron Gibson's serialized story "Herm and I" (1894) and David Klass's young adult novel *California Blue* (1994). In spite of the massive changes that have taken place concerning social and scientific attitudes about the relationship between humans and nature during the hundred years separating these texts, they offer strikingly similar views on the subject: "In both stories, Nature and humans are presented in an adversarial position—first, Nature is represented as uncharted wilderness to be conquered, controlled, commodified; later it is depicted as a vulnerable ecosystem, fragile, a landscape that invites—even requires—human protection and intervention" (Apol 110). Even more disappointingly, she continues, these beliefs precipitate another and arguably more lamentable shared trait: oppositional antagonism. The nineteenth-century text paints a portrait of a seemingly endless bounty ripe for the taking; by contrast, the twentieth-century novel depicts an image of growing scarcity in need of conservation. In each book, "those who stand in the way of the protagonists' (and the authors') goals for Nature are assigned a corresponding stereotypical Otherness: they are portrayed as evil, ignorant, warring, aggressive, vindictive" (110). Both *California Blue* and "Herm and I" adopt a firm "us-versus-them" attitude about the environment that pits humans against nature and creates what Apol describes as a series of "binary oppositions . . . clear cut first-growth timber *or* lose your livelihood, rescue a butterfly *or* preserve a town" (111; italics in original).

Although *The Lorax* and *Truax* take opposite stances on issues like environmental conservation, clear-cut logging, and the protection of endangered species, they share these assumptions. Throughout the books by Seuss and Birkett "nature is constructed for a purpose" (108), a concept that echoes Apol's remarks. The authors differ in their opinions about who ought to be the steward of nature; *The Lorax* names the next generation of children, and *Truax* assigns this task to industry. But they both agree that the environment is in need of management by humans, a viewpoint that ironically overlooks the fact that humans do not exist above or even outside the ecological environment. Adhering to the environmental philosophy known as deep ecology, humans constitute simply another species in it.[7] Furthermore, with Seuss's negative portrait of the profit-driven Once-ler and Birkett's equally disparaging representation of the hysterical Guardbark, each work demonizes those who challenge their viewpoints. These shared traits lead to one final and equally illuminating area of common ground. With their dueling green and anti-green messages, both books aver journalist China Mieville's observation, "Ecology is always political, and young people know it" (par 7).

Children's Literature, Inc.: The Corporate Production of Books for Young Readers

While Terri Birkett's *Truax* is clearly shaped by the message of Seuss's *The Lorax*, it has another equally powerful influence: its corporate publisher, the National Oak Flooring Manufacturers Association. As even Birkett would likely concede,

NOFMA is hardly a neutral printing venue. To be sure, the organization does not attempt to obfuscate its involvement with *Truax* or its investment in the book's message. A shaded box that draws the reader's eye on the inside page of *Truax* flatly admits that "This book is provided to you through . . . the National Oak Flooring Manufacturers Association." In addition, NOFMA identifies itself as a collective "made up of hardwood flooring manufacturers who are dedicated to quality in the industry."

Terri Birkett is equally candid. She could have written *Truax* using a pseudonym to obfuscate her ties to the wood products industry, but she did not. Moreover, in the "About the Author" section that appears inside the front cover of *Truax*, the first characteristic that she reveals about herself is "active member of the hardwood flooring industry." As a result, *Truax* begins, perhaps somewhat appropriately, with details that collectively constitute a *caveat emptor.*

Given the way in which *Truax* wears its corporate connections quite literally on its jacket sleeve, the book illuminates the growing entanglement between private industry and printed narratives in the United States. Birkett's book vividly illustrates the way in which company slogans and creative stories increasingly merge and combine in the nation's contemporary literature for young people. As the line separating laissez-faire commerce from literary creativity blurs, readers and critics have increasingly wondered—to borrow Philip Nel's title, "Is There a Text in this Advertising Campaign?"

Of course, the corporate involvement and even production of books for young readers are far from new phenomena. From the beginning, children's narratives have been published by companies interested in making a profit. John Newbery, one of the first successful commercial publishers of books for children, not only released many titles for young readers but frequently composed these books himself. Likewise, Catherine Van Horn has written how the popular periodical *St. Nicholas Magazine* openly encouraged its child readers to pay close attention to the promotional pages. In columns, articles, and letters, the editors entreated boys and girls to show their support for the magazine by showing their support for the companies who advertised in its page—namely, by buying their products (Van Horn 126–127). Finally, and perhaps most famously, during the 1930s, the Stratemeyer Syndicate—under the direction of founder Edward Stratemeyer and his daughters—produced numerous book series, including Nancy Drew, the Hardy Boys, and the Bobbsey Twins. Although the Syndicate attributed these texts to a single author—such as Carolyn Keene in the case of Nancy Drew, and Franklin W. Dixon on the covers of The Hardy Boys—the books were actually written by the company itself. Hiring a bevy of various freelance ghost writers and using a proven plot formula, the novels were created for the express purpose of making money.

While the corporate involvement in, and even production of, children's literature is not new, the way it in which this relationship is being conceived, configured, and constructed has shifted dramatically. Narratives released by John Newbery, *St. Nicholas Magazine*, and the Stratemeyer Syndicate may have been produced to make a profit, but they were not created for the sole purpose of improving the public image of a specific industry or promoting a certain line of commercial products. For instance, the Nancy Drew mystery series may have been written by a company with an eye on generating sales rather than producing art, but the books do not engage in either product placement or public-relations spin. The title character frequently refers to her beloved roadster, for example, but she neither offers laudatory comments about American car manufacturing nor mentions any specific model. In short, she is not trying to sell cars nor wax poetic about the many wonders of the automobile industry. Similarly, Nancy may often discuss her father's work as a criminal lawyer, but she is trying neither to improve public attitudes about the profession of law nor generate business for the specific firm where he works.

This is not the case for more recent corporate-sponsored texts. Narratives like Terri Birkett's *Truax* are merely a conduit for the messages that they contain. To disseminate their viewpoint, organizations like the National Oak Flooring Association could have produced a commercial, filmed an education video, or distributed an information pamphlet. But, they decided to sponsor a children's book instead. While the text claims to offer a fun and imaginative story, what it really offers is a public-relations campaign. *Truax* may be one of the more well-known corporate-sponsored books for young readers because of its parody of Dr. Seuss and the publicity that this connection has generated, but it is far from the only one. In examples ranging from Geoffrey N. Swinney and Kate Charlesworth's *Fish Facts* (1991), published by the Sea Fish Industry Authority, to the nonfiction *The World of Plastics* (1986), written and released by the British Plastics Federation, many other companies, trade businesses, and corporations have written children's narratives to promote their industries.

The books prepared and packaged by Alloy Media & Marketing take this phenomenon one step further. In best-selling series like The Clique, A-List, and Gossip Girl, they do not simply offer a positive portrait of a particular industry, they encourage their young readers to purchase specific products. As journalist Michael Winerip has written, "Massie, the lead 'Clique' character, doesn't wear miniskirts and sandals. She wears Moschino minis, Jimmy Choo sandals, and Chanel No 19 on her thin wrists, rides in a Range Rover, drinks Glaceau Vitamin Water and totes her books in a Louis Vuitton backpack" (L1). Alloy claims that it does not accept payment from companies for mentioning a product in their books, but a blurb on their website in 2006 asserted: "Advertisers have the opportunity to get their products or services cast in these best-selling books. The value of these mentions far exceeds the hundreds of thousands of readers, creating a viral product buzz" (qtd in Winerip L1). Although *Truax* does not plug specific items in the text—like hardwood flooring or venetian blinds—it does provide a mailing address where individuals can write for more information about "products made from wood."

During the past few decades, the reach of corporate-produced reading materials for young people has extended from the local bookstore to the public school system. Capitalizing on the woefully undersupplied nature of many elementary school teachers, companies have begun providing free instructional materials, offering paid training sessions, and funding educational research projects—all of which offer a positive portrayal of their industry and its products. Consequently, as journalist Chris Moran has written, many of the nation's children are learning "about our food supply with a lesson plan developed and donated by Monsanto. And the video on how oil is formed? An Exxon production" (A1).

Not surprisingly, the logging industry is a major participant in this trend. Pacific Logging Congress "distributed a brochure at a recent science teachers conventions in San Diego that has photos of what's described as environmentally responsible clear cuts" (Moran A1). In a message that is remarkably similar to that of *Truax*, the document "shows how Douglas firs grow better after the removal of other plants and trees that compete with them for sunlight" (Moran A1). Meanwhile, Weyerhauser—the nation's second largest private owner of softwood timber and one of the world's largest paper and pulp companies—has taken this idea even further. The corporation offers teachers a paid six-week summer research retreat at their newly constructed science center (Moran A1). While there, educators learn about the role that logging plays in the forest ecosystem and the many important products made from timber.

These companies share the same motivation for providing no-cost materials to teachers as that of Birkett and the National Oak Flooring Manufacturers Association in producing *Truax*: "The information schoolchildren have access to is of utmost importance to the groups that have a direct stake—whether in profits or in dues-paying memberships—in the outcomes of the classroom debates" (Moran A1). Industries like logging, mining, and oil, "have figured out what fast-food restaurants have long known: 'If you start educating people at young ages around these facts, then they accept it as truth'" (qtd in Moran A1). Far from seeing their materials as propagandistic or even one-sided, corporations justify them as simply representing their side of the issue. "Kathleen deBettencourt, executive director of the Environmental Literacy Council, said businesspeople have a legitimate reason to try to disseminate research-based science in defense of their industries. She said corporate America's environmental education efforts represent a counteroffensive to decades of a movement that has characterized big business interests as rapists, murderers, and pillagers of the land" (Moran A1). It is no coincidence, for example, that soon after Weyerhauser was named the world's forty-second largest corporate producer of air pollution in a study conducted by researchers at the University of Massachusetts at Amherst (Political Economy Research Institute), it began offering science retreat seminars that showcased, among other things, the company's many green practices. Even in the face of such seemingly transparent public relations moves, deBettencourt maintains that "corporate-sponsored teaching tools are excellent teaching tools" (qtd in Moran A1).

Terri Birkett and the National Oak Flooring Manufacturers Association would enthusiastically agree. When *Truax* was first released in 1995, the company offered the book for sale as a stapled softback; however, with both the author and its publisher eager to disseminate the book's message, the narrative soon became available at no cost. Teachers can receive a free copy of *Truax* from NOFMA "when the request is made on school letterhead" ("Book Review: *Truax*," par 13). Concerned parents can likewise solicit copies of the book for use in their child's classroom. As the NOFMA website instructs, "you can send a list of your local schools to the NOFMA office and they will send them a copy" ("Book Review: *Truax*," par 13). Finally, *Truax* is also now available as a free download from the NOFMA website. Through commercial sales, online print-outs, and direct mailings, more than 400,000 copies of *Truax* had been distributed by July 2001 ("Horton Hears" 26).

The National Oak Flooring Manufacturers Association does not simply provide free copies of Birkett's book for parents and teachers to read to kids; they also provide a reproducible set of discussion questions, a student worksheet, and a lesson plan complete with a list of possible classroom activities. Some questions on the discussion sheet include "why the woodcutter thought it was reasonable and necessary to cut trees" ("Lesson Plan"). Significantly, the first response listed on the answer key is "his livelihood" ("Lesson Plan"). Similarly, one of the suggested classroom activities is "Visit a nearby sawmill, furniture factory, or flooring plant. Talk about the number of people who have jobs because of wood products" ("Lesson Plan"). Finally, the student worksheet includes such leading prompts as discuss "how the TRUAX scenario more closely represents American forest management than the scenario described in THE LORAX" ("Lesson Plan"). The worksheet ends by informing children "you can write to the following address for true facts on how America's forests are being managed" ("Lesson Plan"). The organization listed is the American Forest & Paper Association, a political lobbying group located in Washington, D.C.[8]

In 2006, the consumer advocacy group Commercial Alert sent an email message to more than three hundred book critics imploring them not to review a new novel, *Cathy's Book*. Two years earlier, the organization explained, the book's author Carole Matthews signed a deal with the car company Ford "to mention [their model] the Fiesta frequently and glowingly in her novels and stories, to help Ford reach its target market of 'spirited young women'" (Sullivan 28). The email argued that the endorsement deal made *Cathy's Book* not an exciting new 'tween novel as it was being touted by its publisher, but "an adjunct of a corporate marketing campaign aimed at impressionable teenagers"

(Sullivan 28). As Commercial Alert flatly stated to book reviewers, "There is a distinction between a novel and an ad; and if you do not uphold the distinction, then who will" (qtd in Sullivan 28).

Such remarks could also apply to Terri Birkett's *Truax*. Although the narrative is described as a parody of Dr. Seuss, it is really a public relations campaign. Commercial Alert's plea for reviewers to maintain the distinction between a creative work and a corporate promotion can ironically be compared with the exhortation to child readers concerning the environment in the closing pages *The Lorax*. The growing presence of corporate-sponsored materials for young children vividly demonstrates to critics, teachers, and parents that "UNLESS someone like you / cares a whole lot / nothing is going to get better. / It's not."

THE YEAR 1995, when Birkett released *Truax*, was also noteworthy in the history of the conservative movement and ascent of the political right: on January 4, the newly elected and—for the first time in four decades—Republican-controlled Congress took their seats. Led by Speaker of the House Newt Gingrich, the cohort represented not simply a Republican majority but what they termed as nothing less than a "Republican Revolution." Indeed, the GOP gained control of Congress in a landslide victory: "The 1994 congressional elections increased the Republican presence in the House of Representatives by 13 percent, resulting in a crucial 53 percent majority, while in the Senate, Republicans rose from a 43 percent minority to a 52 percent majority" (Judd 125). Putting these numbers into some perspective, James E. Campbell observed that "the 1994 midterm election produced the largest seat shift since 1948" (698).

The next chapter examines another crucial component in the expansion of the conservative movement and the rise of the Republican Right: the role played by evangelical Christians. Originating during the 1970s but increasing exponentially after Pat Buchanan's well-received opening speech at the Republican National Convention in 1992, evangelical voters along with their viewpoints played an important part in the late twentieth-century composition of the GOP and especially its rise to power. As J. Christopher Soper has written, a national exit poll conducted by Mitofsky International revealed that "27 percent of all voters identified themselves as a born-again or evangelical Christians, up from an estimated 18 percent in 1988 and 24 percent in 1992" (118). In an even more telling statistic, he continued: "Republican House candidates outpolled Democrats among white evangelicals by 76 to 24 percent" (Soper 118).

The pages that follow examine the cultural platform and political power of the Christian Right by spotlighting the wildly popular Left Behind novels for young readers. In so doing, they also represent the moment when the messages contained in this genre of conservative books become so radical and their social commentary so extreme that they can no longer accurately be characterized as simply right-leaning but are considered instead as part of the right-wing.

3

Not Just Christianity, But the Christian Right

The Battle over Public Education and the American Sunday School Movement in the Left Behind Series for Kids

In 1998, U.S. evangelical minister Tim LaHaye and prolific Christian writer Jerry B. Jenkins released the first novel in the Left Behind series for kids. Called *The Vanishings*, it was modeled after their tremendously successful Christian-themed narratives for adults. Briefly, *The Vanishings* follows the experiences of four young people who are left behind on earth when the end of the world approaches and those believers who have accepted Jesus ascend into heaven. The event, which is discussed in the first book of Thessalonians in the New Testament and commonly termed Rapture,[1] happens as quickly as it does unexpectedly. As the blurb on the back cover of the first *Left Behind* novel indicates, "In one shocking moment, millions around the globe disappear." Taken as only flesh and bone, they shed all of their material adornments and, as the books repeatedly reiterate, "vanish right out of their clothes." When LaHaye and Jenkins's four central characters realize what has happened, they are left to grapple with the despair of knowing that they missed their chance to accept Jesus and thereby enjoy eternal life.

With Rapture taking place in the opening novel of the Left Behind series for kids, the subsequent books follow the experiences of the protagonists—sixteen-year-old Judd Thompson, fourteen-year-old Vicki Byrnes, thirteen year-old Lionel Washington, and twelve-year-old Ryan Daley—during the seven-year period known as Tribulation that encompasses the time between the ascension of God's faithful and the arrival of the four horsemen of the Apocalypse. Tribulation is a time of great trials, tests, and tragedies. These four young people are orphaned by the Rapture, because their parents were either true Christians who are now in heaven or, in the case of Ryan's mother and father, they were nonbelievers who were killed in the many fires, accidents, and related catastrophes that occur in the wake of the disappearances. Adding to these difficulties, a series of biblically-related plagues, disasters, and scourges begins breaking out worldwide. From earthquakes, locusts, and tidal waves to meteor showers, volcanic eruptions, and water turning into blood, these calamities kill millions around the globe and make daily life ever more treacherous. Finally, and by far most threatening, the group witnesses the rise of the Antichrist. This demonic figure takes the form of a handsome Romanian named Nicolae Carpathia whose personal charisma, eloquent public speaking skills, and hypnotic charm cause him to be elected as the U.N. secretary-general within days after the disappearances. Upon assuming office, Carpathia quickly begins to consolidate power. Not surprisingly, one of his first tasks is to systematically eradicate Christianity.

Within this environment of physical peril and spiritual persecution, LaHaye and Jenkins's four central characters struggle both to maintain their newfound faith and to save as many other souls as possible before Armageddon. In an effort to do so, they form an underground Christian resistance group, which they call the "Young Tribulation Force" (or simply the Young Trib Force). Whereas their counterparts in the series for adults use globe-trotting jets, the latest high-tech computer gadgetry, and even various forms of military weaponry to fight the Antichrist, the juvenile characters in these novels employ a more age-appropriate method: they write, publish, and distribute a Christian newspaper at their public school. This seemingly mundane activity, however, proves to be anything but ordinary. Each book is packed with an array of page-turning events: mistaken identities, near-escapes, covert actions, secret hideouts, frequent kidnappings, clandestine meetings, high-speed chases, and—at one point—even a haunted house. Many chapters end with thrilling cliff-hangers, and each installment contains exciting teasers about the next volume; thus, the books are both plot-driven and episodic.

The Left Behind series for kids has been a tremendous success in the United States. Initially feeding off the anxiety generated by the impending turn into the new millennium and accompanying fears about Y2K, and then being greatly reenergized by the attacks of September 11 and resulting concerns over homeland security, the books have tapped into a powerful cultural vein and catered to a strong psychological need. However, the success of LaHaye and Jenkins's books cannot be attributed simply to historical circumstances. As even my brief plot overview indicates, the novels draw on a clever combination of action, suspense, mystery, romance, adventure, sci-fi, and detective fiction in their appeal to adolescent readers. Indeed, while the popularity of most book sequences wanes after the first few installments, the opposite has occurred with LaHaye and Jenkins's texts. The Left Behind series for kids now boasts forty titles, and thus far the novels have collectively sold an astounding eleven million copies.

Almost as popular as the books themselves is their related merchandise. Young adult fans of the series can purchase Left Behind–themed board games, clothes, comic books, audio tapes, screen savers, greeting cards, calendars, and computer video games.[2] Moreover, in February 2001, a feature-length film was made about the books. Starring former television teen idol Kirk Cameron, the movie earned $2.1 million at the box office during its opening weekend, making it the nation's top-grossing independent film to date for that year (Smith, par. 1). In the wake of this success, five more cinematic productions have followed. While the films mainly spotlight characters in the adult version of the series, they always include plotlines about their children, the focus of the Left Behind version for kids. In 2005 journalist Colleen O'Conner noted in the *Denver Post* that the Left Behind product empire now exceeds more than $60 million in annual sales (par 2).

Since the release of the first Left Behind book for kids in 1998, cultural commentators have attributed the success of the novels to the strong evangelical Christian youth movement in the United States. Emerging during the 1990s, it embodies one of the most rapidly expanding as well as commercially powerful groups in the nation. Evidence of the movement's popularity can be seen in various aspects of popular and commercial culture during the late twentieth and early twenty-first centuries. The new musical genre of Christian rock has grown exponentially, with sales increasing more than 318 percent from 1989 to 2005 (Sandler x). Summer "youth for Christ retreats," such as the one depicted in the popular 2006 documentary *Jesus Camp*, have appeared across the country. Sales of the biblically-themed *Veggie Tales* animated movie have exceeded 50 million copies to date, which make it "one of the most popular children's video series—Christian or secular—of the past 15 years" (Radosh 118). Finally, novelty t-shirts with sayings like "Jesus is My Homeboy" have become ubiquitous in American cities. As even these few examples indicate, the evangelical youth movement is a commercial phenomenon—and accompanying cultural demo-graphic—experiencing mega-growth. Daniel Radosh contends that "depending on your definition, between 44 and 126 million Americans are evangelical Chris-tians" (3). The fastest-growing contingent among these is the cohort of young people. According to a study conducted in 2005, a full "one-third of American teens identify themselves as born-again Christians" (Radosh 133).

This massive rise in the evangelical youth movement during the past ten years prompted journalist Lauren Sandler to revise the generational moniker assigned to young people in the United States today. While this demographic is commonly referred to as the "Millennials," she argued that a more accurate descriptor would be the "Disciple Generation" (Sandler 5). Some historians speculate that this growing legion of new converts has helped precipitate another religious Great Awakening—or a time of religious revival, enthusiasm, and fervor. At the very least, the Disciple Generation has given rise to what can be termed an "alternative Christian explosion" throughout the nation (Sandler 1).

This chapter simultaneously builds on and breaks from this common interpretive lens. I argue that in spite of their obvious biblically based subject matter, clear Christian content, and undeniable evangelical perspective, the Left Behind novels for kids are not simply religious books; they also promote political messages. LaHaye and Jenkins may claim that their narratives are interested in sharing the good news about Jesus for the sake of the future, but they are equally concerned with offering commentary on contentious cultural issues in the present. These topics include such perennially hot-button concerns as abortion, sexual promiscuity, and homosexuality. But, given their adolescent readership, the fact that the four central characters start an underground Christian newspaper at their local high school, and the ongoing conservative crusade concerning the issue of school prayer, they are especially preoccupied with the place of Christianity in general and evangelical faith in particular in public education.

To accomplish this goal of educating youth about school prayer and related topics, LaHaye and Jenkins use a potent blend of significant past events in evangelical church history as well as the movement's late twentieth-century engagement in direct forms of sociopolitical activism. Especially in the first ten novels of the series, the authors rehash the arguments offered by many evangelicals to combat the prohibition against prayer in public schools. These include the question of freedom of religion, the absence of the specific phrase "separation of church and state" in the U.S. Constitution, and the power of the First Amendment to protect speech. Far from simply limiting their argument to elements from the present, LaHaye and Jenkins also employ a key event from the past: the nineteenth-century American Sunday School Movement. In a commonly forgotten facet of American educational history—and one that forms a new, additional challenge to the current prohibition against school prayer—these free, open-access Sabbath schools became the model for the public education system in the United States. In so doing, they provide an important historical precedent for the general presence of Christianity in the nation's public school system and evangelical faith specifically.

Through these and other tactics, the Left Behind series for kids serves as a platform not simply for evangelical Christianity but, more accurately, for the agenda of the Christian Right in the United States. LaHaye and Jenkins are as interested in encouraging young people to get to the right of the political spectrum as they are in persuading them to "get right" with God. Their forty-novel series may do battle over the ostensible fate of young adult souls, but the real conflict in which they are engaged is the U.S. culture war.

Evangelical Minster Turned Special Interest Lobbyist: Tim LaHaye and the Christian Right

In the "About the Author" section, which appears in the back pages of each Left Behind book for kids, Tim LaHaye describes himself solely in terms of his evangelical faith and Christian labors. The opening sentence of his biography, for example, asserts: "LaHaye . . . is a noted author, minister, and nationally-recognized speaker on Bible prophecy." The section continues with a list of his theological credentials—"Dr. LaHaye holds a doctor of ministry degree from Western Theological Seminary and a doctor of literature degree from Liberty University"—and an account of ministerial activities: "For twenty-five years he pastored one of the nation's outstanding churches in San Diego, which grew to three locations."

The penultimate paragraph of LaHaye's "About the Author" page concerns his work as a writer. "Dr. LaHaye has written over forty books, with over 30 million copies in print in thirty-three languages." For those who might be curious about the "wide variety of subjects" that he has addressed in his writings, LaHaye offers three sample subject areas: "family life, temperaments, and Bible prophecy." The paragraph also offers his more notable nonfiction books, which include *Spirit-Controlled Temperament*; *How to Be Happy Though Married*; *Revelation Unveiled*; *Understanding the Last Days*; *Rapture Under Attack*; *Are We Living in the End Times?* LaHaye concludes his biography with a discussion of his family: "He is father of four grown children and grandfather of nine."

Although all these details are factual, they paint only a partial portrait of the man who masterminded the Left Behind series for kids. In his "About the Author" statement, LaHaye focuses on the evangelical Christian aspects of life and work to the exclusion of his extensive cultural, social, and political activities. Amy Johnson Frykholm observed that "Timothy LaHaye is unquestionably a political figure" (*Rapture* 178). LaHaye's résumé reads like a who's who of the evangelical Religious Right during the past thirty years. In *Rapture, Revelations, and The End Times*, Bruce David Forbes and Jeanne Halgren Kilde highlight some of LaHaye's most impressive political connections: "He was a board member of Jerry Falwell's Moral Majority, created the Council for National Policy (a coalition of leaders of the religious right), and became head of the American Coalition for Traditional Values" (13).

LaHaye's involvement with these and other political action groups has secured him invitations to the White House to meet with every sitting president since Jimmy Carter. By the mid-1980s—when LaHaye was a frequent advisor to Ronald Reagan on family issues—his work on various political causes had become so extensive that they eclipsed his preaching and ministering: LaHaye moved his family home from southern California, where he had founded a series of churches, to Washington, D.C., where the bulk of his lobbying organizations was based. Given LaHaye's extensive involvement in conservative politics during the past forty years, "Mark Noll, a noted historian of American evangelicalism, lists LaHaye along with Jerry Falwell and James Dobson as examples of conservative religious leaders who 'entered politics with a vengeance during the 1970s and 1980s.' They 'created the New Religious Right and have made conservative evangelical support so important for the Republican Party since the campaigns of Ronald Reagan'" (Forbes and Kilde 13–14).

Not surprisingly, LaHaye's interest in politics is reflected in his writings. In his *The Unhappy Gays* (1978),[3] LeHaye was one of the first conservatives to speak out against the growing acceptance of homosexuality. In addition, in *The Hidden Censors* (1984), LaHaye discussed what he perceived as the leftist control of news, television, radio, and film in the United States. As he asserts in the book's preface, "we no longer have free media in America. They have been captured by a combination of liberals, socialists, atheists, humanists, and Marxists who are using media to change our nation and destroy traditional moral values" (9).

The politically charged topic on which LaHaye has written most frequently and passionately, however, is secular humanism. In *The Race for the 21st Century* (1986), LaHaye offered the most detailed discussion of what he perceives as this pernicious personal philosophy:

> Secular humanism is the philosophic base of liberalism and is easily defined. I call it a Godless, man-centered philosophy of life that rejects moral absolutes and traditional values. It makes man the measure of all things rather than God. It is usually hostile toward religion in general, with a particular hatred toward Christianity. I consider this worldview to be the most harmful, anti-American, anti-Christian philosophy in our country today. Most of society's current evils can be traced to secular humanist thinkers or liberals whose theories originated in that philosophy. (*Race* 139–140)

LaHaye first tackled the question of secular humanism and its harmful effects on American culture in his 1980 book, *The Battle for the Mind: A Subtle Warfare.* However, the book does more than simply detail the evils of secular humanism; it also embodies a call to action. Whereas evangelical Christians had removed themselves almost completely from politics during the 1960s and 1970s—seeing this arena as inherently corrupt and hopelessly amoral—LaHaye makes a case that the time has come for them to reverse this position:

> The growing coalition of pro-moral Americans is a sleeping giant that is gradually awakening to the realization that it has largely ignored the electoral process for decades. Unless it asserts itself and elects pro-moral people to office, America in the twenty-first century will be a humanist country, for the morals and philosophy of the public-school system of today will become the moral philosophy of our nation, in twenty to thirty years. (*Mind* 46)

Lest any lingering doubts remain about the personal duty and even moral obligation that evangelical Christians in the United States have to slough off their former distaste of politics and become involved in various issues, LaHaye concludes *The Battle for the Mind* with the following quote from Dante: "The hottest places in Hell are reserved for those who, in times of moral crises, maintain their neutrality" (190).

While LaHaye feels that every American citizen is vulnerable to the evils of secular humanism, he believes that one demographic of the population is especially vulnerable: children. As he lamented in *The Battle for the Mind*, "Millions of parents have already lost their children's minds to rock stars, atheistic-humanist educators, sensual entertainers, and a host of other anti-God, amoral and anti-man influence" (17). The evangelical minister-turned-cultural-activist felt so strongly about this issue that he wrote an entire series on the topic under the *Battle* moniker. Each book spotlighted a different issue that affected the nation's young people. The first of these titles was *The Battle for the Family* (1981), which identified feminism, rock music, divorce, television, pornography, and homosexuality as primary among the contemporary "forces that relentlessly attack your family" (28).

But his second text, *The Battle for the Public Schools* (1983), is most salient to this study. The book details the ways in which secular humanism threatens our institutions of learning, and, in so doing, it contains some of LaHaye's strongest and arguably most extreme viewpoints to date. The opening page sets the tone for LaHaye's entire argument: "Secular educators no longer make learning their primary objective. Instead our public schools have become conduits to the minds of our youth, training them to be anti-God, antimoral, antifamily, anti–free enterprise and anti-American" (LaHaye *Public* 1). Akin to his previous political writings, LaHaye does not simply bring this social ill to light; he calls on his readers to take action. The closing paragraph of his introduction to *The Battle for the Public Schools*, in fact, asserts: "This third book in my *Battle* series is sent forth with the prayers that it will ignite in the taxpayers' hearts a fire to reclaim control of public education and that it inspire thousands of parents to protect the minds of their children" (10).

LaHaye's extensive involvement in politics, however, is far from a detail of his past. LaHaye continues to play a tremendously influential role in the shadowy Council for National Policy (CNP), an organization that ABCNews.com deemed "the most powerful conservative organization in America you've never heard of" (qtd in Goldberg, par 3). The group functions in a similar way to the now-defunct Moral Majority but, as its name implies, it is especially focused on issues regarding national public policy. *Rolling Stone* writer Richard Dreyfuss noted in a 2004 article that the CNP has not only "funneled billions of dollars to right-wing Christian activists," but it has been credited with leading "the right-wing jihad against President Clinton in the 1990s"; indeed, Dreyfuss continued, "The impeachment effort was reportedly conceived at a June 1997 meeting of the CNP in Montreal" (Dreyfuss, par 6, 14).

During the past few decades, LaHaye's longstanding involvement with issues of interest to evangelical Christians has been formally recognized by his peers. "The Institute for the Study of American Evangelicals named him the most influential evangelical leader of the past twenty-five years, more influential than Billy Graham, because of his ability to mobilize the political energies of evangelicalism" (Fryholm 178). In addition, Jerry Falwell has publicly asserted that "more than any other person" LaHaye persuaded him to get involved in politics (see Dreyfuss, par 10). Finally, Republican political strategist Paul Weyrich has remarked: "Without [LaHaye], what we call the Religious Right would not have developed the way it did, and as quickly as it did" (qtd in Krieger, par 10). Indeed, in the words of Dreyfuss once again: "LaHaye has been the moving force behind several key organizations of the Christian right that have redrawn the boundaries of American politics" (par 6).

Chipping Away at the Wall of Separation between Church and State: The Left Behind Series and the Conservative Crusade for Christianity in the Classroom

Tim LaHaye continues both his corpus of political writing and his calls for personal activism in his Left Behind series for kids. Although he and Jenkins are listed as authors of the books, LaHaye is their self-professed mastermind. He conceived of the idea to fictionalize an account of end-times, and has frequently acknowledged his role as architect of the series.[4] LaHaye may cast his Left Behind series for kids as religious fiction about biblical end-times. But, given his engagement in various conservative crusades during the past thirty years—coupled with his belief that children are acutely vulnerable to pernicious social influences—it is not surprising that the novels are awash with current cultural commentary. As he undoubtedly learned from the success of the Left Behind books for adults, fiction has the potential to reach a much larger audience than nonfiction. By embedding his ideas in exciting plots, intriguing characters, and page-turning events, he is able to get his message to many more young people—exceeding eleven million by 2009.

Indications that the Left Behind series for kids is going to be about something other than evangelical Christianity and end-times theology appear as early as the first novel. The speed with which the four characters convert, along with the enthusiasm with which they embrace their newfound faith, calls into question the series' ostensible focus of bringing young people to Christ. Lionel Washington, for instance, accepts Christ as his savior within hours after learning about the Rapture. Meanwhile, Judd Thompson and Vicki Byrne do so by the end of the next day. The youngest character, twelve-year-old Ryan Daley, is the longest holdout. Even so, he waits less than one week. In the chronology formed by the novels, this period extends only to the opening chapters of the third book.

If readers wonder what will occupy the remaining thirty-plus novels of the series, they don't have to wait long. Evidence of the not-so-subtle thread of political commentary permeating the series emerges in the opening volume. Illustrating how LaHaye uses his fictional series as a conduit for an array of factual conservative causes, the cultural issues that appear in the Left Behind books for kids reflect nearly every subject that he has discussed in his many previous nonfiction works for adults. For instance, given the centrality of pro-life issues to the Christian Right—as well as LaHaye's involvement with anti-abortion groups like the American Coalition for Traditional Values (ACTV)—the books affirm that human life begins at conception. While only selected children and adults go missing during Rapture, all babies and, even more important, all unborn infants do.[5] Similarly, LaHaye uses his Left Behind books for kids to criticize the degenerate nature of the entertainment industry. In volume fifteen—appropriately titled *Battling for the Commander*—Judd and Lionel turn on the television only to see the following horrific programs: "One game show allowed the winner to kill the other contestant. The next channel showed the torture and murder of innocent people" (24).

Of all the politically charged social issues that appear in the Left Behind series for kids, by far the most frequently and fervently discussed is the question of religion in public education. In *Religious Fundamentalism and American Education*, Eugene F. Provenzo Jr. contends that this issue has been central to the Christian Right since the 1980s. From the classroom display of the Ten Commandments and the curricular use of biblical passages to the teaching of sex education and the question of school prayer, evangelical leaders like Jesse Helms, Jerry Falwell, and Tim LaHaye have fought to keep Christian ideas, practices, and materials in the nation's education system. Indeed, as LaHaye lamented in *The Battle for the Family*, "in the public schools when I was a boy . . . we could have religious assemblies, prayer meetings, and youth Bible clubs; Christian teachers could share their faith openly, without fear of being fired. . . . All that has changed, as you well know" (91).

The "change" to which LaHaye alludes was occasioned by two landmark Supreme Court cases: *Engel v. Vitale*, in 1962, held that state-authored prayer had no place in the public education system, and *Abington Township School District v. Schempp*, in 1963, declared that mandatory readings of the Bible and required recitations of the Lord's Prayer were similarly unconstitutional. Taken collectively, these two rulings precipitated a profound transformation to the culture, climate, and even curriculum of American public education. Prior to *Engel* and *Abington*, the nation's classrooms were theoretically supposed to be nonsectarian. However, as one watchdog group has noted, "In reality, schools often reflected the majority religious view, a kind of nondenominational Protestantism. Classes began with devotional readings from the King James Version of the Bible and recitation of the Protestant version of the Lord's Prayer. Students were expected to take part whether they shared those religious sentiments or not" (Americans United, par 17). Challenges to this practice emerged as early as the mid-nineteenth century. Catholic parents, for example, objected to the Protestant bias of the materials used. As a result, by the 1890s, some states had eliminated certain religious elements from their public schools (Mondale and Patton 31–41). The two Supreme Court rulings in the 1960s, however, settled the issue decisively. In the ensuing decades, an array of cases has elaborated on, added to, and clarified the language of *Engel* and *Abington*, but these rulings remain the legal benchmarks concerning the broad question of school prayer.

LaHaye has made it clear in his previous nonfiction writings for adults that he sees the elimination of required recitations of the Lord's Prayer and mandatory readings of Bible passages as further evidence of the nefarious forces of secular humanism at work within American society. In *The Battle for the Family* he lamented: "Now academic freedom means that humanists and other atheists are free to teach their atheistic beliefs, but Christians may not teach theirs" (91). As a result, far more than any other social ill, he dedicates a significant portion of his Left Behind books for kids to the topic. The subject of religion in public education, in fact, quickly dominates the early portion of the series, eclipsing the books' ostensible focus on end-times theology and transforming them into extended polemics about the misguided nature of the separation of church and state, the constitutional right to freely practice one's religion, and the ability of the First Amendment to protect both.

This theme first emerges in book five, *Nicolae High*. The novel takes place several weeks after the Rapture, when some semblance of normalcy returns for the four central characters as the public schools reopen. Initially, Vicki scoffs at the prospect of returning to class. After all, she argues, what is the purpose of getting an education or training for a future profession when the world is going to end in seven years? Judd, however, sees a new reason for attending school: the chance to proselytize about Christ. He excitedly tells Vicki, "Everybody at that high school needs to know what we know. . . . They were left behind just like we were. We'll probably meet some believers, but I'll bet not many" (*Nicolae* 27).

The four central characters quickly realize that this plan is going to be hampered. The high school that Judd and Vicki attend, formerly known as Prospect High (after their town Prospect Heights) has been renamed Nicolae Carpathia High, in honor of the charismatic new leader of the United Nations; unbeknownst to almost the entire world, Carpathia is the Antichrist. Given this fact, the school has become an inhospitable place for those who believe in Jesus, and it thus serves as a thinly disguised metaphor for what many evangelicals see as the current conditions within American public education. LaHaye and Jenkins draw on several actual headline-making events regarding the issue of faith in public education in the new millennium. Echoing an incident that occurred at a Texas middle school in 2000,[6] a teacher confiscates Bibles at an all-class assembly held during homeroom period on the first day. When Judd asks Coach Handlesman why he took the items away, Judd is made vividly aware of the climate of zero tolerance toward Christianity: "'Mind your own business, Thompson,' Handlesman said. 'We haven't allowed Bibles here since before you were born'" (*Nicolae* 75).

As the assembly progresses, such sentiments become even more pronounced. Before dismissing the students to their first period class, the principal acknowledges, "After an international tragedy that has struck so close to home, it's only natural to want to talk about it. It's therapeutic, and our counselors have advised me to let you have at it" (*Nicolae* 76). In spite of this seeming encouragement for students to share their thoughts openly, she mentions an important caveat regarding any discussions: "I must remind you of the strict rule of the separation of church and state that has helped make this country great. We are a public institution, and this is not a forum in which we should espouse religious views" (*Nicolae* 77). Of course, almost immediately, the teacher violates this rule herself. In a passage that reflects LaHaye's assertions in his nonfiction writings that secular humanism occupies a privileged place in American society, she remarks: "Even if I believed with all my heart that this [Rapture] was the best explanation for the disappearances—which, you may rest assured, I emphatically do not—I would maintain that this is the wrong venue in which to propagate that view" (*Nicolae* 77).

This double standard does not go unnoticed. Judd raises his hand and asks Mrs. Jenness to clarify one detail regarding the statement she just made: "Why freedom of speech is extended only to those who hold certain views of what has happened?" (*Nicolae* 78). Clearly annoyed by his inquiry, the teacher responds by simply reiterating, "This is not a freedom-of-speech issue, young man. It's a church-and-state issue" (78).

The remainder of *Nicolae High* reiterates arguments about how freedom of speech ought to trump the separation of church and state. Later during that first day back at school, for instance, Vicki muses about the injustice and even idiocy of the "gag order" regarding religious discussion: "The explanation that made sense [about the disappearances], that most people were aware of, that many had been warned about, was the one they were not allowed to discuss. And why? Because of the separation of church and state. Vicki suddenly felt very old" (*Nicolae* 96).[7] A few pages later, when the subject of faith is broached again, she wonders aloud: "isn't somebody going to get me in trouble with the church/state police? I guess my freedom of speech only goes so far" (*Nicolae* 98–99).

These sentiments reach a climax near the end of the novel. The closing pages of the penultimate chapter read like a catch-all for thirty years of Christian arguments advocating for prayer in public school. When a classmate accuses Vicki of "pushing [her] personal religious beliefs on us, and that's wrong," she can restrain herself no longer:

> Vicki was mad. "I don't accuse you of forcing your beliefs on me when you tell me it was aliens or *Star Trek* scientists. Don't you have a brain? Can't you think for yourself? Do you need to hide behind some rule about the separation of church and state, so you don't hear something that might mess up your mind?" (*Nicolae* 100)

The young woman does not stop there. Vicki points out that the phrase "separation of church and state" does not appear in the Constitution (*Nicolae* 101). This remark, of course, is true: the phrase originated in an 1802 letter written by Thomas Jefferson. The spirited fourteen-year-old uses this fact to strengthen her argument that the protections afforded by free speech ought to trump those regarding the separation of church and state: "Even if it was a law, which it's not, it would be no good if it violated the right to free speech. I have the right to say whatever I want, except here" (*Nicolae* 101–102).

Such passages, and others like them, mirror LaHaye's longstanding practice from his nonfiction texts of highlighting a social, cultural, or religious injustice and then offering a call to action. The Left Behind books provide their young adult readers with a script for questioning, critiquing, and even openly challenging existing policies regarding faith at their local public school. Novels like *Nicolae High* first discuss controversial issues that a teacher might raise, such as separation of church and state, and then Vicki and Judd's comments provide the counterarguments that young readers can make to challenge such assertions.

Book eight, *Death Strike*, expands on this script, by adding suggestions for acts of civil disobedience to accompany verbal challenges. In an event that forms the centerpiece of the novel, Judd uses an invitation to speak at the high school graduation ceremony to proselytize about Jesus. His speech occupies an entire chapter and more closely represents a word-for-word guide to religious conversion than a passage from a fictional novel: "There is one way, one truth, one path to life and peace, and that is through Jesus Christ. . . . I beg you to consider him! He died that you might live" (66). During one well-timed moment in his speech, Judd dramatically unfurls a banner placed behind him, revealing the text from John 3:16: "For God so loved the world that He gave His only begotten Son, that whoever believes in Him should not perish but have everlasting life" (70).

Constitutional Law Left Behind: Misrepresenting Freedom of Religion, the Establishment Clause, and the Supreme Court

Together with using their end-times books as a conduit for commenting on religion in public schools, Jenkins and LaHaye also inaccurately portray the meaning and implications of both the *Engel* and *Abington* rulings, not to mention the First Amendment. In direct contrast to LaHaye's portrayal of a gag order surrounding discussions of faith in the Left Behind books for kids, these decisions did not outlaw voluntary prayer in public schools, forbid students from bringing their own personal Bibles to school, or mandate that classrooms be a "religion-free zone." As Terry Eastland, Kathleen Sullivan, and Gerald Gunther have written, the Supreme Court ruling in *Engel* and especially *Abington* merely removed government-sponsored, sanctioned, or required forms of worship according to the opening phrase of the First Amendment: "Congress shall make no law respecting an establishment of religion" (Constitution). Commonly known as the "Establishment Clause," this section prohibits the U.S. government from adopting any official religion, from giving preference to one faith over another, or promoting "religion over nonreligion or vice versa" (Keynes and Miller 179). Justice Tom Clark asserted in the majority opinion for *Abington* that the government must maintain a firm stance of neutrality in matters of religion "while protecting all, prefer[ring] none, and disparag[ing] none" (qtd in Sullivan and Gunther 1479–80). In so doing, the Supreme Court affirmed Thomas Jefferson's belief, from his oft-mentioned 1802 letter, that the First Amendment was intended to create a "wall of separation" between the church and the state.[8] That said, students still have the right to pray voluntarily during their free time. As Sullivan and Gunther have pointed out, such activities are actually protected by two other clauses of the First Amendment: the one protecting the free exercise of religion and the one safeguarding free speech (1436).

A similar ethos applies to pupils who bring their personal Bibles to school or wish to discuss their faith. Not only are American public school students permitted to possess a Bible, but they are also free to read and talk about it on their own. *Abington* simply forbade the recitation of Bible passages as a required classroom activity. In a similar vein, the Supreme Court justices made clear that their rulings in both cases did not make public schools a place where discussion of religious belief was forbidden. Justice Clark wrote for the court in the 1963 *Abington* ruling, "Nothing that we have said here indicates that such study of the Bible or of religion, when presented objectively as part of a secular program of education, may not be effected consistent with the First Amendment" (qtd in Americans United, par 13). Once again, teachers are simply prohibited from proselytizing about any one faith tradition.

Finally, in direct contrast to LaHaye's view that secular humanists despise religion in general and Christians in particular, Justice Clark added that the government could not force the exclusion of religion in schools "in the sense of affirmatively opposing or showing hostility to religion" (qtd in Sullivan and Gunther 1470). He concluded: "The place of religion in our society is an *exalted one*, achieved through a long tradition of reliance on the home, the church, and the inviolable citadel of the individual heart and mind" (qtd in Sullivan and Gunther 1470; italics in original). The esteemed status as well as intensely personal nature of faith practice dictates, according to Justice Clark, that "in the relationship between man and religion, the State is firmly committed to a position of *neutrality*" (qtd in Sullivan and Gunther 1470; italics in original). This standard of neutrality "requires indifference rather than hostility toward religion" (Keynes and Miller 179).[9]

Because attempts by Jenkins and LaHaye's four protagonists to speak openly about Jesus and the Bible at school are thwarted, they engage in these efforts covertly: via a self-published Christian newspaper. Vicki, who initially conceived of the idea, excitedly explains the venture: "We can use lots of prophecy and stuff from [Pastor] Bruce, and we can just leave piles of them around where anyone can get them. . . . Who knows how many kids might become believers!" (*Nicolae* 114–115). Echoing Lauren Sandler's observation that the current evangelical youth movement casts itself as countercultural because it exists in opposition to what it sees as the liberal mainstream, the Young Trib Force calls their publication the *Underground*.

The hostility toward Christianity at their public school causes the *Underground* to encounter far more criticism than converts. In an absurd distortion of *Abington*—not to mention an egregious violation of the First Amendment—the initial issue is confiscated by the administration only minutes after being placed in the school newspaper racks. Meanwhile, when the Young Trib Force attempts to sneak the next installment into the school after hours, they are caught on the campus security cameras. Averring Daniel Radosh's assertion that "somehow the more powerful the religious right grows, the more desperately Christians cling to the fantasy that they are only one act of Congress away from being herded into concentration camps" (93), Vicki is incarcerated at a juvenile detention facility for her involvement with the newspaper.[10] Meanwhile, when suspicions arise about Judd's possible involvement with the *Underground*, he is arrested by the police.

By the start of book eight—*Death Strike*, in which the Antichrist commences the initial bombing attacks of what becomes World War III—Nicolae Carpathia High has become a totalitarian state with regard to religion. Principal Jenness informs the students at an all-class assembly to start the new school year, "Any student, faculty member, or other employee" who is perceived to "push their beliefs on others . . . will suffer quick and severe punishment" (*Death* 7).

FIGURE 1. Cover image for Terri Birkett's *Truax* (1995). Courtesy of Terri Birkett.

FIGURE 2. The kindly logger Truax and the scary, tantrum-throwing environmentalist Guardbark, from one of the opening pages to Terri Birkett's *Truax* (1995).

Courtesy of Terri Birkett.

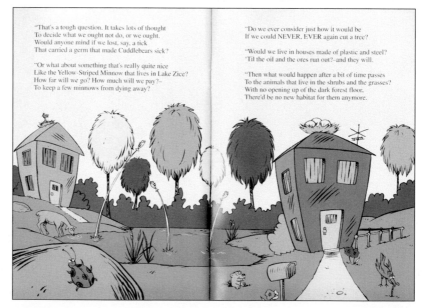

FIGURE 3. Passages from *Truax* where the title character minimizes the endangered species crisis by framing it as a cost-benefit analysis: "How far will we go? How much will we pay?—/ To keep a few minnows from dying away?" Note the Seuss-like trees.

Courtesy of Terri Birkett.

FIGURE 4. Cover image for *Help! Mom! There Are Liberals under My Bed!* (2005). Courtesy of World Ahead Publishing.

FIGURE 5. Mayor Leach, who could be a clone of Ted Kennedy, from *Help! Mom! There Are Liberals under My Bed!* (2005). Courtesy of World Ahead Publishing.

FIGURE 6. Congresswoman Clunkton, who bears a striking resemblance to Hillary Clinton, making the emphatic point, "It takes a village to get kids to eat their vegetables!" From *Help! Mom! There Are Liberals under My Bed!* (2005).

Courtesy of World Ahead Publishing.

FIGURE 7. The lawyer from the LCLU (the "Liberaland Civil Liberties Union") replaces the boys' picture of Jesus with one of a big toe, created with support from public funding. From *Help! Mom! There Are Liberals under My Bed!* (2005).

Courtesy of World Ahead Publishing.

FIGURE 8. Cover image to *Help! Mom! Hollywood's in My Hamper!* (2006). Note the journalist on the far right of the illustration, who takes the politically significant form of a donkey.

Courtesy of World Ahead Publishing.

FIGURE 9. Janie and Sam decked out in their silly, celebrity-sponsored items. A familiar-looking neighbor boy taunts them, and a few other "friends" look on. From *Help! Mom! Hollywood's in My Hamper!* (2006).

Courtesy of World Ahead Publishing.

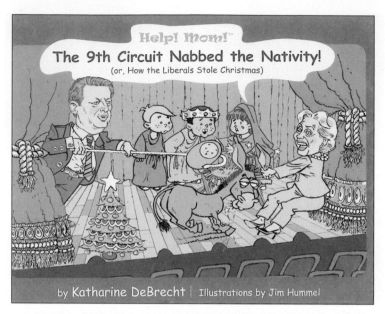

FIGURE 10. Cover image for *Help! Mom! The 9th Circuit Nabbed the Nativity! (or, How the Liberals Stole Christmas)* (2006). Note that, unlike on previous covers, the terms "Help! Mom!" have been trademarked.

Courtesy of World Ahead Publishing.

FIGURE 11. The almost complete cast of characters in *Help! Mom! The 9th Circuit Nabbed the Nativity!* (2006). The cone-headed men in dark suits in the background are judges from the Ninth Circuit.

Courtesy of World Ahead Publishing.

FIGURE 12. Cover image for *Why Mommy Is a Democrat* (2005).
Courtesy of Jeremy Zilber.

FIGURE 13. Sample page from *Why Mommy Is a Democrat* (2005). The large careless elephant recurs throughout the book and is a tacit symbol for the "other" political party, the one to which the mother squirrel does not belong.

Courtesy of Jeremy Zilber.

FIGURE 14. Cover image of *Mama Voted for Obama!* (2008). Courtesy of Jeremy Zilber.

FIGURE 15. A typical page from *Mama Voted for Obama!* (2008).
Courtesy of Jeremy Zilber.

FIGURE 16. However, some passages are more politically pointed. From *Mama Voted for Obama!* (2008).
Courtesy of Jeremy Zilber.

She continues: "Students will be expelled, their records destroyed. Hopes for higher education will be lost" (*Death* 8). The most egregious violators—such as individuals who engage in proselytizing activities like distributing a Christian newspaper—will be sent to the ominous-sounding "Global Community reeducation facility" (*Death* 8).

This atmosphere of religious persecution takes its toll on the four young protagonists, and one cannot help but wonder about its effect on the books' adolescent readers as well. Ryan begins breaking into abandoned homes looking for used Bibles and hoards them in anticipation of the day when the Good Book is outlawed. Meanwhile, Pastor Bruce Barnes offers instruction sessions about how to operate a "home church" for the day when congregational worship is forbidden. By the start of book sixteen, *Fire from Heaven*, the group has been compelled to hide out in a cave to avoid the relentless pursuit of anti-Christian storm troopers from the Global Community and their seemingly ubiquitous helicopters. Finally, during the closing ten novels of the series, the Antichrist has begun executing anyone—man, woman, or even adolescent child—who refuses to pledge complete loyalty to him; they are publicly beheaded on the guillotine.

If these events seem too far-fetched to have much relevance to today, LaHaye and Jenkins pair them with more contemporaneous occurrences. In book eight, *Death Strike*, members of the Young Trib Force "scoffed at the upcoming 'winter holiday' and how far the school went to ensure that the word *Christmas* was never mentioned" (*Death* 34). In so doing, the novels place more extreme examples of the perceived assault against Christianity on a continuum with current cultural controversies. By implying that seemingly small societal changes will eventually—and even inevitably—lead to other more severe forms of persecution, the Left Behind series for kids sends a message to its young readers that a slippery slope exists.

Going Back to the Future: The American Sunday School Movement and Recouping the Evangelical Origins of American Public Education

Not all of the passages advocating for the place of Christianity within public education are this direct or explicit. Together with tapping contemporary arguments gleaned from community challenges and Supreme Court cases since the 1990s, the Left Behind series for kids draws on a more subtle and more historical phenomenon: the American Sunday School Movement. In a frequently recounted history, these largely evangelical Sabbath schools first emerged in the United States during the 1790s. Imported from Great Britain after the tremendous success of Robert Raikes's pioneering efforts during the previous decade, they quickly became, as historian Jack L. Seymour notes, "the nursery of the church" (34). Developing in both urban and rural areas, servicing both poor and middle-class students, and enrolling both adults and children, Sunday schools were proselytizing efforts aimed at bringing nonbelievers to Christ. In weekly lessons held on the Sabbath, students learned about the life of Jesus, heard an overview of his major teachings, and received instruction in how to read and understand the Bible. In this way, Sunday schools not only converted many students to evangelical Protestantism, but they also added to the church membership rolls. According to Seymour, "By 1880, denominational leaders had statistics that showed that 80 percent of all new members came into the church through the Sunday school" (34).

The American Sunday School Movement occupies not merely a passing presence but a central plot point in the Left Behind series for kids. In the opening pages of book one, for example, readers learn that Judd Thompson attended church as well as Sunday school every week from the time that he was a child (*Vanishings* 7). Although the then-nonbeliever scoffed at this institution—sulking during class, deliberately forgetting his Bible, and openly mocking the more enthusiastic pupils—he relishes it in the wake of the disappearances. One of Judd's first actions after the Rapture is to rush back to his church and join a Sunday school–like study group about Jesus and the Bible (138–139).

Akin to their nineteenth-century predecessors, these Sunday school sessions form the cornerstone for the religious instruction of Judd, Vicki, Lionel, and Ryan, as well as a gateway to their church membership. The following passage from book five, *Nicolae High*, offers a representative example of the way in which Pastor Barnes walks the Young Trib Force—and, by extension, the readers of Jenkins and LaHaye's series—through an interpretation of the Bible:

> "So, Judd, read Revelation 7:9."
> Judd took the Bible from Ryan and read, "After this I beheld, and, lo, a great multitude, which no man could number, of all nations, and kindreds, and people, and tongues, stood before the throne, and before the Lamb with white robes, and palms in their hands."
> "That's enough," Bruce said. "Anybody catch it?"
> Vicki said, "I don't know who they're talking about, but it's a crowd so big nobody can number it."
> "Exactly. That's how we know there will be a huge soul harvest. This is talking about the people who come to Christ during the Tribulation."
> (*Nicolae* 38–39)

Pastor Barnes, echoing the main pedagogical technique used in the nineteenth-century Sunday school, explains biblical passages concerning the end times, and then he asks the young people to commit them to memory. Especially when the Young Trib Force is engaged in proselytizing efforts or when another biblically related plague or disaster strikes, they recite these passages; in fact, significant portions of some pages are merely extended quotations of scripture. Finally, reflecting the initial proselytizing purpose of the Sunday school, the Young Trib Force uses their Sabbath sessions to bring into their ranks new pupils, from their public school classmate Shelly and recent convert Conrad to new friend Charlie and converted Jew Chaya. In so doing, the Young Trib Force expands the numbers of evangelical Christian believers.

The presence of elements from the American Sunday School Movement is as much about establishing a historical lineage in the Left Behind series for kids as it is about making a strategic political maneuver. Early Sunday schools in the United States were founded by evangelical Protestant denominations, but religious conversion was not their sole purpose. Anne Boylan has written that, akin to their British counterparts, "most [Sunday schools] were designed to provide rudimentary instruction to poor working children on their only free day of the week" (6). George Schneider has explained the sacred objective behind this seemingly secular mission: "the value of literacy was generally acknowledged, for salvation depended on reading and understanding the Bible. Nevertheless, particularly in remote and sparsely settled regions, it was possible for a young person to grow up without learning how to read" (4). For these reasons, Sunday schools provided a twofold public service: they not only offered literacy instruction to the nation's poor, but they also provided boys and girls with a chance at moral salvation. Pupils who enrolled in Sunday schools did not simply learn how to read; they learned how to read the Bible.

First emerging during the late eighteenth and early nineteenth centuries, Sunday schools predated the advent of free public education in the United States, which did not appear until the 1840s and was not established in some rural areas until as late as the 1870s (Schneider 8). These evangelical-based institutions were the only places where many young people from the lower and lower-middle classes could learn how to read and write. As a result, they had a tremendous attraction and grew exponentially fast: "In Philadelphia alone . . . there were 41 evangelical Sunday schools in 1818. When the American Sunday School Union was organized in 1824, it comprised 723 affiliated schools (others chose not to affiliate), including 68 in Philadelphia. By 1825 the Union had affiliates in twenty-one states, two territories, and the District of Columbia; by 1832 it had expanded to all twenty-four states" (Boylan 10–11). Placing these numbers in a more concrete context, "more than 7,400 students were enrolled in union schools there by 1825. That figure represented approximately 20 percent of the city's five-to-fourteen-year-old population" (Boylan 11). Such figures were replicated in regions throughout the United States: East and West, North and South, urban and rural.

By the outbreak of the Civil War, the rapid growth of Sunday schools made them one of the most powerful religious forces and important cultural institutions in the United States. Indeed, these free, open-access schools became the model for the nation's fledgling system of public education. According to Jack L. Seymour, when state-run "common schools," as they were known, began to appear around the 1840s, they fashioned themselves after the popular, effective, and efficient system of Sabbath schools: the public schools copied the Sunday schools' methods, mimicked their approaches, and even adopted their pedagogical techniques. Through these influences, the origins of American public schools were anything but secular, an often forgotten facet of the nation's educational history:

> The Sunday schools provided a specifically evangelical religious educa-
> tion, but this is not to say that pupils in free schools and later in public
> schools received a purely secular education. They did not. Throughout
> the nineteenth century the curricula of publicly supported schools were
> heavily infused with Protestant precepts and assumptions, yet these
> represented a kind of lowest-common-denominator Protestantism,
> acceptable, for example, to both Unitarians and Baptists. (20)

In a complete reversal of current cultural attitudes, not to mention Supreme Court rulings, public education and Christian content were not seen as mutually exclusive. On the contrary, as George Schneider has written, "Since Sunday schools and education were originally the creation of churches, the general public expected education to be religious and undoubtedly would have been disappointed had it not been" (5).

Tim LaHaye is a longtime scholar of evangelical theology as well as church history. As a result, he is undoubtedly familiar with the critical role that the American Sunday School Movement had in developing public education in the United States. While LaHaye has never explicitly mentioned this fact in any of his published writings, he does frequently discuss the work of Rousas John Rushdoony, who "has contributed more than any other writer or scholar to the fundamentalist interpretation of American educational history" (Provenzo 5). Rushdoony's *The Messianic Character of American Education* promotes reinstituting Bible study and recitations of the Lord's Prayer in American public schools. Rushdoony believes that recovering the Sunday school origins of public education forms the ultimate refutation to claims about the separation of church and state. In *The Race for the 21st Century*, LaHaye has expressed similar sentiments in language that mirrors that of Rushdoony: "That America is *not* a secular nation needs to be officially reaffirmed. This would not only allow voluntary school prayer but would make it possible for our teachers to introduce character training into their curricula" (LaHaye 132; italics in original). He ends his book with a call for readers to "Reaffirm America as a religious country rather than a secular nation" (*Race* 131). Of course, what LaHaye really means by "religious country" is a Christian one: "The noisy liberals who claim that America was not founded on religious principles have never opened a history book or toured our nation's capital, where hundreds of Biblical or religious inscriptions appear on our official monuments" (LaHaye *Race* 131).

The Left Behind series for kids makes a tacit but traceable case for recouping and reclaiming the evangelical root of the public school system in the United States. In book twelve, "the earthquake of the Lamb" physically destroys many public schools or, as in the case of Nicolae Carpathia High, causes them to be converted into temporary shelters and emergency hospitals. However, the Young Trib Force's Sunday school endures. Although their regular meeting schedule is interrupted by the chaotic conditions, the main characters continue to gather together to learn about the life of Jesus and the biblical prophecies concerning end-times. Even the death of Pastor Barnes does not halt instruction. After their teacher is killed in book eight, *Death Strike*, first Judd and then Vicki, assuming leadership roles, conduct the Sunday study sessions and take responsibility for their lessons and curriculum. By book sixteen, *Fire from Heaven*, the Young Trib Force's Sunday school acquires added legitimacy when it relocates to an old, abandoned boarding school that is owned by the family of one of their adult friends. The previously informal Bible study sessions now have an institutional setting, along with a bevy of supplies, courtesy of an adult friend, a former biker known as "Z." "Underneath [a handwritten note in a large box] was a huge stack of spiral notebooks, pens, colored pencils, and other materials" (*Terror in the Stadium* 91).

At this point, the Global Community has discontinued the former system of public education, which leaves only the Sunday school. The GC continues to operate paramilitary training centers that they call, in Orwellian double-speak, "satellite schools." But, as the pamphlets for the institutions themselves assert, they do not teach the three "R's": "You don't need math and science right now. You don't need tests in English composition" (*Horsemen* 121). As a result, although the Young Trib Force initially intends to admit only pupils who are already believers to their Sunday school, they soon revise this policy and welcome those who have yet to accept Jesus. As Vicki tells Melinda, a young girl in dire need of a safe haven from the GC, about the boarding school's system of operation: "Everyone pitches in . . . Plus, you'll attend our studies" (*Terror in the Stadium* 15). Although LaHaye and Jenkins's books claim to look ahead in time, they actually make a case—to appropriate the title of a popular film from the 1980s—for going "back to the future." The Left Behind series for kids returns readers to a time when evangelical Protestant Sunday schools are the only open, free-access forms of education in the United States.

Jerry Falwell, in his 1979 book *America Can Be Saved*, opined: "I hope to live to see the day when, as in the early days of our country, we won't have any public schools. The churches will have taken them over again and Christians will be running them. What a happy day that will be" (53). Tim LaHaye, who worked closely with Falwell during the past thirty years and considered him a close personal friend, has already begun turning this dream into a reality. During his career, LaHaye founded no fewer than twelve evangelical-based elementary and secondary schools along with a Christian college (Dreyfuss, par 9). Now, in his Left Behind series for kids, the evangelical minister turned political activist strives to complete Falwell's vision. Instead of simply establishing faith-based schools that exist in tandem with public ones, LaHaye merges and combines them, blurring their ideological distinctions and bringing the system of open, free access education back to its nineteenth-century roots in the evangelical church. With sales of the novels in the Left Behind series for kids at more than eleven million copies by 2009, the books present to many young adult readers an array of current arguments as well as past precedents allowing for Christianity in the American public schools. One can only imagine LaHaye's hope that this fictional vision will soon become a factual reality in the United States.

From the American Evangelical Community to the World Religious Community: The Left Behind Series for Kids in a Global Context

In an oft-quoted remark, Mahatma Gandhi wrote, "those who say religion has nothing to do with politics do not know what religion means" (67). While the Indian philosopher/political activist was of course not describing the Left Behind series for kids when he penned this statement, he might have been. The series demonstrates the way in which Christian religion and conservative politics are deeply imbricated in the United States. Even the way in which LaHaye and Jenkins's series discusses evangelicalism is, not surprisingly, intensely politically charged. Not only does a strong "us versus them" attitude pervade the books, but they also possess an "I told you so" sense of smugness. A passage from book three, *Through the Flames*, provides a representative example: "Those oldest three kids realized their tragic mistake immediately when the vanishings had taken place. . . . [T]hey had to admit they had been wrong—as wrong as wrong could be" (4). Such comments serve a dual purpose: a scare tactic for nonbelieving readers—the message exhorts the students to give their hearts to Jesus today lest they live to regret it tomorrow—and validation or even wish fulfillment for the evangelical Christian audience.

Given this attitude, the Left Behind books for kids characterize other religions in disparaging ways. With evangelical Protestantism repeatedly cast as "the truth," any other faith is presented, unequivocally, as a "false religion." Unitarianism is discounted in book five, *Nicolae High*; new age spirituality is debunked in book nine, *The Search*; Roman Catholicism is discredited in almost every book, but especially volume six, *The Underground*; and Islam—which is repeatedly used to demonstrate the difference between mere religion and true faith—is disregarded in various books throughout the second half of the series.

Of all the religious traditions criticized in the Left Behind books for kids, Judaism fares the worst. Soon after the Rapture, two biblical-times witnesses, Eli and Moishe, appear at the Wailing Wall in Jerusalem. For twenty-four hours a day, the two men proselytize about Jesus, largely by renouncing Judaism. In the opening pages of book eight, for example, they proclaim: "Israel has rebuilt the temple to hasten the return of their Messiah . . . not realizing that the true Messiah has already come!" (*Death* 18). Lest this point remains unclear, it is uttered by several Jewish characters themselves. First, Rabbi Tsion Ben-Judah, an Israeli scholar who has spent decades studying the Torah, Talmud, and various theological documents, concludes that Jesus is "the true Messiah of the Jews" (*Darkening Skies* 102). His "discovery" is broadcast on all the major news channels. Then, in numerous novels throughout the series, several Jewish characters convert, including Chaya Stein and her formerly recalcitrant father, Mitchell: "'My daughter was right. I believe Jesus is the only way and that I cannot come to God except through him. . . . I am ashamed to have been so blind.' . . . Tearfully, Mr. Stein completed his prayer. 'Oh God, please forgive me'" (*Battling the Commander* 29).

The tone of religious intolerance reaches an arguable all-time high—not to mention a shocking level of candor—in book twenty-three, *Horsemen of Terror*: "God does not permit murder. It is one of his commandments. But there are certain circumstances, in warfare for instance, where God tells his people to kill those who are against him" (114). To be fair, this comment is uttered during a conversation contemplating a possible assassination attempt on the Antichrist. But the distance between justifying the use of lethal violence against the devil incarnate and justifying its use against anyone who disagrees with your beliefs is bridged in the very next novel. In book twenty-four, *Uplink from the Underground*, Vicki talks about God with religious skeptic Marjorie and, in doing so, conveys her absolutist stance regarding nonbelievers: "Jesus said that anybody who isn't for him is against him" (52).

This antipathy toward religious difference and hostility for multiculturalism forms the premise for the series-inspired PC-based video game. Called *Left Behind: Eternal Forces*, the item was initially released in March 2006, and Max Blumenthal provided an overview of the product in *The Nation*. The game's premise is so over-the-top that it is difficult not to see it as a parody. Blumenthal describes the action: when a "*Left Behind* player kills a UN soldier, their virtual character exclaims, 'Praise the Lord!' To win the game, players must kill or convert all the non-believers left behind after the rapture" (par 1). The game is rated "T" for teen by the Entertainment Software Rating Board—the governing body for video game content in the United States—which means that is approved for players as young as thirteen. Even more astoundingly, the FAQ page on the product's official commercial website offers the following endorsement: "The millions of parents—and many casual players of games—that are looking for entertainment that also *offers positive, inspirational content* will flock to this title" (Left Behind Games, par 1; my emphasis). Apparently, such plugs have been successful, for the initial Left Behind video game now boasts a sequel, *Left Behind: Tribulation Force.*

The Left Behind video games appeared in the news again in 2007, when Operation Straight Up (OSU), an evangelical organization that provides Christian entertainment and materials to U.S. troops, planned to include the sequel game in their "Freedom Packages" to personnel serving in Iraq. Public outcry—as well as government pressure—ultimately prompted the organization to remove the item (see Blumenthal). Nonetheless, given their negative and even murderous messages about international cooperation, multiculturalism, and religious diversity, these games—and the books on which they are based—have alarming implications for not simply the American evangelical community but also the global religious community. The role that rhetoric concerning religious righteousness and Christian rectitude has played in U.S. foreign policy during the opening years of the new millennium provides just one vivid example. President George W. Bush—himself a born-again Christian—repeatedly claimed that "God is on our side" both in the war on terror and in the invasion of Iraq (see "Bush Slammed" and Toohey). Tim LaHaye's remarks on these subjects have been even more pointed. In the issue of his magazine *Pre-Trib Perspectives* that was published a few months after the terrorist attacks of 9/11, LaHaye proclaimed that he was not surprised by the events because "the religion of Islam has always been a terrorist religion" (1). In an earlier issue—the first one to appear in the wake of 9/11—LaHaye predicted that the attack would "contribute to the fulfillment of several . . . end-times signs" (3).

IN RELIGIOUS FUNDAMENTALISM AND AMERICAN EDUCATION: The Battle for the Public Schools, Eugene F. Provenzo Jr. offers his assessment of the McCollum case: "Justice Felix Frankfurter argued in *McCollum v. Board of Education* that: 'The public school is at once a symbol of our democracy and that most pervasive means of promoting our common destiny'" (91). As Frankfurter's comments suggest, the real question being asked in disputes concerning the content, aim and objective of classroom curricula is not simply "What should our children know?" but rather, and more important, "Who should our children—and, by extension, our nation—become?" In this way, arguments over the inclusion (or exclusion) of certain reading materials are really arguments over the nature of national identity and the composition of a collective cultural character.

The chapter that follows both continues and extends this argument. It examines a series of patriotic-themed picture books penned by then-Second

Lady Lynne Chency that reignited longstanding cultural debates concerning the "correct" presentation of U.S. history, the "appropriate" way to teach about socio-cultural events from previous eras, and the "proper" portrayal of foundational American figures and texts. Whether discussing the United States today or yesterday, Cheney's message to young people is clear. Throughout books like *America: A Patriotic Primer*, *We the People*, and *Our 50 States*, the second lady equates patriotism with conservatism.

4

Patriot Acts

Fighting the War on Terror via the Canon Wars in Lynne Cheney's Picture Books

While evangelical figures such as Tim LaHaye and movements such as the Christian Right, discussed in chapter 3, played an important role in the expansion of conservative thought and right-wing politics since the 1970s, another less publicly visible but equally powerful influence was also instrumental: the proliferation of think tanks.

Public policy research institutes, or "think tanks" as they are more popularly known, are, in the words of James McGann and Erik K. Johnson, "nongovernmental and nonprofit organizations that perform research and provide advice on public policy" (11). Staff members at these organizations seek to bridge the perceived gap between the Ivory Tower and Capital Hill by providing analysis about social, economic, and political issues with the ultimate—and ideal—goal of helping elected officials make wiser, more informed decisions.

Think tanks first emerged in the United States in the early 1900s—out of the philanthropic impulses of the Progressive era—but the number of these organizations, the political power that they wielded, and the ideological leaning to which they subscribed radically changed during the latter half of the twentieth century. Arising in part from the increasing fragmentation of U.S. politics during the 1970s and in part from the large-scale shift of American businesses to more conservative viewpoints, a "wide range of corporations and foundations supported a growing network of conservative think tanks and policy centers" (Himmelstein 148). In statistics as impressive as they are eye-opening, "two-thirds of all the think tanks in existence today were established after 1970 and over half were established since 1980" (McGann and Johnson 11). Donald Abelson, attaching more precise numbers to this general trend, noted how "until the outbreak of World War II, less than two dozen policy institutes existed in the United States. . . . By the end of the twentieth century, this number exceeded sixteen hundred" (17). Perhaps it is not surprising, given that think tanks are generally founded by individuals who have amassed their wealth through capitalism, that "overwhelming majority . . . have been broadly conservative, producing work that favors limited government, free enterprise, and personal freedom" (Rich 10). In fact, after conducting a statistical analysis of public policy research institutes operating during the late 1990s, Rich estimated that conservative-leaning organizations outnumbered liberal groups by more than two to one; moreover, he continued, they outspend them at a rate that exceeds three to one (22).

The size, scope, and mission statements of conservative think tanks vary widely; some institutions focus on a single policy area and have a budget of less than a hundred thousand dollars, while others operate as what Rich characterizes as "full-service" organizations that tackle a broad range of issues and enjoy a budget in the tens of millions (17). Nonetheless, think tanks share a common purpose. In activities ranging from drafting policy proposals, organizing conferences, and hosting speakers to testifying before Congress, appearing as commentators on television and radio programs, and writing newspaper, magazine, and scholarly articles, conservative think tanks work both to shape public opinion and to influence policy makers. Often, the institutes reflect the libertarian strain within conservatism. For instance, "beginning in 1977 the John M. Olin Foundation, founded by former head of the Olin Corporation, spent about $5 million a year to support 'scholarship in the philosophy of a free society and the economics of a free market'" (Himmelstein 149).

Especially since the Reagan administration, conservative think tanks have exerted tremendous influence. The success of "these institutions stems from an unavoidable weakness in all modern political systems—the constraints of time. Decision makers simply do not have the time to conduct in-depth research into all of the topics for which they must formulate and evaluate policies" (McGann and Johnson 12). Hence, they rely on the statistical information, research analysis, and ready-made legislative materials provided by think tanks. The more than one-thousand-page *Mandate for Leadership: Policy Management in a Conservative Administration* that the Heritage Foundation delivered to Ronald Reagan when he took office in 1981 forms a poignant example. The report, which was compiled with "the assistance of over three hundred academics, consultants, lawyers, and former government officials divided into twenty project teams," contained more than "two thousand proposals on issues ranging from how to streamline the government bureaucracy to ways to improve U.S. national security" (Abelson 134). By 1982, Edwin Feulner, the president of Heritage, estimated "that more than 60 percent of Heritage's proposals had been adopted by the Reagan administration" (qtd in Abelson 135).

Public policy research institutes also play a more direct role in government. Cabinet members and other high-level appointees in the executive branch are frequently drawn from the ranks of the larger and more influential organizations. Consider one presidential administration as an example: "In Reagan's first-term alone, fifty [appointees] came from Hoover, thirty-six from Heritage . . . and eighteen from the Center for Strategic and International Studies" (Himmelstein 151). Conversely, when an administration leaves office, key figures routinely take up residence at various think tanks. Such institutions provide these men and women with an operational base, steady funding, and a public platform from which they can continue their legislative agenda. Edwin Meese, the U.S. attorney general during Reagan's second term, for example, accepted a position as distinguished visiting fellow at the Hoover Institute. Likewise, William Bennett, the former secretary of education as well as, of course, the subject of chapter 1, has been a fellow at the Heritage Foundation since leaving his post as director of National Drug Control Policy in 1991.

Of the numerous and diverse conservative think tanks in the United States, the American Enterprise Institute (AEI) is one of the oldest and most influential. Indeed, both Jerome Himmelstein and John S. Saloma have called the organization "the flagship" among conservative public policy research institutes (Himmelstein 147; Saloma 12). Founded in 1943 as a counterpart to the left-leaning Brookings Institute, AEI has been an intellectual hub for the conservative movement for more than six decades. Reflecting a wide range of conservative viewpoints, it seeks, in the words of its mission statement, "to defend the principles and improve the institutions of American freedom and democratic capitalism—limited government, private enterprise, individual liberty and responsibility, vigilant and effective defense and foreign policies, political accountability, and open debate" ("AEI's Organization and Purpose," par 2).

The American Enterprise Institute remains a fixture in the contemporary conservative movement and political activities of the right. As Sally Covington has documented, the organization "actively sought to influence the economic, regulatory, welfare, health, and other social policies, appearing on national media several times a day throughout the 1995–1996 period" (16). On behalf of these causes, "AEI and affiliated scholars also produced over 600 articles and studies" (Covington 16). Indicating the influence that the think tank possessed inside the Beltway, AEI President Christopher DeMuth commented in the institute's 1994 annual report: "We are delighted to be members in good standing of the Washington Establishment, called upon many times each day for Congressional testimony, media commentary, and advice on all manner of policy issues" (qtd in Covington 16).

AEI attained prominence in the opening decade of the twenty-first century as the mastermind of George W. Bush's public policy during his second term. AEI counts former U.S. Deputy Secretary of Defense Paul Wolfowitz, former Republican Speaker of the House Newt Gingrich, and no fewer than twenty other past or present members of the Bush administration as staff members. When not engaged in direct lobbying efforts, AEI sponsors a bevy of academic lectures, conferences, and book readings. In 2008, for example, they hosted a panel discussion about Mark Krikorian's *The New Case Against Immigration*, a nonfiction work that argues that "America has reached maturity as a nation and thus simply has no need for immigration, legal or otherwise" so therefore "it's time to lock down the gates to all but the most select few" (Kirkus 99). These and other activities have earned the American Enterprise Institute the reputation for providing "a home and launching pad for arch-conservative scholars" (Media Transparency, "American Enterprise Institute," par 9). By 2004, the net worth of the organization had grown to more than $56 million (Foundation Center). With these ample assets, AEI funded more than seventy scholars and fellows, along with "four journals and a monthly television show" (Himmelstein 147).

In May 2002, the American Enterprise Institute expanded its repertoire of sponsored activities to a new realm—picture books for children—when the then-second lady and longtime senior fellow in education and culture at AEI released *America: A Patriotic Primer*. Beautifully illustrated by Robin Preiss Glasser, the text had an unmistakably didactic purpose and clear conservative message. As its title suggested, *Primer* combined a survey of the alphabet with a historical overview of the United States. With the letter A standing for America, C for the Constitution, and J for Jefferson, and so on, Cheney's book offered to the next generation a laudatory view of America's past, a spotlight on "classic" figures and texts in U.S. history, and a clear demonstration of the undeniable greatness of the nation's heroes.

While these issues have always been at the heart of the conservative movement, they assumed added urgency at the time when Cheney's book was written and released: the aftermath of the terrorist attacks of September 11, 2001. The events of 9/11 unified the cause and energized the force for conservatives in the United States. The twenty-first-century goal of combating terrorism filled the void left by the now-defunct twentieth-century focus on combating communism. Released into a public atmosphere that witnessed a massive surge in patriotism, a growing interest in American history, and a heightened veneration for heroism, *America: A Patriotic Primer* was an instant commercial success. By June, "the book held the top slot on children's lists from *Publisher's Weekly*, BookSense, and the *New York Times* (having charted *USA Today* and the *Wall Street Journal* as well)" (Maughan 26). Encouraged by this reception, by 2009 Cheney penned four additional picture books: *A Is for Abigail: An Almanac of Amazing American Women* (2003), *When Washington Crossed the Delaware: A Wintertime Story for Young Patriots* (2004), *Our Fifty States: A Family Adventure Across America* (2006), and *We the People: The Story of Our Constitution* (2008).

In numerous interviews and press releases, the former second lady has repeatedly pointed to her delight in being a grandmother and her desire to entertain young children as the inspiration for her new career as a children's author. Discussing *When Washington Crossed the Delaware*, for instance, she remarked how much she "likes to tell her grandchildren the story of George Washington crossing the Delaware River on Christmas 1776 for the Battle of Trenton" and wanted to share "that historical story with children nationwide" ("Cheney" par 1). Reinforcing these sentiments, all of Cheney's picture books are dedicated to her various grandsons and granddaughters. Furthermore, the back cover to each narrative contains a large color photograph of the former second lady surrounded by a gaggle of cute, happy youngsters. These details have placed Cheney in dialogue with the numerous other celebrities who have penned books for children during the past few decades and who cite similar reasons for their sudden decision to write for young people (see Kakutani).[1]

In this chapter I offer another, far less philanthropic and sentimental motive. Although the former second lady claims to have written her picture books as a gift for the families of the nation, they can be more comfortably seen as the product of the growing reach of conservative think tanks. In a detail that Cheney announces directly in the acknowledgments to *America: A Patriotic Primer*, the narrative was an official project for her at the American Enterprise Institute; so, too, were all of its sequels.

Cheney's first and by far most popular picture book reveals how the commencement of the U.S. foreign war on terror prompted her to resume her previous battle station in the domestic canon wars. From 1986 to 1993, Cheney served as chairman of the National Endowment for the Humanities (NEH) where she waged a very public fight against changes to the canon of U.S. history that were being precipitated by the growing interest in multiculturalism. After leaving the position, Cheney accepted a post at the American Enterprise Institute where she continued this crusade through op-ed pieces, speeches, and mainstream media appearances.

This chapter charts the process by which Cheney began at NEH, moved to AEI, and finally, with the publication of *America: A Patriotic Primer*, ended up at ABC. Although the acronyms associated with Cheney's institutional affiliation have changed, her ideological message has remained the same. The continuity of Cheney's viewpoints across time periods, cultural media, and target audiences points to an even more important implication. Whereas conservative think tanks like AEI formerly limited their advocacy work to an adult audience, the appearance of *Primer* signals a move into a new demographic: children. Thus, Cheney's picture book is more than an altruistic gift from a loving grandmother or selfless public servant; ultimately, it is a think tank solution to a perceived national problem.

From NEH to AEI to ABC: Lynne Cheney's Previous
Career in the Alphabet Acronym Soup

While Lynne Cheney is perhaps currently most well known as the wife of former Vice President Dick Cheney, she is famous in her own right. Prior to becoming second lady, Cheney was chairman of the National Endowment for the Humanities. Appointed by President Reagan to the position in 1986, she succeeded fellow public-figure-turned-children's-author William Bennett. Cheney, Bennett's chronological as well as ideological successor, continued his battle against changes to the canon of Western literature, history, and philosophy. In a series of public reports that Cheney wrote as head of the NEH, she railed against what she saw as a misguided change in focus. Her very first report, titled *Humanities in America*, argued that the elimination of required courses in Western civilization and the new emphasis on the contributions from gender, racial, ethnic, and socioeconomic minority groups in the teaching of U.S. history was crowding out more "classic" and, in her view, "essential" areas of study (4). Cheney discussed, for example, how "a 1988 survey funded by the National Endowment for the Humanities shows . . . it is possible to graduate now, as it was five years ago, from *more* than 80 percent of our institutions of higher education without taking a course in American history" (5; italics in original). As a result of this trend, Cheney believed that U.S. students were becoming increasingly ignorant of key elements from the nation's past. She cited with alarm, for example, how a 1986 survey funded by the NEH and conducted by the National Assessment of Educational Progress showed that "the plurality" of students at "the 55 most elite colleges in the country" could not identify "the commanding general at Yorktown" (12–13).

Such sentiments became the theme for all of Cheney's future work as chair of the NEH. Her 1990 report, for instance, bore not only the eye-catching title *Tyrannical Machines*, but the even more explicit subtitle, *A Report on Educational Practices Gone Wrong and Our Best Hopes for Setting Them Right*. On almost every page of the document, Cheney peppers the reader with statistics that point to the perceived erosion of knowledge regarding "classics" or "masterworks" of Western literature, history, and philosophy:

> A 1989 survey, also funded by the NEH, showed one out of four college seniors unable to distinguish Churchill's words from Stalin's or Karl Marx's thoughts from the ideas of the United States Constitution. More than half failed to understand the purpose of the Emancipation Proclamation or *The Federalist* papers. (*Tyrannical* 2)

Cheney's third and final NEH report was the most polemical. Under the revealing title *Telling the Truth* (1992), it broadened her attack against changes in the humanities to include the emerging field of women's studies. In comments that ignited a firestorm both within the academic world and throughout the culture at large, Cheney accused college and university professors of using their classrooms not to disseminate knowledge, but to "break down student resistance to feminist ideology" (*Telling* 15). As Cheney had written earlier: "It might seem obvious that all students should be knowledgeable about texts that have formed the foundations of the society in which they live" (*Humanities* 12). The nation's largely liberal academics, she continued, denigrated documents like The Declaration of Independence and the U.S. Constitution, which, because they were "mostly written by a privileged group of white males, are elitist, racist, and sexist" (*Humanities* 12).

For her efforts, Cheney was the first person in the history of the NEH to be confirmed for a second term, by a unanimous vote of the Senate in 1990. Although her tenure as chair did not expire until April 1995, she resigned sixteen months early, on January 20, 1993, the day that Clinton was inaugurated. U.S. presidents do not have the power to dismiss a sitting NEH chairman, but Cheney, a longtime Republican, did not wish to work with the new Democratic commander-in-chief or his administration.

Cheney's resignation from the NEH did not end her work as "an attack dog for the right"—as Elaine Showalter once quipped (par 25). That same year, she accepted the position as the W. H. Brady Scholar at the American Enterprise Institute and used the post to continue her crusade against the perceived assault on U.S history by multiculturalism, feminism, and postmodernism. One of her first projects, for example, was to compose a book-length version of her NEH report, *Telling the Truth*.[2] The expanded text was published in 1995 and bore the inflammatory subtitle *Why Our Culture and Our Country Have Stopped Making Sense—and What We Can Do About It*. Moreover, its strong sales and equally strong public reaction helped Cheney earn a promotion to the rank of senior fellow in education and culture ("Lynne Cheney Returning," par 3).

From her new post at AEI Cheney did not simply carry on her work in the canon wars; she actually expanded on it. In a detail that is often overlooked by commentators, some of Cheney's most notorious acts on behalf of defending the nation's so-called "common culture" occurred while she was a staff member at the conservative think tank. In 1994, one year after she arrived at AEI, Cheney made headlines when she denounced the proposed new National Standards in United States History. In op-ed pieces that appeared in the *New York Times* and the *Wall Street Journal*, Cheney declared that the standards, which outlined five broad subject areas for students in the United States, embodied "the gloomy, politically driven, blame-the-West-first revisionism that is all too common today" ("Mocking" A29). Cheney believed that the proposal was far too critical of Western culture. "Reading the world history standards," she remarked, "one would think that sexism and ethnocentrism arose in the West" ("Mocking" A29). Cheney objected to the praise lavished on the "achievements and grandeur of Mansa Musa's court, and the social customs and wealth of the kingdom of Mali" in West Africa but lamented that "such celebratory prose is rare when the document gets to American history itself" ("End" A22). On the contrary, the Standards focus on national failings and missteps, such as the U.S. genocide of American Indian tribes and the "unethical and amoral business practices" of capitalists like John D. Rockefeller ("End" A22). In her closing comments, Cheney bemoaned how foundational documents like the U.S. Constitution are relegated to the appendices of supporting texts rather than given prominence as required areas of knowledge on their own.[3]

Cheney's displeasure with the proposed National History Standards was a contributing factor in another of her most infamous acts: advocating for the elimination of the National Endowment for the Humanities itself. In 1995, from her position at the American Enterprise Institute, Cheney wrote articles, gave speeches, and even appeared before the newly elected Republican Congress to argue that this organization, which she had enthusiastically chaired for an unprecedented two terms, vociferously championed in the public eye, and on whose behalf she had successfully lobbied for an increase in federal funding, should be dismantled. In a dramatic change in attitude, shared by fellow former NEH chair William Bennett and attributed by many more to partisan politics than a genuine shift in viewpoint, Cheney declared that it was time to "cut funding for cultural elites" (qtd in Cashburn 12). Instead, the future second lady argued that support for the arts should come from the private, not the public, sector (qtd in Cashburn 12). The recommendations of Bennett and Cheney were largely heeded; in 1996, the Republican Congress voted to cut the budget of the NEH by 36 percent ("Scholarly Editions" 12).

Even when not battling specific issues, Lynne Cheney has remained very much in the spotlight. She served as a cohost from 1995 to 1998 for the Sunday edition of CNN's political debate program *Crossfire*. Her on-air bio and on-screen byline frequently mentioned both her former chairmanship of the National Endowment for the Humanities and her current post at the American Enterprise Institute. Moreover, in a telling tagline, she signed off many episodes with the remark: "From the right, and right on every issue, I'm Lynne Cheney" (see Henneberger A1).

Taken collectively, Cheney's public actions and the ideology that fueled them have earned her the nickname the "Wicked Witch of the West" (Showalter, par 2). Meanwhile, Jonathan Chait in *The American Prospect* dubbed the future second lady "the leading policy assassin for the right-wing cultural warriors" (par 2). Finally, Jon Wiener in an article that appeared in *The Nation* called Cheney nothing less than an "ideological pugilist" who is "a master at getting herself into the limelight" (par 4). "Making war on liberals is her forte," he concluded (Wiener, par 4), and this assessment was more than accurate; Cheney built a career largely by doing so.

The Perfect Storm: The Terrorist Attacks of 9/11, the Surge in U.S. Patriotism, and Revival of Lynne Cheney's Celebratory View of American History

Given Cheney's outspoken nature and her stalwart conservative credentials, many Republicans were thrilled when her husband was named as the vice presidential nominee in 2000. Cheney's predecessor at the NEH, William Bennett, in fact, "openly rejoiced at the prospect of a tough-minded second lady who would defend the Western canon and lash out at women's studies and multiculturalism" (Showalter, par 2). Bennett gleefully informed *The Washington Post*, "She'll be hard to muzzle" (qtd in Schmidt A1).

In spite of this seemingly reasonable prediction, both during the 2000 presidential campaign and after she moved into the residence of the vice president, Cheney scaled back her public role. Out of an oft-stated desire not to overshadow the first lady—not to mention the Bush administration as a whole—Cheney showed such a moderate side of her personality that *Newsday* called her "the woman with the sock in her mouth" (Winer D2). Whereas Cheney was previously ridiculed for being a "Republican cultural warrior" (Wolfe, par 15), she was now chastised, in an article that appeared in the *Chicago Sun-Times*, for feeling "compelled to portray herself so, well, lamely" (Neal and Sweet 22). Far from mere hyperbole, the woman who had formerly been called "strident," "combative," and an "ideologue" was now posing for photo-ops that showed her cheerfully ironing her husband's shirts (Wiener, par 4). Although Cheney retained her position as senior faculty fellow of education and culture at the American Enterprise Institute, it seemed increasingly nominal.

Whatever detente Lynne Cheney brokered for herself in the canon wars, the events of September 11, 2001, brought this truce to an end. The terrorist attacks on New York and Washington ended her days on the cultural sidelines and marked her return to the spotlight. Both her words and her actions in the aftermath of 9/11 revealed that while she may have scaled back her advocacy efforts during the 2000 presidential campaign and early days of the Bush administration, she did not fundamentally change who she was or what she believed. This fact was evident in the very first speech that Cheney gave after the attacks. Delivered in late November at the James Madison Program of Princeton University, Cheney used it to lament the widespread lack of general knowledge about U.S. history among students at the nation's elite campuses. In statistics that mirror those contained in her various reports as NEH chair and her many subsequent writings as a fellow at AEI, she asserted: "A 1999 survey of elite college seniors—that is seniors at schools like Princeton and Yale and Stanford—showed that only one out of five knew that the words 'government of the people, by the people, for the people' came from the Gettysburg Address. Forty percent did not know that the Constitution established the division of power between the states and the federal government." To the question of who was the American general in command at Yorktown, the most popular answer was Ulysses S. Grant ("Mrs. Cheney's Remarks," par 11–12). Cheney attributed this lack of "essential knowledge of our nation's past" to the same culprits as in previous eras. In a comment that seems taken directly out of Cheney's previous reports at the NEH, she asserted, "surely a contributing factor to the lack of knowledge highlighted by the survey is that not one—not a single one—of the fifty-five elite colleges and universities whose students were polled required a course in American history" ("Mrs. Cheney's Remarks," par 13). Having lost hope that colleges and universities would remedy this situation anytime soon, she encouraged her audience to take matters into their hands for the sake of the nation's students: "They will continue to place Ulysses S. Grant at Yorktown—unless we come up with extracurricular ways to encourage them to know the men and women and events and ideas that have shaped this country" ("Mrs. Cheney's Remarks," par 15).

Such comments were only the beginning. In the months that followed, the frequency as well as ferocity of Cheney remarks on the subject increased. Journalist Susan Page reported in *USA Today*, "Some educators have said the attacks underscore the need to teach more about other cultures. But Cheney, a veteran of the wars over political correctness during her tenure as head of the National Endowment for the Humanities, takes a different lesson" (Page 1D). In that first public interview after 9/11 Cheney herself asserted that "it seems to me that the most important thing to do now is to look at the neglected area of American history teaching. . . . When we're in a state of war . . . we need to be sure our children and that we ourselves understand what's at stake, what is worth defending. When you know the story of this country, that makes it pretty clear what it is we're standing for." (Page 1D). *America: A Patriotic Primer* was written in direct response to these sentiments. The picture book emerged from Cheney's longstanding belief that the nation's children always need to have a firm knowledge about U.S. history and government but especially during a time of sociopolitical crisis. Indeed, in a prepared statement that formed part of the pre-release media blitz for *Patriotic Primer*, Cheney asserted: "It is now more important than ever that our children and grandchildren know the foundation of America's freedom and understand why we hold this nation dear" (qtd in "Newsmakers" A2). After years of arguing that children should be exposed to more positive views of the United States, Cheney composed a book that accomplished this task. Indeed, as Anastasia Ulanowicz has observed, *America: A Patriotic Primer* put into practice her call from the November 2001 speech at Princeton to "come up with extracurricular ways" to convey information that was not being taught in the nation's schools (348). Cheney told journalist Beth Gillin in an article about her new book: "'When teaching about America, [. . .] it is wrong to disguise the greatness of our national story. We've achieved mightily'" (D1).

The mode of production for *Patriotic Primer* was just as significant as its message. Cheney could have written an op-ed piece, given a speech, or published a position paper to disseminate her views about the renewed need for U.S. history instruction for young people, as she had done in the past. In a significant divergence from these previous tactics, she decided instead to write a picture book. Using the financial resources, staff support and—perhaps most important—marketing machine provided by her position at the American Enterprise Institute, Cheney repackaged the message of her previous and more vitriolic writings for adults into a more palatable and cutely illustrated narrative for children. In so doing, Cheney moved from simply advocating for an idea to staging an intervention.

CHENEY MAKES NO ATTEMPT to obfuscate the connection between *America: A Patriotic Primer* and her work at a conservative think tank. Far from a detail that readers can discover only from investigating the internal operations at AEI, this fact can be gleaned simply from reading the acknowledgments in Cheney's picture book. Located on the left—or verso—side of the text following the title page—and sharing space with the publisher's imprint, copyright material, and Library of Congress cataloguing information—the acknowledgments are easily overlooked. However, the list is exceptionally revealing. Cheney devotes the largest portion of this segment—six out of the thirteen lines—to thanking her colleagues at AEI, thus spotlighting the tie between the think tank and her narrative for young readers. In a comment that reveals her high esteem for the conservative think tank but not for the field of children's literature, Cheney says of her AEI colleagues: "All of them together create a rich intellectual environment in which all kinds of ideas thrive, *even an idea for a children's book*" (my emphasis).[4]

In the same way that Cheney makes no attempt to conceal the connection between her work at the conservative think tank and her production of a picture book for young readers, she also does not try to hide the politically charged nature of *America: A Patriotic Primer*. On the contrary, Cheney announces its culturally combative component via the illustration that she elected to display on its cover. The image shows a group of children raising an American flag in a manner that is reflective of Joe Roesenthal's Pulitzer Prize–winning photograph of soldiers at Iwo Jima. By having elementary-aged children replace adult soldiers, and the present day stand-in for the era of World War II, Cheney is not only making a statement about how young people currently occupy the field of battle, but she is also piggy-backing on a time of unquestioned patriotism, strong pride, and supreme confidence in the United States. As books like Clifton Daniel's best-selling *America's Century* attest, the twentieth century in general and 1940s in particular are routinely cast as the apex of U.S. influence. Moreover, the Second World War is commonly viewed as an unquestionably justified conflict and one that demonstrated American military prowess, catapulting the United States to the status of a global superpower. It is no mere coincidence that Cheney draws on these associations during a new time of national conflict. In *America: A Patriotic Primer*, she is trying to conjure up the feelings of jubilant patriotism, strong national pride, and unquestioned politico-military supremacy that permeated the 1940s. In so doing, she is making the tacit argument that the justified war against Hitler and the Axis powers corresponds to the current conflict against Osama bin Laden and al-Qaeda in the wake of 9/11.

Lest readers miss this message in the cover image, Cheney announces it directly in her prefatory comments to *Patriotic Primer*. In a remark that encapsulates the triumphant view of American history presented in her book, she declares in the opening line, "We live in a land of shining cities and natural splendors, a beautiful land made more beautiful still by our commitment to freedom." Although the sentences that follow are ostensibly addressed to her grandchildren, it is clear that they apply to all of the nation's young people. In remarks that combine her belief in a positive portrayal of national history with her oft-stated assertion that the West in general and United States in particular embody the greatest civilization ever known, Cheney remarks: "I wrote this book because I want my grandchildren to understand how blessed we are. I want them to know they are part of a nation whose citizens enjoy liberty and opportunity such as have never been known before. Generations have passed from the earth never dreaming that people could be as fortunate as we Americans are." Later, she reiterates these sentiments even more directly. In a comment that is as saturated with national pride as it is ethnocentrism, Cheney asserts: "We have benefited from the freedom we have enjoyed, and so has all of humankind."

As Cheney's prefatory comments progress, her language moves away from a broadly celebratory portrayal of the United States and closer to the arguments she posited while chair of the NEH in the 1980s and a new faculty fellow at AEI in the 1990s. Akin to her advocacy for the teaching of traditional texts and more conservative approaches to humanities curricula, she asserts in the introduction to *Primer*, "I hope that parents and grandparents will use this book to teach children about Washington's character, Jefferson's intellect, and Madison's wide-ranging knowledge. The upcoming generation should know about these men and their thoughts and aspirations." For these reasons, Cheney concludes her prefatory comments to *Patriotic Primer* with the following call to action: "We should all commit ourselves to seeing that the children of this blessed country understand these reasons from their youngest years."

This is exactly what *American: A Patriotic Primer* aims to accomplish. From its opening page to its final panel, Cheney wraps the book in the stars and stripes to convey not only a strong sense of the nation's past, but, as Anastasia Ulanowicz has so aptly phrased it, a "cheerfully aggressive insistence upon the categorical truth of America's greatness" (346). Although illustrator Robin Preiss Glasser uses a full color palate for the images that she creates, the shades of red, white, and blue are sufficient for many pages. The opening vignettes, for example, in which "A is for America, the land that we love" and "B is for the Birthday of this nation of ours" sets the tone for the rest of the book. The two-page spread presents a panoramic view of New York harbor on the Fourth of July. With the Statue of Liberty occupying a place of visual prominence, fireworks illuminate the sky, boats dot the water, and a jubilant crowd waves American flags. Accompanying these images are lyrics from the song "America the Beautiful" as well as a quotation from a letter by John Adams about how America's birthday ought to be celebrated with "illuminations from one end of this continent to the other from this time forward and forever more." If Cheney is not depicting how the Fourth of July is actually celebrated, then she is surely presenting her view of how it should be commemorated.

Coupled with instilling feelings of national pride, *Patriotic Primer* incorporates plenty of information about the "foundational" documents and "essential" areas of knowledge that Cheney repeatedly identified during her work as chair of the NEH and her lobbying efforts afterward at AEI. The letter C, for example, is for the Constitution "that binds us all together." Likewise, D is for "the Declaration that proclaimed we were free." Moreover, R is for "the Rights we are guaranteed." The protections that Cheney chooses to spotlight are as instructive as her decision to include this category in the book. Together with profiling the expected elements of freedom of speech and freedom of the press, Cheney includes two that have been at the heart of many conservative causes and Republican crusades over the past few decades: the right to bear arms and the freedom of religion.

Even the letter X—arguably one of the most difficult letters to connect thematically with America—serves Cheney's didactic purpose. Cheney chooses "X marks the spot," pinpointing various geographic places where important events in U.S. history have occurred. In addition to profiling locales such as Philadelphia "where the Declaration of Independence and the Constitution were signed" and Washington, D.C., "where our nation's capital has been for more than two hundred years," the page also spotlights a site that was the source of an oft-cited statistic from her days as chair of the NEH and her earlier advocacy work at AEI: Yorktown, Virginia, the location of the final battle of the Revolutionary War.

It is not surprising that many letters in *Patriotic Primer* are devoted to the nation's founding fathers and elder statesman. The letter J is for Jefferson,

L is for Lincoln, M is for Madison, and W is for Washington. Both Cheney's text and the illustrations that accompany it offer a plethora of information about each figure—from his political accomplishments and major writings to his terms in office and impact on American history. The page on Thomas Jefferson, for example, discusses how he was the author of the Declaration of Independence, the first secretary of state, and the third president. In addition, it mentions that he was the mastermind of the Louisiana Purchase, the founder of the University of Virginia, and an accomplished inventor, engineer, and architect, listing a copying machine and the design of his estate Monticello among his many achievements. Given her oft-expressed disdain epitomized in an op-ed piece about the National History Standards, for "the gloomy, politically driven, blame-the-West-first revisionism that is all too common today" ("Mocking" A29), Cheney omits any information that is negative. For example, neither the page itself nor the supplemental information in the back of the book mention Jefferson's ownership of slaves or the confirmation through DNA testing in the late 1990s that he fathered at least one child with slave Sally Hemings.

As one might imagine, the terrorist attacks of September 11 and the surge in patriotism that followed them form the backdrop to many of her pages and shape her view of the United States. As mentioned above, the opening page, "A is for America," is not only set in New York harbor, but it bears a lyric from "America, the Beautiful" that is especially resonant in the aftermath of 9/11: "beautiful for patriotic dream that sees beyond the years / Thine alabaster cities gleam undimmed by human tears!" In addition, the letter H stands for Heroes. Together with featuring teachers, astronauts, and pioneers, the page also contains police, firefighters, and members of the U.S. military—figures who attained special prominence after 9/11. Likewise, the letter V in the book is dedicated to the concept of Valor. The page profiles men and women who have been awarded the Navy Cross, Silver Star, or Medal of Honor from the Revolutionary War through the present day. Given the book's release after the commencement of the war on terror, the page could be used an advertisement for the U.S. military. Perhaps the quotation that has the most resonance with 9/11 appears, appropriately, on the page "P is for Patriotism." Attributed to John Adams and appearing in a banner at the very top of the page, it reads: "Our obligations to our country never cease but with our lives." This message, consonant with the nation's entrance into a time of war, is ironically held aloft by four doves.

Cheney's picture book ends on a note that is as politically charged as its beginning. In a passage that makes the partisan leanings of her narrative even more evident, she awards the final quote in *Patriotic Primer* to her former boss and Republican icon, Ronald Reagan: "I know that for America there will always be a bright dawn ahead." Cheney couples these remarks with her own analogous sentiments: "Strong and free, we will continue to be an inspiration to the world."

A banner on the lower-left corner of the opposing page contains the closing lyrics from the song "America! the Beautiful": "America! America! God shed his grace on thee and crown thy good with brotherhood from sea to shining sea!" Meanwhile, the box containing the letter "Z" on the upper left side shows a child wearing a t-shirt that says "USA" and saluting. Above her are two American flags with their poles crisscrossed, a shield with the stars and stripes on it, and a Revolutionary-era style drum and military trumpets. When the images are taken collectively, the page looks like an Uncle Sam recruiting poster for the elementary-aged set.

Even the narrative format that Cheney chose for her children's book can be connected to her desire not simply to educate children about a celebratory portrayal of American history but to inculcate them with this viewpoint. As Michael Heyman, George Bodmer, and Katherine Capshaw Smith have all written, from the appearance of primers in the United States during the sixteenth century, they have served a twofold purpose: teaching young children the rudiments of literacy—that is, their ABCs—while simultaneously conveying information about their culture's religion, political structure, or social organization. Indeed, in the words of Bodmer, "the alphabet book has always reflected the time and culture from which it springs" (115). *The New England Primer*, which likely originated around 1680s and was in wide circulation throughout the American colonies by the 1720s, forms perhaps the most well known example. In the most frequently quoted passage from the *Primer*, the initial two letters informed its child readers:

A   In Adam's Fall,
             We Sinned All.

B (BIBLE)   Thy Life to Mend
             This Book to Attend.

By yoking letters of the alphabet with biblical events and moral values, *The New England Primer* combined literacy education with religious instruction and imprinted these elements simultaneously. While child readers learned their ABCs, they also learned about Adam, original sin, and the centrality of the Bible to one's life.

Cheney uses the genre in the same way. Although penning *Patriotic Primer* more than three centuries later, she undoubtedly hopes that her picture book will cause young readers to forever associate the letter A with America, C with Constitution, and D with Declaration of the Independence. Indeed, an article in the magazine *Time for Kids* commented on the *Patriotic Primer*'s potential: "You may have learned your ABCs in kindergarten, *but Lynne Cheney will teach you the alphabet in a whole new way*" (Winchester 7; my italics). If this strategy is successful, then the next generation will never allow documents like the U.S. Constitution to be ignored, figures like Thomas Jefferson to be maligned, or events like the Revolutionary War to be overlooked—phenomena that Cheney believed had occurred in previous eras and which, of course, she has made a career combating.

"Multiculturalism Done Right" (Pun Undoubtedly Intended): Change as a Form of Stasis in *Patriotic Primer*

Admittedly, *America: A Patriotic Primer* does not exactly mirror Cheney's previous writings. She does modify or at least soften some of her formerly steadfast opposition to multiculturalism. The letter K, for example, is dedicated to Dr. Martin Luther King. Similarly, the letter N in *Primer* stands for the Native Americans who, Cheney's text notes, "came here first." Finally, and perhaps most surprising given Cheney's previous attacks on feminism and the women's movement, the letter S is "for Suffrage." The illustrations that ring the page depict some of the leading figures in the fight for women's votes, including Lucretia Mott, Elizabeth Cady Stanton, and Harriet Tubman.

These elements have caused some critics to praise the nonpartisan nature of Cheney's book. Journalist Karen MacPherson noted in a review of *Patriotic Primer*: "What may be surprising to Cheney's political critics, however, is how well she has managed to cast aside her strong conservative credentials. Overall, 'America' is refreshingly nonpolitical in its celebration of the many facets of American history" (D4). Meanwhile, Alexander Stille went one step further in the book review section of the *New York Times*; after reading Cheney's picture book, he declared, "There may be a truce in the culture wars" (20).

Any truce, however, was merely imaginary. Elements of multiculturalism and feminism in *Patriotic Primer* do not signal far-reaching social change; rather, they maintain the status quo. It is significant, for instance, that Cheney chose to spotlight the safely historical suffragist movement instead of the more contemporary, and controversial, feminist movement. Likewise, Cheney elected to profile Martin Luther King as an example of the civil right movement instead of "the equally influential, though comparatively more divisive figure of Malcolm X, whose longtime membership in the Nation of Islam and involvement in the Pan-African movement would certainly disrupt its depiction of America as a colorblind nation" (Ulanowicz 355). Similarly, Clare Bradford pointed out that Cheney's classification of Native Americans as a group "who came here first" rather than as indigenous inhabitants ascribes them the same immigrant status, arguably, as Anglo-European settlers (1–2). Just as revealing, her profile of influential American Indians omits more controversial figures "like Sitting Bull or the 1969 occupants of Alcatraz, whose deeds did not explicitly lead to—and, indeed, challenged—the advancement of dominant American culture" (Ulanowicz 356). Cheney instead focuses on undeniably important but less contentious individuals like Pocahontas, Tecumseh, and Sacajawea.

The way in which Cheney's ostensibly progressive multicultural vision does not actually support a progressive social vision reaches its apex on the page "U is for the United States." One of the most discussed passages in *Patriotic Primer*, the segment presents a large illustrated map of the nation that is framed by holidays celebrated by various cultures, religions, and peoples. Together with expected civic celebrations like President's Day, Veteran's Day, and Labor Day, Cheney includes less expected holidays such as the Islamic period of Ramadan, Hindu Diwali, Mexican Cinco De Mayo, Chinese New Year, Jewish Hanukkah, and African American Kwanzaa. The seemingly inclusive nature of these images, however, is undercut by both their spatial arrangement and their rhetorical framing. The large map of the United States, which occupies the centerpiece of the page and thus first draws the reader's eye, "suggests that diversity does not so much constitute the general character of the United States as it remains (literally) marginal to it" (Ulanowicz 351). This reading is reinforced by the other letter that shares this page and the theme that Cheney chose for it: "T is for Tolerance." Although this concept may seem to recognize diversity and even applaud difference, it can also be read as reinforcing existing racial hierarchies. Indeed, the concept of "tolerance" does not denote the coexistence of equals, but rather an inherent imbalance of power—whereby the dominant group elects to recognize or acknowledge a minority group, a decision that could be reversed at any time (Ulanowicz 352). Moreover, by writing the caption for Tolerance as "Free to think and believe and pursue happiness in our own way, we recognize the rights of others to do the same" Cheney places the reader of her book "in opposition to unnamed 'others' whose beliefs she must graciously condone" (Ulanowicz 352).

For children who may resist this classification as other, the inclusion of the Seal of the United States, along with its motto "E Pluribus Unum," reminds them that the many are ultimately—and even inevitably—assimilated into the one (see Ulanowicz 351). In a final irony, Cheney has characterized her unexpected inclusion of racial, ethnic, cultural, and gender minority groups in *Patriotic Primer* as "Multiculturalism done *right*" ("Multiculturalism Done" 66; my emphasis), and one cannot help believe that her suggestive word choice is far from simply coincidental—especially given her CNN *Crossfire* signoff.

Cheney does not make a secret of the continuity between *Patriotic Primer* and her previous work on behalf of American history and the canon wars. In an article that appeared in the *Washington Post*, she "chuckled at a question about how much more controversial her writing used to be" (Allen A27). As she told journalist Mike Allen:

"It's kind of a matter of perspective. You know, I didn't say anything different when I was chairman of the National Endowment for the Humanities from what I'm saying now. It's just that then I said it in an academic setting, where the idea that colleges and universities ought to teach a version of American history that helps students understand how fortunate we are to be Americans. . . . Now, I'm saying the same thing but I'm saying it in a more mainstream—to a more mainstream audience. . . . So I'm not sure I've changed. Maybe the place from which I'm saying those things has changed." (qtd in Allen A27)

"I Decided, Let's Start with Them While They're Little": Cheney's Picture Book America and the Ever-Expanding Reach of Public Policy Research Institutes in the United States

The positive critical reception and strong commercial sales of *America: A Patriotic Primer* prompted Lynne Cheney to write two more books with illustrator Robin Preiss Glasser: *A Is for Abigail: An Almanac of Amazing American Women* was released in 2003, and *Our Fifty States: A Family Adventure Across America* hit bookstore shelves in 2006. Although the subject matter of these narratives differs from that of *Primer*, they follow the same formula. Both present a laudatory view of the United States and offer young readers a plethora of information on what Cheney feels are "essential" areas of knowledge concerning American history, culture, and government. In keeping with Cheney's belief that history is one of the most grossly neglected areas of American education, all of the women profiled in *A Is for Abigail* were born before 1950. Moreover, reflecting her conservative approach to presenting the nation's past, she includes largely traditional or at least uncontroversial figures. For example, one page features Anna Jarvis, who "loved her mother very much" and therefore lobbied successfully to make Mother's Day a national holiday in 1914. Meanwhile, another profile depicts Fannie Peck, a seven-year-old girl who walked the Mormon Trail in 1852, primarily barefoot, because she wanted to save her shoes for Sunday. Peck is Cheney's great-great-grandmother.

   A Is for Abigail enjoyed even greater levels of critical acclaim and commercial success than *Patriotic Primer*. The book reached the number-two sales spot on the *New York Times* picture book bestseller list only two months after its release, and by mid-summer, "the book held the top slot on children's lists from *Publisher's Weekly*, BookSense, and the *New York Times* (having charted high at *USA Today* and *Wall Street Journal* as well)" (Maughan 26). In a telling comment, when Cheney was asked why she decided to publish another patriotic-themed picture book and also why she chose to structure it—akin to *Patriotic Primer*—as an alphabet text, she responded: "I decided, let's start with them while they're little" (Gillin D1).

Cheney's third picture book, *Our 50 States: A Family Adventure Across America*, puts these words into further practice. The text chronicles the experiences of a family of five as they take a cross-country road trip that makes a stop in every state plus the District of Columbia and, in so doing, conveys an even more celebratory portrayal of the United States than in her previous books. Cheney packs the narrative with historical information, cultural highlights, and detailed maps. Akin to her previous texts, the messages that her book conveys about multiculturalism, difference, and diversity are mixed. On the page dedicated to New Mexico, for example, the seemingly progressive information about how "On the floor of the capitol building is an image that combines the sun symbol of Zia Pueblo with the state seal of New Mexico" is undercut by the description that the seal "shows a large eagle shielding a smaller one," a detail that perpetuates white paternalistic attitudes toward American Indians.

Finally, the historical focus and patriotic message of Cheney's latest two picture books—*When Washington Crossed the Delaware: A Wintertime Story for Young Patriots* (2004) and *We the People: The Story of Our Constitution* (2008)—is plain. So, too, is their connection to Cheney's previous work in the canon wars.

Akin to *America: A Patriotic Primer*, all of Cheney's picture books have been projects for her at the American Enterprise Institute. As before, she makes no attempt to obfuscate this fact; she reveals the sponsorship openly and at some length in the acknowledgements section of each text. In *A Is for Abigail*, for example, Cheney expresses her gratitude "to AEI President Chris DeMuth for his fine leadership and for his support of scholars who take on all manner of projects—even children's books." Cheney also singles out another colleague at the American Enterprise Institute for her "knowledge, insight, and clarity of expression" while crafting the text: former U.N. ambassador and foreign policy advisor to Ronald Reagan, Jeane Kirkpatrick. Conversely, Cheney's biography on the website for the American Enterprise Institute includes all of her picture books. Because the page only provides a chronological list of titles and does not separate genres or distinguish among audiences, a casual browser will not realize that certain texts are not policy briefs but narratives for children.

While reviewers and critics have often attributed Cheney's release of picture books to the phenomenon during the past few decades of well-known actors, singers, sports figures, and politicians who have written narratives for young readers,[5] her new identity as a children's author embodies far more than simply another celebrity figure jumping on the latest pop culture bandwagon. This general trend points to the increasing commercialization of children's literature,[6] but Cheney's participation has even more socially serious implications. The picture books written and released by the second lady signal an important shift in her public advocacy approach and—in an even more significant ramification—the cultural reach, power, and influence of conservative think tanks in general and the American Enterprise Institute in particular.

In this much discussed phenomenon, conservative-focused public policy research institutes underwent a significant shift in their operating style and research tactics in the final decades of the twentieth century. During their emergence in the 1900s, these organizations produced analysis that genuinely strove to be nonpartisan and that was simply made available to, not pushed on, policy makers. Reflective of the Progressive impulse out of which think tanks were first founded, both the early research fellows who worked at these organizations and the donors who funded them believed that to achieve their overarching goal—"to alleviate human suffering and improve government efficiency" (McGann 3)—they needed to consider all viewpoints. Thus, the analysis from think tanks during the early twentieth century sought to be objective, unbiased, and politically impartial. The American Enterprise Institute, founded largely in accordance with these principles, thus had a longstanding commitment to offering research on public policy issues; they sought neither to directly lobby politicians or the general public.[7]

The new crop of think tanks that emerged during the 1970s, however, took a vastly different approach to operations. In fact, Edwin Feulner describes how he and Paul Weyrich formed the Heritage Foundation in 1973 in direct response to AEI's hands-off tactics:

> "Weyrich and I were having lunch together and he showed me a study that had the pros and cons on the SST (Supersonic Transport). It was a good analysis, but it arrived on his desk the day after the vote took place. We both kicked that around and said, 'Wouldn't it be great if there were an institution that delivered the kind of timely, usable policy analysis so that those of us working on the Hill could really make use of it?' I immediately called up the President of the organization to praise him for this thorough piece of research and asked why we did not receive it until after the debate and the vote. His answer: they did not want to influence the vote. That was when the idea for the Heritage Foundation was born." (Feulner qtd in Abelson 39–40)

Instead of passively sitting by and hoping that policy makers would come upon their research, staff members at Heritage took a more active approach. Through radically new and even completely unorthodox practices (at least at times), Heritage staffers distributed free copies of their research to members of Congress, released it to major media outlets, organized conferences to discuss and disseminate it, and published it not only in scholarly journals but also in nationally circulating newspapers and magazines. As the organization's former executive president Phillip Truluck commented: 'We certainly spend as much money on marketing our ideas as we do on research. We keep these two functions in balance because we believe that the process doesn't end when a paper is published. . . . We cannot just put out a study and hope that it gets into the right people's hands" (qtd in Abelson 40).

Heritage revolutionized the think tank industry in other important ways. The organization dispensed with the longstanding practice by public policy research institutes to produce mainly book-length, academic-style publications; instead, Heritage offered short, timely, and more accessible briefs on current national policy issues. Jean Stefancic and Richard Delgado have noted, "Most of their publications are designed to meet the 'briefcase test'—succinct enough to be read in the time it takes for an official to be driven from Washington's National Airport to a congressional committee hearing on Capitol Hill (about twenty minutes)" (53). In yet another radical departure from the overall operating procedure of think tanks, the Heritage Foundation made no attempt to obfuscate either their conservative ideological leaning or their desire to sway lawmakers to this viewpoint: "Our aim is to change public policy—not merely to comment on it" (Truluck qtd in Abelson 40).

These new strategies proved exceedingly effective. As David Ricci has documented, "The conservative Heritage Foundation appeared in 1973 with a budget of only $250,000. By 1983, Heritage had moved into its own building, worth $9.3 million, and was carrying out a yearly schedule of activities costing $10 million" (2). Today, Heritage is routinely cast—by members of Congress, journalists, and political scientists alike—as one the most powerful conservative think tanks in the United States. By the 1990s, in fact, a survey conducted by Andrew Rich found that "more than three-quarters of congressional staff and journalists (80 percent) named the Heritage Foundation as among the three most influential think tanks" (80). Thus, "the Heritage Foundation has become the type of policy institute other advocacy-oriented think tanks have sought to emulate" (Abelson 39).

The American Enterprise Institute was one such organization. After witnessing the remarkable success of this new conservative think tank—and the subsequent waning of its own political influence—AEI modified its tactics in the 1970s. The organization moved away from the largely behind-the-scenes, book-based, and academic-style research and adopted the Heritage Foundation's more aggressive, opportunistic, and activist approach. Karilyn Bowman, a staff member at AEI, explained this shift: "We're pretty convinced that people just don't read books in the way that they once did. You can produce things more quickly that are shorter . . . and I think that you can perhaps be more influential" (qtd in Rich 68). Akin to the Heritage Foundation, this new approach achieved almost instant success and sparked a renaissance for AEI. In the years that followed, the think tank greatly expanded its personnel size, financial scope, and political influence. In 1970 Ricci noted that "the American Enterprise Institute had a budget of only $1 million. It then grew so rapidly throughout the 1970s that by 1982 program expenses at AEI reached almost $12 million annually" (1). By 2002, total assets for AEI were more than $39 million; four years later, in 2006, that number had climbed to over $77 million (Foundation Center).

Although AEI changed their research approach and operating tactics during the 1970s, they did not mimic the new conservative think tank completely. Whereas the Heritage Foundation was soon devoting as much of their budget to marketing as it was to research, AEI still kept its primary focus on analysis. Indeed, as James McGann noted in the mid-1990s, "Heritage and AEI, for example, share the same conservative orientation but their methods for reaching policy makers and influencing debate are radically different" (128). Almost a decade later, Andrew Rich echoed this observation. In *Think Tanks, Public Policy, and the Politics of Expertise* (2004), he lists AEI as a "non-marketing" think tank, while he classifies the Heritage Foundation as a "marketing" institution (90).

The American Enterprise Institute's involvement with Lynne Cheney's picture books blurs the line separating these two organizations even more by moving AEI even closer to the aggressive marketing tactics and activist public relations methods of the Heritage Foundation. *America: A Patriotic Primer*, along with all of its sequels, possess many qualities that James McGann and others have identified as being hallmarks of Heritage's policy analyses—as well as the key to their astounding success. Cheney's books for children, for example, are "direct and timely," contain "topical research on current issues," employ a "successful marketing strategy," embody an "innovative product line," "exhibit a *low* degree of specialization in terms of its target customer segment," and reflect "very high *push* ratings for [their] effective approaches to creating significant brand identification" (McGann 98–100; all italics in original). In a final hallmark, advocacy-based think tanks like the Heritage Foundation are known "more for marketing and repackaging ideas than for generating them" (Abelson 20). Cheney's picture books likewise largely recycle her earlier messages about the teaching of American history rather than introduce new material to the conversation.

Moreover, given that Cheney's narratives are written for a child instead of an adult audience, AEI pushes Heritage's aggressive public relations efforts even further; AEI takes these approaches to a public audience and potential political constituency that no previous think tank in the United States has ever targeted. In this way, AEI can be seen as "out-Heritaging" the Heritage Foundation. While this organization has become known for their "innovative product line" (McGann 99), it has been limited to policy briefs, mass mailings, and occasional monographs. Heritage published books intended for a mass audience or general public readership, but the group never released texts intended for children. AEI alone now claims this groundbreaking but nonetheless dubious distinction.

The American Enterprise Institute's move into picture books may be not only an opportunistic seizure of a popular culture moment but also a strategy in the fight to remain politically relevant. Amy Wilentz observed that "AEI, once Washington's most influential citadel of mainstream conservative policy research has been the most seriously injured by the rise of advocacy think tanks," such as Heritage (22). Indeed, Howard J. Wiarda, among others, has detailed AEI's financial troubles and near collapse during the late 1980s owing in part to what Wiarda characterizes as being "Outflanked on the Right" (241). He explained: "The rise of the Heritage Foundation in the 1970s and 1980s drew a lot of conservative money away from AEI. Especially big donors like Richard Scaife and Joseph Coors began giving far more to Heritage than AEI" (Wiarda 241). Although the American Enterprise Institute survived this period of difficulty, they have never returned to their former, pre-Heritage power. Andrew Rich, in a chart ranking the most influential think tanks during the 1990s, reveals that AEI has been moving steadily downward while Heritage, by 1997, had ascended to the top spot (81).

In light of the critical acclaim and commercial success of *America: A Patriotic Primer* and its sequels, one wonders whether the American Enterprise Institute has established a new paradigm. William Bennett's children's text *The Book of Virtues* was a separate project, unconnected to his work at the Heritage Foundation.[8] Given the critical acclaim and commercial success enjoyed by Lynne Cheney's picture books, this detail may change. In the same way that Cheney followed in Bennett's footsteps when she took over for him at the NEH, someday he—along with other right-leaning political figures at think tanks—may follow in her footsteps at AEI by producing conservative-themed narratives for children.

In fact, this process already seems to have begun. In 2008, William Bennett expanded his children's book repertoire beyond *The Book of Virtues* franchise to other conservative themes and sociopolitical subject matters. In late November 2008, he released the very Lynne Cheney–sounding *The American Patriot's Almanac: Daily Readings on America*. In the acknowledgments at the back of the book, Bennett and his coauthor, John T. E. Cribb, express their indebtedness "to a few people in particular who gave indispensable aid" (503). The first person they name is Seth Leibsohn: "Our friend . . . [who] always supplied excellent advice and shared his wisdom" (503). They neglect to mention, however, that Leibsohn is a fellow at the Claremont Institute, a conservative think tank in California, where—according to the biographical profile posted on the organization's own website—he "specializes in issues related to the war on terrorism" ("Seth Leibsohn," par 2). In a detail that furthers the connection between *The American*

Patriot's Almanac and the conservative think tank, the website also reveals that Bennett himself is a staff member at Claremont. He joined the organization as their new Washington Fellow in 2003 (see *Hannity and Colmes*).

IN THE OPENING PAGES of *Do Think Tanks Matter?: Assessing the Impact of Public Policy Institutes*, Donald Abelson observed that, at least since the transformations to these organizations during the 1970s, "the nostalgic vision of think tanks as idea factories, or brain trusts created to address society's most pressing social, economic, and political problems" is just a wistful view of the past, not an accurate characterization of their aims and operations in the present (Abelson 9). Lynne Cheney's picture books contribute to this major shift. David Rich succinctly describes the phenomenon: "The firewall [that once separated conservative think tanks from policy makers] is gone, and the change in the role and behavior of experts in recent decades suggests a need for fundamental revision in how scholars treat them in accounts of policy making" (209). With the appearance of *America: A Patriotic Primer*, a second and even more alarming barrier has fallen; in the past, children were separate from the ideological interest and material reach of these organizations. In the process of blurring these distinctions, the already formidable political power and cultural influence of think tanks expands even more.

The chapter that follows furthers this theme by examining not a right-leaning organization but a right-leaning figure whose cultural power and social scope is also ever-increasing: political pundit Bill O'Reilly. Television and radio host, nationally syndicated columnist, recurrent political commentator, and best-selling author, O'Reilly has become—as rival personality Howard Stern once said about himself—the veritable "King of all Media" in the new millennium. O'Reilly may be most commonly associated with his popular television program, *The O'Reilly Factor*. But, in the pages that follow, I demonstrate how especially in the wake of his 2005 advice book for young kids, he can perhaps more accurately be characterized, in the apt words of journalist Tom Lowry, as "The O'Reilly Factory." O'Reilly expands the material reach and cultural influence of his conservative viewpoints and right-leaning political opinions not through a position at a conservative think tank like Lynne Cheney, but via the use of a commercial strategy known as brand marketing. It is to these issues that this project now turns its attention.

5

Pundit Knows Best

The Self-Help Boom, Brand Marketing,
and *The O'Reilly Factor for Kids*

"The more polite you are, the more responsive the other person will be.
Remember that in any debate."

–Bill O'Reilly, in *The O'Reilly Factor for Kids*

Few other media personalities have enjoyed more success during the past
decade than Bill O'Reilly. His nightly current events and political talk program
The O'Reilly Factor, which first aired in 1996, is the most popular cable news show
in the United States, routinely attracting more than two million viewers (Crupi).
Likewise, its guest list is a veritable pantheon of well-known journalists, cultural
commentators, and prominent politicians. Among the figures who have made
repeat appearances on *The O'Reilly Factor* since 2000 are civil rights activist Al
Sharpton, Pulitzer Prize–winning journalist Bob Woodward, and public figures
Newt Gingrich, Hillary Clinton, Karl Rove, Condoleezza Rice, Laura Bush, Barney
Frank, John McCain, Barack Obama, and George W. Bush.

The radio version of the program—called *The Radio Factor with Bill O'Reilly*—
is just as successful. According to a report about talk radio prepared by the
Pew Research Center in 2007, the show enjoyed an audience of 3.25 million
listeners in 2006, an increase of 1.5 million since 2003 ("Talk Radio Audience").
In addition, as Westwood One, the distributor for *The Radio Factor*, reveals, the
program is carried on "over 390 radio stations, in 100 of the top 100 markets"
(Westwood).

Together with appearing on the show that bears his name, O'Reilly is
both a frequent political commentator on various television programs
concerning politics and culture and a regular columnist for various nationally
circulating periodicals. O'Reilly can regularly be seen as a "talking head" on
current events and news analysis shows like *Hannity & Colmes*, John Gibson's
Big Story, and segments of Fox News. Meanwhile, his weekly syndicated column
appears in newspapers around the country, including the *Boston Herald*, the

Washington Times, the *New York Post*, and the *Chicago Sun-Times* ("Newspaper Column List").

O'Reilly is an equally popular and prolific author. From 2000 to 2006, he released four books: *The O'Reilly Factor* (2000), *The No-Spin Zone* (2001), *Who's Looking Out for You?* (2003), and *Culture Warrior* (2006). Each title flew off the shelves and sold millions of copies to reach the number one spot on the *New York Times* nonfiction best-seller list.[1] In late September 2008, O'Reilly added a fifth book to his oeuvre, the memoir *A Bold Fresh Piece of Humanity*. *Bold* debuted at number fourteen on *USA Today*'s best-seller list for nonfiction. Moreover, the *New York Daily News* reported that O'Reilly received an astounding five-million-dollar advance from his publisher for the memoir (Kelly, par 24)—a figure that indicates his continued esteemed cultural status and strong commercial appeal in American print and visual media.

At the same time that Bill O'Reilly has attained a level of success enjoyed by few other media personalities during the past decade, he has also achieved a level of notoriety that is almost equally unparalleled. From the moment of his debut on the national broadcasting stage, O'Reilly has generated at least as much controversy and criticism as he has ratings and recognition. First, the live-to-tape format that he uses for *The O'Reilly Show* has sparked accusations that he edits material—including comments by his own guests—to affirm his viewpoint or suit a particular political agenda rather than simply to fit in the time allotted. A representative example of such editing occurred in June 2005 when O'Reilly omitted segments of George Stephanopoulos's interview with Joseph Biden regarding the Abu Ghraib scandal and then criticized the Democratic senator from Delaware for failing to address these exact issues (*O'Reilly Factor*, 6 June 2005).

In addition, O'Reilly's confrontational on-air style—in which he routinely interrupts guests and callers—has come under attack for being combative, promoting incivility, and generally lowering the level of public discourse. People have similarly complained about his frequent use of the term "pinhead" for individuals whom he thinks are misinformed, have behaved inappropriately, or disagree with him;[2] he also has a predilection for telling interviewees to "shut up" or ordering their microphones cut off. Perhaps the most infamous example of this kind of behavior occurred when O'Reilly was interviewing Jeremy Glick, the young man whose father was killed in the terrorist attack on the World Trade Center and who appeared on *The O'Reilly Factor* on February 4, 2003, to discuss the antiwar petition Not in Our Name, which protested the U.S. invasion of Afghanistan.[3]

O'Reilly's brusque style has even been directed at well-known public leaders and prominent politicians. On his radio program on September 25, 2008, O'Reilly not only called Congressman Barney Frank a "big fat toad," but expressed a desire to hit him, along with fellow Senator Christopher Dodd (*Radio Factor*).[4]

Likewise, complaining that Senator Tom Daschle had repeatedly declined to appear on *The O'Reilly Factor*, he asserted, "Daschle has been and remains too frightened to appear. So with all due respect, Senator, shut up" (*O'Reilly Factor*, 17 May 2002).[5] Given O'Reilly's frequent use of this phrase, Jack Shafer has noted, "Fox News channel talk show host Bill O'Reilly says 'shut up' the way other people say 'um.' On his daily show, *The O'Reilly Factor*, he uses it as a place-holder for an idea still formulating in his brain. As a way to begin a sentence, end it, or punctuate it" (par 1–2).

When observers aren't criticizing O'Reilly for insulting his opponents or interrupting his guests, they are often accusing him of presenting inaccurate information. In his book-length study about *The O'Reilly Factor* (published in 2003), Peter Hart documents dozens of episodes in which the host misused statistics or stated facts that were simply false. In the three successive shows that aired from February 5 to 7, 2002, for example, O'Reilly quoted vastly different numbers for the percentage of households headed by a single mother and receiving welfare support. First, he offered what he claimed was the "dead-on" statistic that "58 percent of single-mom homes are on welfare" (see Hart 97). Then, the next night, he stated that "52 percent of families receiving public assistance are headed by a single mother" (see Hart 97). Finally, during the show on the following evening, he said that around 14 percent of single mothers receive federal welfare benefits (see Hart 97). O'Reilly never referenced the data that he cited on the earlier night, nor did he ever say that he was making a correction to previously quoted information (Hart 97).

These misrepresentations assume an added irony given the tagline for *The O'Reilly Factor*: the "no-spin zone." O'Reilly claims to cut through the partisan rhetoric, personal opinions, and distorting slants on his program to get to the truth of matters. However, as Hart has written, "In truth, it's an *all*-spin zone, where the host absurdly denies the show's conservative political slant and 'facts' are manipulated in order to win arguments against O'Reilly's opponents" (12). For many media commentators, the cable news host's record of misleading and even erroneous reporting has earned him the nickname Bill "Oh Really" (see Hart).

Even when the facts are not in dispute, O'Reilly often comes under fire for making inflammatory comments. When the city of San Francisco passed the "College Not Combat" ordinance, which protested the presence of military recruiters at public schools, O'Reilly was outraged by what he viewed as their un-Americanism. On his November 8, 2005, radio program, he blasted the city:

> I say listen, citizens of San Francisco, if you vote against military recruiting, you're not going to get another nickel in federal funds. Fine. You want to be your own country? Go right ahead. And if Al Qaeda comes in here and blows you up, we're not going to do anything about it. . . .

We're going to say, "Look, every other place in America is off limits to you, except San Francisco. You want to blow up the Coit Tower? Go ahead." (qtd in Garofoli, par 8)

O'Reilly has also repeatedly made racially insensitive comments, remarking on the radio version of his program that aired on September 19, 2007, about a recent dinner he had at Sylvia's restaurant in Harlem with Reverend Al Sharpton: "I couldn't get over the fact that there was no difference between Sylvia's restaurant and any other restaurant in New York City. I mean, it was exactly the same, even though it's run by blacks, primarily black patronship" (*Radio Factor*, 19 September 2007). The topic of his show that day was racial stereotypes.[6]

O'Reilly's personal life has been just as controversial as his professional one. Both on and off of the air, he has made repeated reference to his working-class background and childhood upbringing in hardscrabble Levittown, New York. "You don't come from any lower than I came from on an economic scale," he has commented (qtd in Gay, par 20). To support this position, O'Reilly has pointed out that his father never made more than $35,000 a year—a claim that has come under considerable scrutiny. According to the media watchdog group Fairness and Accuracy in Reporting (FAIR), "O'Reilly's father's $35,000 income in 1978 is equivalent to over $90,000 today [2003] in inflation-adjusted dollars" (qtd in Hart 119). O'Reilly responded by saying that his father's $35,000 income came near the end of his career when "I had been out of the house at that point for 10 years" (qtd in Sheff 59). The geographic location of O'Reilly's childhood home has likewise been disputed. During an interview with the *Washington Post*, the cable news host's mother told the reporter that the family lived not in the lower-class region of Levittown but in the more middle-class neighborhood of Westbury (see Farhi C1). O'Reilly first insisted that the newspaper misquoted her (see Franken 73–74). Then, he modified his statement to say that his family's home was located in the "Westbury section of Levittown" ("Bill O'Reilly's Bio," par 3)—a claim that remains part of his official biography on Fox news website even though critics have questioned whether such a region actually exists.

O'Reilly's most public and arguably most injurious personal controversy unfolded in fall 2004 when Andrea Mackris, a former producer of *The O'Reilly Factor*, sued him for sexual harassment. O'Reilly, who was married at the time and had two small children, vociferously denied the charges and even filed a countersuit, claiming extortion. However, Mackris's court papers quickly found their way to the Internet and her complaint contained so many lengthy quotations of the sexually explicit phone calls that O'Reilly allegedly made to her that the media concluded that she had tape recordings of them. In one particularly damaging conversation, which quickly became the subject of many late-night jokes and water-cooler jests, the caller described a sexual fantasy involving a loofah sponge and falafel. The fallout from the suit led the political

commentator to cancel several public appearances and even to take a temporary hiatus from hosting *The O'Reilly Factor*. O'Reilly settled with Mackris two
weeks after she filed her suit for an undisclosed sum and the stipulation that he
had engaged in "no wrongdoing in the case whatsoever" (qtd in Kurtz "O'Reilly,
Producer Settle" C1).

Given both the fame and the infamy that Bill O'Reilly has attained during
the past decade, David Sheff aptly dubbed him "the man who is most revered
and most loathed on television these days" (59). Indeed, Peter Hart summarized
O'Reilly's intensely polarizing effect: "fans see him as a tireless truth-seeker
taking on the elites. Critics see him as a boorish, arrogant host who's never
wrong" (11). Whether individuals love or hate O'Reilly, he is an undeniable media
force—and one whose cultural influence is unlikely to fade any time soon.

With the publication of *The O'Reilly Factor for Kids* in October 2004, Bill
O'Reilly expanded his multi-media prowess and cultural influence into a new
realm—books for young readers. Written with Charles Flowers, *Kids* is an advice
and self-help text aimed at children aged ten through sixteen. Subtitled *A
Survival Guide for America's Families*, the book is divided into four sections that
address what O'Reilly feels are the most difficult personal, social, psychological,
and relational issues that young people face today. The first segment, titled
"People in Your Life," has chapters devoted to the subjects of friends, bullies,
parents, siblings, divorce, and disagreements. The second segment, called "Your
Private Life," examines the topics of money, smoking, alcohol, drugs, sex, television, music, and fun. Meanwhile, the third portion, dubbed "Your School Life,"
focuses on the issues of clothes, cheating, reading, self-esteem, sports, teachers,
and the future. Finally, the closing section, "Things to Think About" tackles
issues of health, work, stereotypes, politics, death, God, and helping others.

Akin to all of O'Reilly's other media endeavors during the past few years,
The O'Reilly Factor for Kids was a phenomenal success. The book debuted at
number six on the *New York Times* best-seller list in the advice genre and spent
seven additional weeks on the chart, ultimately peaking at number four.[7] His
publisher released a revised paperback edition of *The O'Reilly Factor for Kids* in
September 2005, with a new closing section on cyber-bullying.

This chapter takes its cue from the tagline for O'Reilly's popular cable
program and "un-spins" the narrative content, cultural commentary, and
commercial success of *The O'Reilly Factor for Kids*. In his 2004 book for young
readers, the cable host brings the popular and rapidly growing genre of advice
literature to young readers, while he simultaneously replicates the genre's many
flaws. From its main title and basic premise to its literary format and specific
chapter discussions, *The O'Reilly Factor for Kids* puts the self in self-help. He may
have written the book with Charles Flowers, and it may be shelved in bookstores
as a nonfiction advice text for young people, but, as its title suggests, the volume
is little more than an extension of the O'Reilly product, brand, and especially

persona—a way to extend his media franchise into a new market and broaden his audience to a new demographic. During this process, *Kids* does push the boundaries of right-leaning, conservative-themed books for children into new areas. But even these seemingly progressive changes serve a reactionary purpose. They demonstrate that however conservatism is defined or discussed, it has commercial potential; its ideas, attitudes, and viewpoints—as O'Reilly has so successfully demonstrated on television, on the radio, and in his books for adults—can be effectively packaged and profitably sold. This time, however, the target market for these viewpoints is young people.

The Doctor Is In Print: The Growth of the Self-Help, Personal Advice, and Self-Improvement Genres

Judith Gero John noted, "There are few activities more human than the desire to offer advice" (52). Tapping into the basic human longing for knowledge and insight, books that offer help and wisdom embody one of the oldest as well as richest literary genres.

Such narratives are arguably especially popular and pervasive in the United States, given the national traits of self-reliance, practicality, and self-improvement. Indeed, Arlie Russell Hochschild has written, from Cotton Mather and Benjamin Franklin to Horatio Alger and Stephen Covey, "America has been the land of self-help" (par 1). On subjects ranging from business success and personal growth to spiritual fulfillment and romantic relationships, "For many, the opportunity for self-improvement is regarded as a national birthright" (Ewart par 1).

If books offering advice are one of the oldest as well as the most popular genres in the United States, then those intended for child audiences would seem even more natural. Not only do boys and girls have much to learn about the world, but all self-help books—even those intended for adults—"establish a parent-child, teacher-student relationship" (John 52). In fact, some of the earliest books that could be placed in the advice or self-help categories—such as the medieval book of manners, *The Babees' Book*—were intended for children (John 52). This legacy continues to the present. While advice books for children do not garner the same media attention as those for adults, they remain a staple of the field, with dozens of titles released annually. For example, *Chicken Soup for the Kid's Soul* (1997), *The Seven Habits of Highly Effective Teens* (1998), *Don't Sweat the Small Stuff for Teens* (2000), and *Unstoppable Me!: 10 Ways to Soar Through Life* (2006) were all extremely popular, and several appeared in various versions and formats targeted to specific youth audiences.

Although the self-help genre has always been a fixture in American print and popular culture, it witnessed one of its biggest booms during the 1990s. Clarissa Estés's *Women Who Run with the Wolves* (1992) was a constant on the

New York Times nonfiction best-seller list for longer than ninety weeks. The following year, Deepak Chopra's *Ageless Body, Timeless Mind* rocketed to the top spot on the *New York Times* best-seller list, which made its author a household name. These events paled in comparison, though, to the performance of John Gray's *Men Are from Mars, Women Are from Venus* (1993). Karen S. Falling Buzzard noted that Gray's book "quickly topped *Publisher's Weekly* charts for the next 4 years, with over 6 million copies sold, and no slow down to date. It has gone back to press every two weeks since its publication" (89).

This spike in self-help books continued into the new millennium. Some of the most commercially successful books released during the 2000s were in the self-help genre. Titles such as Dr. Phil McGraw's *Self Matters: Creating Your Life from the Inside Out* (2001), Dr. Laura Schlessinger's *The Proper Care and Feeding of Husbands* (2004), Greg Behrendt and Liz Tuccillo's *He's Just Not That Into You* (2004), and Rhonda Bryne's *The Secret* (2006, which was first released on DVD and later adapted into a book) enjoyed phenomenal popularity and prompted Inger Askehave to comment: "Never before have the bookstore shelves been so loaded with [self-help] books . . . and never before have so many 'ordinary' people been consulting these books to find a way to lead a 'meaningful' life" (7). Indeed, in 2005, Anne Whitney reported this amazing statistic: "eight of the top fifteen titles on the *Publisher's Weekly* best-seller's list for hardcover nonfiction . . . are self-help books" (196). Such strong sales translated into equally strong profits. A 2006 report released by Marketdata Enterprises, an independent research publisher, found that the total self-improvement market—including books, audiotapes, seminars, infomercials, personal coaching sessions and support groups—exceeded $9 billion in 2005, an increase of more than 24 percent since 2003 (LaRosa, par 3). Moreover, the firm projected that sales would expand further, gaining another 11.4 percent, to rise to a total value of $13.9 billion by 2010 (LaRosa, par 3).

Self-help books may have been among the most commercially successful genres in the United States, but they are not universally praised. Critics of the genre say these texts do at least as much harm as good, perhaps more so. The charge most frequently levied against self-help books is that they are too simplistic. The tips, suggestions, and formulas that they offer might be catchy, but they are not comprehensive. Marcia Ford offers a blunt assessment: "most of life's problems cannot be solved in seven steps" (2).

Not only are self-help books overly simplistic, but they are also often excessively formulaic. Many self-help and advice books offer one basic idea that they state at the beginning and then reiterate throughout (Askehave 16). As a result, their content is quite thin. Even many of the most well known books suffer from this flaw. As a review of Deepak Chopra's *Ageless Body, Timeless Mind* in *Publisher's Weekly* cautioned, "alert readers will finish the book with unsettling questions, the result of a book that is rife with inspirational conviction but at times thin on substance" (McQuade and Steinberg 74).

In an even more serious problem, self-help books also largely ignore or, at least, minimize personal differences. The advice they offer is presented as universal, or "one size fits all." Henry Giroux and Cynthia Schrager contend that these authors address their audience as a monolithic entity, a method that overlooks the way in which the root of many personal problems is just that, personal and arising from the individual's particular racial, cultural, ethnic, socioeconomic, familial, psychological, geographic, or generational circumstances. Giroux, for instance, has written about the damaging effects that the "pull yourself up by your bootstrap" ethos has had on many minority groups because it ignores or, at least, minimizes the very real obstacles posed by race and class. "The doctrine of self-help is invariably bolstered by allusions to a few African Americans—Tiger Woods and Michael Jordan, for example—and is aimed at youth who allegedly can achieve the American dream if they quit whining and 'just do it'" (Giroux 529). On a related note, advice books also suggest that the solution to all personal and professional difficulties rests with the individual, not with larger social problems like racism, sexism, classism, or homophobia. Cynthia Schrager has commented on the gender bias that has historically permeated self-help books about commerce and enterprise. Given men's traditional place in the public sphere, the advice that these books offer is not always applicable to a businesswoman whose career difficulties may stem from gender discrimination as well as the struggles of balancing work and home life. In this way, advice books overemphasize individual responsibility and personal autonomy. In the words of one critic, they "disregard the systemic social inequalities . . . that cause individual discontent and do not acknowledge social solutions that might actually help" (Dwyer 106).

At least some self-help books suffer from such societal myopia because they rely heavily on personal anecdote and individual experience rather than broad-based research. Norman Vincent Peale's *The Power of Positive Thinking* (1952)—one of the most successful titles in the modern self-help movement—has been criticized for this quality. Not only does Peale base many of his points on his own subjective experiences, but he also takes much of his supporting research from vague, unidentified sources. At various points, he buttresses his claims by drawing on either a commentary by an unnamed "famous psychologist" (52) or a testimonial from an unidentified "prominent citizen" (88).

Equally problematic is the speed with which many self-help writers release new titles—rates that seem too swift for any book to be carefully conceived, thoughtfully constructed, and intellectually inspired. In a memorable joke from his late-night television show, for example, David Letterman satirized the frequency with which Dr. Phil cranked out his best-selling texts, which totaled thirteen in the eight years from 1999 to 2006. In his typical dead-pan seriousness, the comedian held up a copy of an alleged new title by Dr. Phil: *More Advice I Pulled Out of My Ass*. Finally, but not inconsequentially, self-help is often accused of being narcissistic, of promoting excessive self-interest, and of overemphasizing the individual—that is, both the individual author and the individual readers. Marcia Ford succinctly summarized this solipsistic tendency: this genre is "Self-help, with its perceived overemphasis on 'self'" (Ford 2).

In light of the many ideological flaws and practical pitfalls associated with the advice movement, Micki McGee has flatly asserted that self-help books do not actually help. Instead, Stuart Ewan finds that "the self-help industry is an obsessional treadmill far more than a path to a better life" (par 1). An advice book about business and finance published in the late 1990s stated the illusion of self-help even more bluntly. At multiple points in *God Is My Broker* (1998) the authors humorously but candidly remark, "The only way to get rich from a get-rich book is to write one" (Ty, Buckley and Tierney 185, 195).

More Self than Help: *The O'Reilly Factor for Kids* and the Promise, as Well as Problems, of the Advice Genre

The O'Reilly Factor for Kids reflects both the commercial boom in self-help litera-ture and its many flaws. Echoing the basic premise of the genre, O'Reilly's book purports to offer young people useful tips about life. O'Reilly promotes *Kids* in the introduction, "It will give you an edge in facing the challenges of this crazy but exciting time of your life. And that edge will make your life easier" (xiii). Reflecting the approach of many self-help books for adults, *The O'Reilly Factor for Kids* often outlines a series of steps for young people to follow as they confront a problem or address an issue. In the chapter dealing with parents, for example, O'Reilly walks his readers through tactics for managing disagreement more effectively. First, he suggests "In Every Argument, You Should Begin by Isolating the Conflict. What are you and your parents really disagreeing about?" (19; bold in original). Then, he cautions them: "Do Not Bring Up Issues of Right and Wrong. Are your parents wrong? According to you, yes. According to them, no. So there's no going there" (19; bold in original). Finally, O'Reilly advises his young readers, "Once You Understand their Reason(s), See What You Can Work Out. Safety concerns? Offer to take a safe driving course. Money? Find a job, or go for the secondhand option" (20; bold in original).

In another hallmark of the self-help genre, O'Reilly stresses the need for self-reflection and self-examination. In the chapter about learning how to compromise, for instance, he includes a fill-in-the-blank worksheet for young people to complete. To aid in this process, O'Reilly offers prompts like "I've compromised/will compromise with my brother/sister by _____" and "I've compromised/will compromise with my parents by _____" (32–33).

Later, in the chapter dedicated to the all-important topic of fun, he asks his readers to "Write down a list of the things you find the most fun to do, even stupid things" (90). He urges kids to include even those activities that are silly, embarrassing, or not very admirable because they can learn from them: "For instance, if you're a bully and you think you enjoy pantsing a kid who's younger or weaker, include that. This little list will ultimately serve as a tool for you to look at yourself and consider what your tastes in fun really say about you. So be honest" (90).

In the same way that *The O'Reilly Factor for Kids* reflects some of the most popular features of the self-help genre, it also embodies many of its fatal flaws. Arguably the most prominent limitation is that, although O'Reilly's text is ostensibly "for Kids," it becomes clear in the opening pages that it really is more focused on the author himself. O'Reilly begins his book by stating that he wrote the nonfiction work at least as much for his adolescent past self as for the kids of today: "I wish I'd has this book when I was a teenager because . . . I had many concerns" (xiii). Then, in a comment that simultaneously dismisses the usefulness of the entire body of children's literature while it simultaneously places the blame for his own personal mistakes on others, he continues: "Unfortunately, no one had written a realistic book for kids. So I made dumb mistakes, got into trouble" (xiii).

O'Reilly openly states that his own childhood problems will not take a backseat to those faced by kids today; on the contrary, they will form the basis for his narrative: "I'm going to tell you about some of those things in this book. Maybe you'll laugh at my boneheaded behavior, but that's okay, as long as you end up smarter than I was at your age" (xiii). Perhaps aware that some young readers may not be persuaded by this explanation, O'Reilly asks, "What does an adult know?" (xiii), and answers: "Well, I have a career that's lots of fun and makes me lots of money" (xiii).

Each chapter of *The O'Reilly Factor for Kids* is based on a story that the author tells about himself, usually from his adolescence. These autobiographical segments are visually set off from the rest of the text in a different font. In addition, they are announced by the moniker "My Story." Moreover, they contain many self-congratulatory comments. The very first "My Story" presented in the opening chapter on friendships forms a representative example. The anecdote concludes with the following assertion: "Even though I am now famous and successful, I still keep my old friends" (4). Many similar remarks pepper later chapters. He ends a "My Story" anecdote in the chapter on alcohol, for instance, with the comment: "Given my highly-public position, I've avoided many problems by not drinking" (62). The focus here, as elsewhere, is more on applauding himself than helping young people.

Although most of the personal stories that O'Reilly offers are at least tangentially related to the theme of the chapter, some seem curiously off-topic. In the chapter concerning God, O'Reilly offers a "My Story" anecdote about serving as an altar boy at Saint Brigid's Catholic Church. Rather than discussing how this position influenced his faith, he relays the effective method that he devised to shake down a member of wedding party for money. O'Reilly writes:

> The best man was expected to tip the boys. If the tip was not forth-coming, he and I would have the following chat:
>
> ME: Excuse me, sir. Are you the best man?
>
> GUY: That's me, son.
>
> ME: Well, I just want to thank you for tipping Father Murphy so gener-ously . . . but you may not know that Father does not share his good fortune with his assistants.
>
> GUY: I didn't know that.
>
> ME: And it's really too bad, because Richie and I will be holding the plates [with the chalice of wine and the host] during the ring cere-mony . . . and that takes strength and stamina. *[Here I looked the guy straight in the eye]*, if you know what I mean.
>
> GUY: *[after a slight pause]* Here's a ten for the two of you. (175; brackets and italics in original)

The advice that O'Reilly culls from these anecdotes is equally problematic. Akin to many other self-help books, the actual advice is often simplistic or reductive. In the friendship chapter, O'Reilly offers such trite platitudes as "In real life, true friends stand by you when things get rough," and "If you have friends who will help you, you'll be a lot better off" (3). Similarly, he urges his readers to avoid befriending kids who are violent, do drugs, lie, cheat, get drunk, and spread "malicious gossip" (though perhaps "non-malicious gossip" is acceptable?). Echoing Inger Askehave's argument that self-help books offer one basic idea that they reiterate endlessly, he repeats these axioms in "O'Reilly's List of True Friendship Factors" near the end of the chapter (7). Many of the other chapters likewise follow this formula. The chapter on sex, for example, ends with the direct announcement, "But I repeat my mantra . . ." (75). Similarly, the section on self-esteem concludes with a recap of the points that he has already made several times: "To sum up . . ." (119). Not only does this reiterative style underestimate the intellectual capacity—or, at least, attention span—of the book's young readership, but it also denies them more substantive content.

In an even more problematic feature—and one that again reflects a common flaw of the genre—*The O'Reilly Factor for Kids* places too much emphasis on individual autonomy and ignores factors like gender, race, class, and culture. Perhaps because O'Reilly is drawing on his own experiences, he seems to be addressing a largely male audience. Indeed, some language that he uses is sexist or at least not gender inclusive. The author frequently uses the male pronoun as universal. Discussing the importance of "dressing to impress," for example, O'Reilly writes: "There's an old saying that 'clothes make the man'" (101). A few pages later, addressing the existence of dress codes at many professional offices, he remarks: "Is that fair? You bet. The guy who signs the checks gets to make the rules. He wants people working for him who actually reflect the image of his company" (103). Likewise, in the chapter on self-esteem, he again fails to use gender-neutral pronouns; instead, he often identifies authority figures—even those in traditionally female professions such as teaching—as male: "In my day, the music teacher would politely say no, as he well should, and that would be that" (117).

Other chapters contain more serious oversights. In the section on drugs, O'Reilly recounts how some of his childhood playmates became addicted to narcotics after they began appearing in their neighborhood during the late 1960s: "Right away, three of my friends got hooked on heroin. One died, two went to prison. Those two were never the same again. Their lives were ruined" (69). O'Reilly's account neglects the myriad physical, psychological, cultural, environmental, social, and even genetic factors that may lead a person to drug use. By overlooking these elements, his book offers a harsh judgment, which implies that the author's childhood friends became drug users because they were either weak or simply because they were bad people.

Likewise, in the chapter discussing relationships with siblings, O'Reilly ignores or minimizes many personal, psychological, and familial unknowns: "You'll forget the struggles [with your brothers and sisters] and remember the good times. It's true. You'll get together to celebrate family joys and to comfort each other in times of tragedy. You'll share the challenges of taking care of your aging parents, the delight of watching the next generation grow up, and many more" (27–28). This rosy picture does not hold true for many individuals, as sibling conflicts do not always reach a peaceful resolution in adulthood.

O'Reilly's minimization of outside factors is by far the most evident in the chapter on work. Echoing Horatio Alger's oft-repeated formula, he repeatedly argues that effort, education, ambition, and personal determination lead to success. To support this point, O'Reilly uses his own life story as an example: "When I was a kid, I didn't spend money foolishly for one very good reason: I didn't have any" (51). Even as a young person, O'Reilly reports, he was determined to rise above his modest origins and make something of himself. At various points throughout the book, the author tells stories about how he babysat, mowed lawns, and painted houses—jobs that earned him money but also motivated him to set higher future goals. In a comment that could have been expressed by the protagonist in a Horatio Alger novel, O'Reilly writes:

"I began to contemplate the relationship between hard work and the money it earns. I also began to realize that I did not want to live the rest of my life on low wages. I began to study harder. I did not, repeat NOT, want to paint houses for the rest of my life" (53).

While the importance of hard work, the need for a good education, and the necessity of having ambition are all worthy of praise, O'Reilly ignores the many real obstacles that often interfere with an individual's ability to succeed. Indeed, the author's own success story does not take into account the many economic opportunities, educational privileges, and personal advantages that he enjoyed by the sheer virtue of his being white, male, heterosexual, and born into a family that was not living in poverty. O'Reilly concludes his chapter on work with the following naïve platitude:

> Hard work rules!
> Don't forget that.
> It's a primary rule of life. (155)

Analogous sentiments form the closing thoughts to the original version of the book. The new paperback edition of *The O'Reilly Factor for Kids* added a new chapter on cyber bullying, but the initial hardback concludes with the following exhortation: "Just remember, life is tough, but it is also full of adventure and joy. Work hard, be honest, help others. Do those things, and you'll get the O'Reilly Guarantee: You will succeed! And I'll be happy when you do" (186). In so doing, *The O'Reilly Factor for Kids* fails to live up to its opening promise of giving young people "an edge. . . . An edge that will make your life easier" (xiii). Instead of offering them the "no-spin" truth, his advice book paints an overly rosy and ultimately distorted view of life in the United States. Some of O'Reilly's young readers, having already encountered firsthand social problems like racism, sexism, and classism, will already be sadly familiar with the inaccurate nature of this portrait.

O'Reilly, Inc.: Brand Marketing and Selling the Self

The self-help genre was not the only publishing formula that experienced a commercial boom during the final decade of the twentieth century and the first few years of the new millennium; so did something known as brand marketing. As Karen S. Falling Buzzard explains, "Brand names help identify the product and brands take on their own meaning and presence because they embody a rich configuration of symbols and meaning. A good brand name should appeal to its customers, be memorable, as well as offer a distinctive image which separates it from competing products" (95). The most popular and successful brands, she continues, include "a wide range of line extensions (also called sub-brands or variants). These are functionally distinct versions of the product but trading under the same name, e.g. diet Coke" (Falling Buzzard 96).

Establishing a brand name has obvious benefits for manufacturers—increasing public recognition, consumer purchasing frequency and, ultimately, profits—but it benefits buyers as well. "Buying a brand name is a matter of habit and convenience. It is reassuring to buy consistency and known quality. It saves the customer time, money, disappointment, and self blame." Over time, brand names come to embody much more than the products that they signify; they also represent a personal attitude, a social image, and a cultural style. Consumers "identify with brands and use them for self-expression. Brands make statements to other people. They are a short-hand communication of who you are." For these reasons, brands engender communal qualities. In fact, "certain brands create a link with other users: owners talk to one another, complement one another on their good taste, and feel validated in their choices. They create social acceptance and mutual recognition" (Falling Buzzard 95–96).

While brand marketing was formerly associated with industries like clothing and car manufacturing, it has permeated the publishing world during the past twenty years. Arising in part from the budgets cuts at even large publishing houses during the late 1980s and in part from the success of Jacqueline Susann's *Valley of the Dolls*—which used a nontraditional marketing campaign to great success—presses began releasing a smaller number of books and promoting them in new and more aggressive ways: via media blitzes that more closely resembled those used by Hollywood studios to promote their latest blockbuster (see Falling Buzzard 95–96). Publishers saturated print, television, Internet, and radio mediums with an author's name, face, book title, jacket cover, and interview sound bites.

Brand marketing is an especially common feature of both contemporary children's literature and the self-help genre. Daniel Hade explains, "The corporate owners of children's book publishing really aren't interested in the business of publishing books anymore. . . . The business of corporate owners is developing brands" (512). He continues that if you read the annual reports from children's publishers,

> you may be surprised to learn that these brands and media assets are Madeline, Curious George, Peter Rabbit, Clifford, and the Magic School Bus. In other words, these corporations are hoping that children are attracted not to books so much as to *any* product that carries the brand's name. To the corporation, a Clifford key ring is no different from a Clifford book. Each is a 'container' for the idea of 'Clifford.' Each

'container' is simply a means for a child to experience 'Cliffordness.' In this world there is no difference between a book and a video or a CD or a T-shirt or a backpack (Hade 512; italics in original).

Operating with this new marketing ethos, "the corporation, then, seeks to expand its brand to as many aspects of a consumer's life as possible. . . . The goal isn't to see as many copies of *Madeline* as possible (though that is still desirable) but to extend Madeline into as many aspects of a child's life as possible" (Hade 512–513). Hade uses Curious George to illustrate this phenomenon, listing the numerous toys, clothes, games, household products, electronic items, food products, dolls, videos, and school supplies available that are based on the books. But the Harry Potter series, with its massive merchandising bonanza, serves the demonstration just as well.

An analogous ethos permeates the world of self-help works for adults. Books like John Gray's *Men Are from Mars, Women Are from Venus* and Jack Canfield and Mark Victor Hansen's *Chicken Soup for the Soul*—to name just a few—have gone from successful single texts to commercial franchises. The books are available not only in hardback and paperback editions, but in audio formats, via CD-ROMs, on calendars, in videos, and—in the case of Gray's book—even as a Broadway show, family board game, weekend retreat, and luxury cruise seminar (Miller and McHoul 137–138). Both books also have numerous sequel or spin-off texts, each with slight variations on the original title so as to capitalize on its name recognition. Gray added *Mars and Venus in the Bedroom* (1995), *Mars and Venus Together Forever* (1996), *Mars and Venus in Love* (1996), *Mars and Venus on a Date* (1997), and *Mars and Venus Starting Over* (1998) within the first five years of the publication of his original. Meanwhile, *Chicken Soup for the Soul,* which was first released in 1995, had ballooned to more than one hundred spin-off titles by January 2006, including many aimed at young people: *Chicken Soup for the Teenage Soul* (1997), *Chicken Soup for the Kid's Soul* (1998), *Chicken Soup for the College Soul* (1999), *Chicken Soup for the Preteen Soul* (2000), *Chicken Soup for the Teenage Soul on Tough Stuff* (2001), *Chicken Soup for the Teenage Soul on Love and Friendship* (2002), *Chicken Soup for the Christian Teenage Soul* (2003), *Chicken Soup for the Preteen Soul II* (2004), and *Chicken Soup for the Girl's Soul* (2005), to name just a few. Some self-help authors—for example, Dr. Phil, Deepak Chopra, and Dr. Laura—embody their own brand. The success of their books arguably depends less on the particular title or specific content than on the fact that their name and picture appear on the cover.

Since the debut of his cable news and talk commentary program in 1996, Bill O'Reilly has become an astute disciple and successful connoisseur of brand marketing. Tom Lowry analyzes the recognition, "Love him or hate him, O'Reilly has done a masterful job of using the groundswell of support for his conservative views to build himself into a multimedia brand" (par 3). With his TV program, radio broadcast, books, newspaper columns, and the Internet, "O'Reilly generates an estimated $60 million a year for his outlets though ad and book sales, syndication fees and merchandising sales" (Lowry, par 3). The success of these venues prompted him to expand his brand franchise into retail goods. On his official website, *www.billoreilly.com*, fans can purchase *The O'Reilly Factor*–themed jackets, hats, t-shirts, key chains, umbrellas, pens, flashlights, bumper stickers, mugs, car mats, lapel pins, doormats, golf balls, and children's clothing, in addition to all of his books.

The O'Reilly Factor for Kids is simply another extension of the O'Reilly brand, product, and persona. The title that he chose for the text foregrounds this element. Rather than selecting a moniker that was original, unique, and tailored specifically for this book and its subject matter, he used a title that simply rehashed his already established success; he simply tacked on "for Kids" at the end. The cover image furthers this association. Although the author asserts in the introduction, "*The O'Reilly Factor for Kids* is not about me. It is about you" (xiv), the book's jacket is comprised of a large photograph of the author himself. Finally, the name "O'Reilly" appears prominently not once but twice on the cover: first, in all-caps and a bold black font against a white background at the top of the page—and, incidentally, the name is much larger than any other word in the title—and then again in all-caps and fire-engine red font at the bottom.

Given the way in which *The O'Reilly Factor for Kids* is pitched and packaged, readers know what they are getting even before they examine the first page. For those who are drawn to *The O'Reilly Factor for Kids* for this exact reason, they are not disappointed. As the author reveals on the opening page of the introduction, the entire project began as an off-shoot of his popular cable talk program. The "Eyewitness Report" that prefaces *The O'Reilly Factor for Kids* contains the following opening quotation from a young girl identified as "Elizabeth from Ohio": "I'm 15½ years old. You said on your show, Mr. O'Reilly, for kids aged 10 to 16 to write in about the biggest problem in their life" (xiii). While the years from ten to sixteen are undoubtedly difficult ones—with the trials of puberty, peer pressure, and parental conflict—they are also a time in which young people collectively possess tremendous consumer power. An article that appeared in *Business Week* in December 2005—one year after *The O'Reilly Factor for Kids* was released—revealed this extent of this lucrative market: "There are nearly 21 million Tweens (ages 6–12) and young teens in the U.S. who control more than $50B in purchasing power" ("Tween Power," par 1). O'Reilly is a savvy businessman who knows demographics as well as their commercial importance. As a result, it seems likely that he is aware of the tremendous purchasing potential of young people. Viewed from this perspective, his book promises to help expand his fan base at least as much as it promises to help young people navigate a difficult period in their lives.

O'Reilly's references to his popular cable show, however, are not simply confined to this opening instance. These references permeate his advice book for kids by appearing at least once per chapter and several times in some chapters. O'Reilly begins the chapter on work, for instance, with the following plug: "Maybe you turn on the TV or switch on the radio and there I am, yammering away off the top of my head. I'm not looking at notes. I'm not reading questions. You don't see an aide handing me a cheat sheet (as if I were a congressman holding a hearing without a clue)" (151). Later, the final "Eyewitness Report" that precedes the chapter on politics offers the following program endorsement from "Danny," a fan of *The Factor*: "I don't understand all the political conflicts going on in the world. I like your GOOD sense of humor. You make politics easier to understand" (161; caps in original). O'Reilly mentions his cable show by name later in the chapter: "If you've ever watched *The O'Reilly Factor*, you know that I spend a lot of time on political subjects" (164). For those who may not be familiar with his cable show, O'Reilly often pauses to urge young readers to contact him via the television network on which it airs: "Remember, you can always reach me via e-mail at O'Reilly@FoxNews.com" (39).

This repetitive pattern underscores the way in which the literary genre for *The O'Reilly Factor for Kids* may technically be self-help but its narrative format is that of his cable news show. References to his program appear in the most unexpected of places, such as during a discussion about the importance of religious tolerance and open-mindedness: "I mean, you do not want to be like one of the mean-spirited, self-righteous maniacs who attack me when I say something that sets them off. If you watch *The Factor*, you may have heard me read one of these angry letters or emails at the end of the program" (177). Moreover, in the chapter on smoking, O'Reilly does not simply mention his cable news show, he quotes himself from it: "As I said one night on *The Factor*, 'Big business sees the ordinary American as a consumer, not a fellow citizen. They want your money even if it means your life. We're there to be had'" (58).

Perhaps the clearest example of brand marketing in *The O'Reilly Factor for Kids* appears in the final "Eyewitness Report" that prefaces the chapter on the "Dressing Game" and is attributed to "Corey in California." The youngster writes: "You should see some of the stares I get when I wear *The Factor* jacket to school!" (98). This comment combines the previous instances of cross-promotion for his cable show with product placement for his merchandising apparel. Not surprisingly, the author also promotes his other nonfiction narratives that are also spin-offs of the O'Reilly brand. An "Eyewitness Report" submitted by "RJ in New York" appears before the chapter on "Reading"; RJ asserts: "Mr. O'Reilly, I am 15. My biggest problem right now is the fact that I cannot find time to go out and buy *Who's Looking Out for You?*" (110). Later, near the closing pages of *The O'Reilly Factor for Kids*, the author directly promotes this book. For kids who are wondering how to "Have a lot of fun, accomplish many things, and associate with good people," he offers the following suggestion: "My last book, *Who's Looking Out for You?*, deals with those themes. If you like this book, you might want to check out that one, too" (169).

The O'Reilly Factor for Kids incorporates many signature elements of his cable program. O'Reilly does not actually begin his book with the verbatim tagline, "Caution: You are Entering the No-Spin Zone" as he does nightly on the air. He does, however, utter numerous variations on it. In the introduction, for example, he writes: "You may have seen me on my daily TV program, *The O'Reilly Factor*, or heard me on the radio. If you have, you know that I tell it straight, no matter what. And I make sure my guests tell the truth, too" (xiv). He offers his readers a similar promise for this text: "I am as honest in this guide as I am on the air. No sugarcoating. This is straight stuff" (xiv). Such comments are reiterated at multiple points throughout the discussion. In an opening paragraph in the chapter on teachers, for instance, O'Reilly vows, "Not all advice books will tell you the truth on this score, but I will" (127). A few pages later, in a "My Story" anecdote about the time when he was a teacher of English and history, he talks with pride about how he "dropped the truth bomb" (131).

The controversies surrounding his use of faulty or misleading information on *The O'Reilly Factor* made these assurances cause for concern. Such problems also appear in the advice book. In the chapter dedicated to the social ill of cheating, O'Reilly writes that "according to research by the Josephson Institute of Ethics . . . nearly 90% of you readily admit to flat-out lying" (105). First, the Josephson Institute of Ethics publishes a report every two years, and O'Reilly does not mention the date of the specific report he is referencing. Even more problematic, the statistics from the two reports that seem the most likely for him to cite—2002 and 2004—do not match up. The data from Johnson Institute of Ethics from 2004, which is the year that O'Reilly's book was published, put the rate of lying at 64 percent (Josephson, 2004). Meanwhile, the figure from the 2002 report is closer—at 83 percent—but cannot be accurately called "nearly 90 percent" even when rounded up (Josephson, 2002).

Such instances of exaggeration recur. In the chapter dedicated to the subject of work, O'Reilly offers a lengthy description of a typical day on his cable and radio shows. The story presents him as not simply an exceedingly hard worker but also a seemingly solo act, who conceives, researches, and writes his programs with little or no outside help:

> Every weekday morning I get up at 7:00 A.M. and read several newspapers so that I can absorb what's going on in the world. Then I write a TV or newspaper commentary giving my opinion on some recent event. . . . After that, I start planning my radio and TV programs. I talk with my staff by phone about setting up interviews. After that I leave home for the TV studios in Manhattan, where I will write the entire script for *The*

O'Reilly Factor. I'll also begin preparing my questions and approaches to the topics that will be discussed on my daily two-hour radio program. Off and on during the day, I will prepare to interview the four or five guests who will be on my nightly hour-long TV program. Some of them will be hostile, so I'll want to be sure I've anticipated every argument and have researched my points well. . . . The radio program is live on the air from 12:00 P.M. to 2:00 P.M. Just before 6 P.M. I go to the TV studio to host *The Factor.* Sometime after 7:00 P.M., unless there's a special nightly program because of some breaking news, I head toward home and my family. (152–153)

In actuality, of course, O'Reilly has a team of script writers, researchers, and fact checkers (see Sheff).

While the phrase "shut up" does not appear in O'Reilly's advice book for kids, he does employ the abrupt tone that has become a signature feature of his broadcast style. In the chapter discussing the benefits and pitfalls of television, for instance, O'Reilly uses sharp language to make his points. In the space of only one page, for example, he tells his readers, "get a grip," "you've been tricked, "watch out," "you've got your priorities wrong," and "step back" (80).

The book also engages in various forms of name-calling. O'Reilly notes the dismissive pronouncement about kids who urge their peers to "ignore their homework or cut class to 'have fun' instead," "That's being a jerk" (91). Later, while addressing personal fashion choices, he partakes in dismissive labeling once again: "Sure, there are computer geniuses and authors who get respect even if they dress like geeks and bums, but they're the exception to the rule" (101). Sometimes, O'Reilly's language gets so sharp that it seems inappropriate for younger readers. In the section on sports, for instance, he tells his readers: "when you get screwed, you should use your anger to become even better at whatever it is you are doing" (122). O'Reilly discusses an experience during his teenage years when he felt that he had been unjustly cut from a local baseball team, not because he wasn't a good player but because, he says, the coach "did not like me at all" (122). In the wake of this "injustice," as O'Reilly calls it (122), he does not follow his own earlier advice to examine possible reasons for why the coach may have disliked his attitude so much that it caused him to disregard his baseball abilities. O'Reilly could have asked himself questions, such as "Was I disrespectful to the coach?" "Did I behave inappropriately?" and "What part did I play in, or what responsibility do I have for, creating this situation?" Instead, he responds in a far different manner: "I vowed I would show that coach who cut me that he was an idiot" (122). While the author's determination and perseverance are admirable, this anecdote nonetheless embodies a missed educational opportunity: not every coach who fails to pick a young person for a sporting team is necessarily an "idiot." Here, as elsewhere, O'Reilly overlooks many possible mitigating circumstances, not the least of which is himself.

O'Reilly's favorite dismissive insult remains, of course, "Pinhead." He uses that designation in *The O'Reilly Factor for Kids* to describe individuals whom he feels have behaved badly and dedicates large portions of the book to the concept. Segments called "Instant Messages" separate the book's four main sections from one another, and they consist of lengthy paragraphs describing actions and attitudes that belong to either that of a "Pinhead" or a "Smart Operator." A typical passage reads "A Pinhead is a kid who is bored. . . ." and "A Smart Operator is a kid who hugs his parents even at this age. . . ." (140). Not only are many of these examples somewhat silly, but they also bifurcate young adult behavior into a reductive and simplistic binary, for obviously not every child who experiences boredom is worthy of scorn, nor is every youngster who shows affection to his parents deserving of praise. Akin to many other passages, O'Reilly simplifies a situation that is much more complex. Even here, however, O'Reilly does not miss a chance for cross-marketing and self-promotion. The closing entry in the final Instant Message section reads "A Smart Operator is a kid who watches *The O'Reilly Factor*" (186). O'Reilly adds the IM-acronym "JJA"—just joking again—but the sheer number of times that he utters these comments cast doubt on that assertion.

Those who take issue with O'Reilly's broadcasting style may find the frequent references to his cable news show ironic. It is difficult not to think of O'Reilly's signature style of interrupting, talking over, and even shouting down guests and callers when reading this discussion about handling conflict with parents: "The more polite you are, the more responsive the other person will be. Remember that in any debate" (19). Similar comments can be made about the entire chapter dedicated to "Striking a Compromise"—an act for which O'Reilly is not particularly well known. The book also includes passages that seem to contradict his television demeanor: "It's hard to make friends when you demand your way all the time. You know the people I mean" (31), and "I don't interrupt in social situations, unless it is absolutely necessary—that is, when somebody is lying or spreading malicious gossip" (30).

In the same way that O'Reilly frequently mentions his cable news show in *The O'Reilly Factor for Kids*, he likewise routinely plugs his advice book for kids on his daily cable and radio shows by repeatedly referring to its title, giving away free signed copies to callers, and updating fans about the text's ranking on various best-seller lists. A significant portion of references to *The O'Reilly Factor for Kids* on databases like LexisNexis, in fact, are from transcripts of *The O'Reilly Factor*. In the cross-promotional world of millennial marketing, this tendency suits his publisher just fine. "'Bill is one of our cherished marquee authors,' says Stephen Rubin, president of Doubleday Broadway Publishing Group, a unit of Random House Inc. that has published four of O'Reilly's titles. 'It doesn't hurt that he shamelessly promotes his books'" (Lowry, par 3).

These plugs have proved eminently successful. *The O'Reilly Factor for Kids* sold more than 240,000 copies within the first eighteen months of its release (McEvoy). The text became the best-selling nonfiction book for juvenile readers of 2005, according to the Book Standard and Nielsen Bookscan (see "*The O'Reilly Factor for Kids*: Winner," pars 1–2).

This astounding commercial success prompted O'Reilly to compose a follow-up text. In October 2007, he released *Kids Are Americans Too*, another ostensible advice book for young readers. Demonstrating the often hastily written nature of sequel texts, many pages in *Kids Are Americans Too* contain nearly as much white space as they do text. Moreover, the book is more of an obvious spin-off of his cable news program and on-air persona than his first text. Not only is the cover image comprised of another portrait of the author, but, this time, it presents him standing beside a studio television camera. In addition, O'Reilly's name is printed in a font that is larger than the title of the book itself. Finally, the format and content of the book more closely mirror his cable and radio program than the earlier volume. In an example that sets the tone for the entire text, *Kids Are Americans Too* begins with "A Quick Bite of Reality TV" in which O'Reilly relays a story about the robbery of single mother and then asks his readers to ponder if this was "justice at work?" and what the occurrence says "about your rights as an American kid" (xv). Throughout, O'Reilly addresses his young readers in his signature brusque style, exemplified in passages such as the following: "Let's face it. Many kids are complete morons. So are many American adults. As I say on TV, the Constitution gives all Americans the right to be a moron, and a lot of us exercise that right every day" (xx).

Putting a Trademark on Traditionalism: Broadening the (Commercial) Boundaries of Conservatism

Unlike all the other authors profiled in the previous chapters, Bill O'Reilly does not consider himself a conservative. In articles, interviews, and broadcasts, he describes himself as a "traditionalist." O'Reilly defines the term, which he claims to have coined, as someone whose opinions do not fall along expected political or social lines but instead are the products of independent thinking. Traditionalists advocate for long-established beliefs and time-honored positions, whether they are held by Democrats or Republicans or supported by progressives or conservatives (see O'Reilly *Culture Warrior* 61–74).

Many critics have questioned the veracity of this claim, given that O'Reilly's views generally mirror other conservative thinkers, given that the guests on his show are generally from the right of the political spectrum, and—most of all—given that traditionalism is a founding theme of the conservative movement itself.[8] Nonetheless, *The O'Reilly Factor for Kids* does reflect a distinction between the author's avowed traditionalism and many classic tenets of conservatism. The book advocates for many conservative causes, including an anti-abortion passage telling kids "Respect your life and the lives of all others, including the unborn" (169). But the book also strays from this truly conservative script. In the chapter concerning God, for example, O'Reilly is much more inclusive or, at least, far less dogmatic than many conservatives. His religious vision not only includes faith traditions outside Judeo-Christianity, but it is also grounded in individual doubt rather than doctrinal conformity. O'Reilly begins the chapter with a series of provocative questions about faith, including "Is there a God? What does He (or She!) want from me?" (173). Throughout his discussion, he encourages healthy skepticism and discourages absolutist beliefs about any one religious tradition:

> Faith never means that I'm always right, or you're always right, or any religious leader is always right.
> We're human.
> That's why some of us believe that we need a God.
> You may not. But the choice, in this society, is always yours. (178)

Likewise, in the chapter titled "Dealing with Divorce," O'Reilly, who is a practicing Catholic, does not condemn the growing phenomenon, nor does he repeat platitudes about the scared nature of marriage. On the contrary, he offers a more nuanced perspective:

> When I was a kid, I rarely heard of divorce. Most of the parents I knew were religious, and believed that marriage was sacred. At least, that's what they told us kids. Also, most of them didn't have enough money to support two separate households. I didn't understand that at the time.
> Nor did I understand that there was probably a lot of anger, distrust, and cheating going on in some of those homes.
> So which is better? Unhappy, toxic marriages that become a prison for both spouses? Or today's situation, where just about half of the marriages in America are likely to end in divorce? (35)

Later, O'Reilly strays even further from the standard conservative message that criticizes performers like Eminem whose lyrics not only use profanity, glorify violence, and convey poor attitudes about women but also engage in homophobia. "They dis women and gays and use gutter language" (84). Later in the book, he defends homosexuals once again: "Speculate that decent, hard-working gays might make good adoptive parents? The bigots foam at the mouth" (178).[9]

By far the most different—and most controversial—section in *The O'Reilly Factor for Kids* is the one addressing drugs. The author begins the chapter by vowing "I promise not to use the same old arguments that everyone else uses" (66), and he does not disappoint. Rather than taking the zero-tolerance, "just say no" approach found in many other conservative-themed advice books for teens, the cable host is more flexible and, ultimately, more realistic. He writes, "I know that you will not be terrorized or moralized into staying away from drugs" (68). Indeed, he acknowledges, "About half of you will never try pot, they say. The other half is going to 'experiment,' knowing that most kids don't become raving maniacs or suicidal depressives because of social use of marijuana" (68). In a comment that has been oft-quoted, he remarks on the subject: "Like a brain surgeon who drinks a martini when he's not on call, the successful kids in your school may smoke pot on occasion, but they are not stoners" (67). He even asserts that the kids who are "the best athletes," "the most active leaders," and "the most original students" are probably no strangers to marijuana: "Like many of you, they have experimented—they may enjoy toking on Saturday nights at a party. But these people are rocking your teenage worlds because they are motivated, healthy, and hard-working kids the majority of the time" (67). Indeed, while O'Reilly flatly states "doing drugs strikes me as such a waste . . . a terrible misuse of time, potential, opportunity, and youth" (68), he also concedes: "many of you can play around with marijuana for a few years, then get on with your lives" (67).[10]

His chapter on sex is equally iconoclastic. Once again, he does not advocate for the typical conservative stance of abstinence before marriage. In a remark that is part realistic and part fatalistic, he writes in the opening pages of the section: "As for me, I'm not going to tell you to avoid sex, because in the end you will do what you want anyway" (75). Instead, he urges young people to wait to have sex at least until they have found love: "For most of us, it's a lengthy search, but the challenge is fun, and the result, when you do find someone you respect, care about, and can laugh with, is the best" (75).[11] Because O'Reilly is aware of the unconventional and possibly even controversial nature of his advice, he remarks to his readers: "Are you surprised by my thoughts on the subject? Did you think that O'Reilly would tell you that sex is off-limits? As you know, things are more complicated than that" (75).

In these and other passages, O'Reilly demonstrates not only the range of conservative thinking in the United States during the first decade of the twenty-first century but its ever-changing nature. Far from a seeming monolith, this mode of thought has variety, multiplicity, and even diversity.

However conservatism is expressed or represented in *The O'Reilly Factor for Kids* though, it retains a strong tie to commercial culture. Whether marketed by O'Reilly via a cable show, a radio broadcast, or a book for young readers, this ideological viewpoint and its attendant cultural movement has given rise to its own merchandise lines and commercial brands. In his introduction's closing paragraph the author describes the purpose of *The O'Reilly Factor for Kids* in the following way:

> About finding the courage and willpower to be who you really are. About standing up for yourself. About doing the smartest thing.
>
> Did you notice what I said? 'The smartest thing.' This guide is not necessarily about what's right and wrong. It's about using your head.
>
> Listen up . . . (xiv)

Although this comment can be read in the iconoclastic way of encouraging kids to engage in a form of moral relativism, it also can be regarded in a more conventional manner when viewed through the lens of brand marketing. Given the way in which *The O'Reilly Factor for Kids* embodies an extension of O'Reilly brand, the idea of "using your head" to the author means being loyal to the O'Reilly name, and "doing the smartest thing" means buying another one of his products. Ultimately, this is the message or the advice that he offers young readers.

In the introduction to *Novel Gazing: Queer Readings of Fiction*, Eve Kosofsky Sedgwick discusses what she describes as a "paranoid" reading of texts. In this type of interpretive practice, individuals encounter ideas and information that they already know. As a result, their beliefs are not challenged, critiqued, or even broadened by the material they encounter; they are simply averred. Sedgwick asks, "What does knowledge do—the pursuit of it, the having and exposing of it, the receiving again of what one already knows?" (4).

The O'Reilly Factor for Kids participates in or, at least, encourages a paranoid reading. The messages contained in his advice book for young people simply replicate the interests, tastes, and attitudes of the adults who have purchased the text for children, if not the children who are intended to read it. Narratives written out of this impulse do not expand knowledge bases and change minds. Instead, they only lead to further entrenchment. It is regrettable that this feature forms the true "straight talk/no spin" facet of the book.

ACCOMPLISHED AUTHOR AND FREQUENT REVIEWER Brooke Allen observed, "The decline of American civilization has been a favorite subject for writers throughout the last half century" (par 1). This issue has become so powerful and pervasive that it crosses the boundaries of race, class, age, ethnicity, and even sociopolitical perspective. Allen notes that those writing about the decay of U.S. society from the left side of the political spectrum generally identify problems like ongoing racial prejudice, persistent cultural ignorance, and entrenched socioeconomic inequality as central factors in this process (par 1). Meanwhile individuals whose viewpoints emanate from the right side of the sociopolitical scale tend to cite different sources: "the '60s, political correctness, and the hijacking of universities by radical feminists and multiculturalists" (Allen par 1).

Allen points out these two seemingly opposite viewpoints regarding the decline of American civilization agree on one issue: "their distrust of television and electronic media and their belief that these technologies are rendering us ever dumb and dumber" (par 1). Both the left and the right assert that various facets of American television, film, the Internet, radio, and even print media contribute to and, on occasion, are even the cause of many of the nation's problems. To illustrate this point, Allen cites the work of commentators ranging from Allan Bloom, David Horowitz, and Bernard Goldberg on the right to Richard Hofstadter, Susan Jacoby, and Al Gore on the left.

Bill O'Reilly, with his massive and ever-expanding multimedia empire, is both a participant in and product of this phenomenon. His cable news show and the Fox News channel on which it airs routinely decry the problems with the media that both the left and the right identify as contributing to the problems in American society while they contribute to them. Audience members can watch the host of *The O'Reilly Factor* condemn the violent, sexual, and vapid nature of television programming that is polluting the minds of our children. But then, later that night on the same network, they can also tune in to watch shows that contain these exact features, such as *Temptation Island* (2001–2003), in which committed couples are separated on a tropical island and their fidelity is tested by an array of alluring men and women; *Who's Your Daddy?* (2005), where an adult woman who was adopted as a child attempts to win $100,000 by correctly identifying which contestant is her biological father; or *The Littlest Groom* (2004), on which a group of average-sized women compete against a group composed of little people for the heart of a diminutive bachelor.

Often these paradoxes occur on *The O'Reilly Factor* itself. In the broadcast that aired on February 2, 2009, for example, O'Reilly criticized the *New York Times* for attempting to distract the nation from the early failures of the Obama administration in general and its bungled handling of the current financial crisis more specifically with divisive issues in the cultural wars, namely that of illegal immigration. As journalist Peter Hart, media watchdog group Fairness and Accuracy in Reporting, and even *The Daily Show* host Jon Stewart have all documented, however, O'Reilly has engaged in this practice himself for years. Indeed, as mentioned above, the cable news host titled his best-selling 2006 book *Culture Warrior*.

The subject of the next chapter—Katherine DeBrecht and her series of *Help! Mom!* books—can be placed on this continuum as well. Akin to O'Reilly and the Fox channel, DeBrecht condemns the noxious nature of the American mass media and the pernicious impact of its popular culture while she paradoxically exploits these elements to her advantage. Indeed, the pages that follow present the growing genre of right-leaning literature for young readers at its most culturally conservative, politically partisan, and—far more importantly—media savvy.

6

"One State, Two State, Red State, Blue State"

Bringing Partisan Politics to Picture Books in Katharine DeBrecht's *Help! Mom!* Series

In 2005, after one of the most divisive presidential elections in U.S. history, a small California-based publishing company called World Ahead released the first title in its new line of children's books: *Help! Mom! There Are Liberals under My Bed!* Written by Katharine DeBrecht and illustrated by Jim Hummel, the story follows the adventures of two young boys who decide to open a lemonade stand to earn money for a much-desired swing set. That night, both boys dream that their stand is a tremendous success until a series of well-known and thinly disguised liberals appear to stymie their efforts. First, Mayor Leach (a Ted Kennedy look-alike) levies taxes so heavy that they eradicate the boys' profit margin. Then, Mr. Fussman, a sallow-faced lawyer from the "LCLU" (that is, the "Liberaland Civil Liberties Union"), demands that the boys remove the "offensive" picture of Jesus atop their stand and replace it with one of a big toe. Finally, Congresswoman Clunkton (a.k.a. Hillary Clinton) mandates that the pair reduce the amount of sugar in their lemonade and also serve a floret of broccoli with each glass.

As even this brief overview indicates, with its over-the-top characterizations, tongue-in-cheek humor, and rigid "good versus bad" dichotomy, *Liberals* seems more like a playful satire for adults than a serious narrative for young readers. Offering support for this viewpoint, the "About the Author" section in the back of the book reveals that Katharine DeBrecht is the pseudonym of a former freelance journalist (DeBrecht 53).[1] Likewise, the drawings that accompany *Liberals* are not the work of an established children's book illustrator, but a multi-award-winning newspaper cartoonist.[2]

In spite of such seemingly strong evidence for viewing *Liberals* as a humor book for adults that is simply written in the style of a picture book for children, both the narrative's author and its publisher adamantly object to this classification. In numerous interviews, articles, and press releases, DeBrecht presents herself as a sincere suburban homemaker who wrote the story because she was concerned about what she felt were the increasingly liberal messages that her three young sons were receiving in contemporary picture books. "I have seen children's books representing the left for several years" (Mapes A1), she asserted in a remark that echoes the attitudes of many other conservative parents. The first-time author cited examples like *Heather Has Two Mommies* (a 1989 picture book that features same-sex parents), *Rainbow Fish* (a fable-like narrative from 1992 about the importance of sharing that has been criticized for promoting socialism), and *King and King* (an illustrated fairy tale that was published in 2002 and features a young prince who wishes to marry another prince). DeBrecht lamented, however, that books for young readers that possess conservative messages have not shown a corresponding increase. As a result, she felt that her book was not simply a new but a necessary narrative for young readers. As she told a reporter soon after *Liberals* was released, "On the children's level, there really wasn't something out there to teach the traditional values" (Mapes A1).

Eric Jackson, the president of World Ahead and the founder of its new Kids Ahead line that released *Liberals*, reinforces DeBrecht's claims. He has explained that the mission of his imprint is "to provide books for families who have traditional values, if you will, and who want to have books to use as a tool to pass on those values to their children" (Cottle, par. 2). Demonstrating the way in which *Liberals* is meant as a conservative response and even antidote to the perceived spike in left-leaning children's books since the 1990s, the promotional plug for the narrative provided by World Ahead publishing on Barnes and Noble.com reads:

> Would you let your child read blatantly liberal stories with titles such as *King & King*; *No, George, No*; or *It's Just a Plant?*
>
> Unless you live in Haight-Ashbury or write for the *New York Times*, probably not. But with the nation's libraries and classrooms filled with overtly liberal children's books advocating everything from gay marriage to marijuana use, kids everywhere are being deluged with left-wing propaganda.
>
> *Help! Mom! There Are Liberals Under My Bed* is the book conservative parents have been seeking. ("Synopsis")

Lest any lingering doubts remain, Jackson himself has emphatically asserted: "The point is not to attack politicians. . . . The point is that the books are teaching a story about values to kids. *Liberals Under My Bed!* is about hard work and being able to live the American dream and family, faith and free enterprise as core values" (Dreher F4).

While Jackson touts the child-centered nature of *Liberals*, he does not deny its simultaneous appeal to adults. A successful businessman who was one of the creators of the popular online transaction site PayPal, he is keenly aware that children's books enjoy increased sales when they reach a dual audience or, as critics of children's literature would say, are cross-written. When choosing the inaugural title for his Kids Ahead imprint, therefore, he consciously selected a manuscript that included hybrid humor: "the goal was to put a lot of satire in the content that would allow adults to enjoy the books as much as children, somewhat akin to the popular *Shrek* movies" ("World Ahead Presses" 4). Accordingly, the World Ahead website touts *Liberals* as perfect "for parents who seek to share their traditional values with their children," as well as "for adults who wish to give a humorous gift to a friend" (World Ahead 2005).

This strategy has worked. Since the publication of DeBrecht's text in September 2005, it has been astoundingly successful. This small book printed by an equally small publisher went through three press runs during its first six weeks of release. In addition, it has been reviewed in major U.S. print venues, including the *Wall Street Journal, Harper's Magazine, Publisher's Weekly*, and *U.S. News & World Report*.[3] Likewise, the book has enjoyed prominent in-store displays at national bookstore chains like Borders and Barnes and Noble. All of this attention has helped *Liberals* sell more than 30,000 copies by 2009, earning it a place on various best-seller lists. During the first month following the book's release, for example, the narrative shot to the top sales spot on Barnes and Noble.com. Meanwhile, it was ranked second on Amazon.com, behind only *Harry Potter and the Half-Blood Prince*, which had been released earlier that year.

The popularity of *Liberals* inspired DeBrecht to expand upon her general concept and create a series bearing the *Help! Mom!* title. Since 2005, she has released two more books with the same basic theme: *Help! Mom! Hollywood's in My Hamper!* appeared in March 2006, and *Help! Mom! The 9th Circuit Nabbed the Nativity!* was released in time for Christmas later that year. DeBrecht has a fourth title in the works, *Help! Mom! There Are Lawyers in My Lunchbox!*

This chapter explores the *Help! Mom!* books as a powerful and growing new trend in American popular, material and literary culture. With their flimsy plots, predictable stereotypes, and propagandistic messages, the books bring U.S. partisan perspectives and the current sharp division between the political left and right from the broadside to the bedtime story. While narratives written for young readers have a longstanding history of being didactic and containing socially minded themes, the *Help! Mom!* series signals a shift in the representation of politics within children's literature and, by extension, cultural attitudes about the purpose or intent of narratives for young readers. Although the ugly slugfest known as contemporary partisan politics is commonly thought confined to adult nonfiction fare such as Ann Coulter's *Slander: Liberal Lies about the American Right* (2003) and its retorts like Joe Maguire's *The Lies and Lunacy of Ann Coulter* (2006), the political urgency as well as social anxiety surrounding events like the perceived erosion of so-called traditional family values and the escalating stakes of the culture wars have moved this battleground to fictional storybooks for young readers. Fueled by the steady growth of sales for children's books over the past several years, the subsequent rise of highly specialized niche markets, and the promotional opportunities made possible by the internet, DeBrecht's *Help! Mom!* series is the most visible and certainly most successful example of this new genre. The books represent conservative-themed narratives for young readers at their most partisan and extreme.

In a related and arguably even more important implication, the success of the *Help! Mom!* books also points to a shift in popular cultural attitudes about children and childhood in the United States. Although DeBrecht claims to be protecting her young, innocent, and seemingly "impressionable" readers from what she sees as liberal vices of the adult world, her books ironically create an environment in which the line separating children from adults has disappeared or, at least, blurred. Whereas the ideological disputes between Democrats and Republicans were formerly issues about which only "grown-ups" were concerned, the *Help! Mom!* series demonstrates that this distinction is no longer the case. The high stakes associated with both current political issues and contemporary cultural debates have caused even elementary-school-aged children to be pulled into the fray. In a throwback to pre-Enlightenment attitudes about childhood, DeBrecht envisions children as nothing more than politicized little adults.

"Once Upon a Time, There Were the Culture Wars": *Liberals under My Bed!* and the Rise of Partisan Parenting

Even before the opening sentence of *Help! Mom! There Are Liberals under My Bed!*, DeBrecht announces the overtly political and highly partisan aim of her book. Her chosen title is neither neutral nor subtle. Especially when seen through the eyes of a child reader, the phrase "There Are Liberals under My Bed" is reminiscent of "There Are Monsters under My Bed." The image created by Jim Hummel to accompany this moniker reinforces the message that liberalism and the individuals who subscribe to it embody a monstrous threat that endangers children. The drawing, which presents caricatures of Hillary Clinton and Ted Kennedy along with a television reporter who is not a person but, appropriately, a donkey emerging from under a child's bed, looks more like a political cartoon than an illustration for a children's book. Moreover, the image shows Clinton holding a plump piggybank by the tail. The purple animal, which is sitting atop the child's bed, has an angry scowl on its face and is trying to wiggle away. With coins scattered about the floor, an untied sneaker lying off to the side, and a cute dog looking plaintively at the reader, one wonders if the trio of liberals haven't cannibalistically eaten, or at least kidnapped, the child occupant of the bed.

This eye-catching image coupled with the dramatics that DeBrecht attaches to her title—using no fewer than three exclamation points in the space of only eight words—makes the cover of *Liberals* unsettling to adults, let alone children. Indeed, one mother who blogs about homeschooling her children wrote that after reading DeBrecht's book to her five-year-old son, "I did have to try to explain in gentle terms that they [liberals] really are not under anyone's bed" (Victoria, par. 3). The divisive agenda and even demonizing intent behind DeBrecht's title becomes more pronounced, given that its scenario is not directly related to the story. The book's two protagonists have a frightful dream about "Liberaland," but at no point do any liberals—either real or imagined—come out from under their beds.

This "good versus evil" or, at least, "us versus them" stance continues in a modified form in the opening sentence of *Liberals*: "Tommy and Lou were brothers who lived in a small house, on a small street, in a small neighborhood, in a small city, in the great USA" (1). Although infused with jingoistic patriotism and even American ethnocentrism, this "once upon a time" beginning ostensibly supports the author's claim that *Liberals* is a narrative for children. Moreover, DeBrecht revives the fairy tale motif at various points throughout her book. Describing how the boys work "hours and hours, day and night, trying to get their [lemonade] recipe just right" (11), she casts them as Cinderella-type figures: "Their little hands ached from squeezing lemons and little Lou even got a blister" (11). Showing a phenomenal concern for customer satisfaction—and absolutely no concern for profit margins—Tommy and Lou open their stand only after they have crafted the perfect lemonade recipe. Like Goldilocks's satisfactory porridge, it was "not too sweet, not too sour" (DeBrecht 11).

As DeBrecht relays the overwhelming success of Tommy and Lou's lemonade stand, her book shifts from iconic myths about fairy tale figures to equally iconic myths about the United States. Before Mayor Leach, Mr. Fussman, and Congresswoman Clunkton appear, Tommy and Lou enjoy a miniature version of the American Dream. In a passage that could have come out of a Horatio Alger novel, DeBrecht writes: "the boys were proud of their hard work and felt good about taking responsibility to earn money for their swing set" (13). Not surprisingly, a refrain throughout the book recalls Benjamin Franklin's now-legendary work ethic outlined in his autobiography: "And each day, after school, after homework, after chores, the boys went on squeezing lemonades, selling lemonade with smiles and thank-yous, like the good little boys they were" (11).

In a powerful indication of the partisan agenda in her book, DeBrecht links these admirable and all-American qualities with a particular political affiliation. When Tommy and Lou initially ask their parents for the swing set, they receive the following disappointing but also character-building response: "Mom and Dad always told them that having everything given to them would not make them feel good about themselves, and that earning things on their own would make them feel proud and become better people" (DeBrecht 3). DeBrecht's narrative makes it clear that the boys' parents could afford to buy them the swing set, but, in rhetoric that recalls conservative critiques of "liberal" social welfare programs, the parents dislike the idea of a "handout": "'Swing sets are an expensive toy,' their Mom explained. 'Would you love it more if we just gave it to you or if you worked hard for it?'" (DeBrecht 5). Lest the politicized subtext of this passage is unclear, a portrait of Ronald Reagan hangs on the wall in the accompanying illustration.

In this and other sections, the partisan focus of DeBrecht's text is amplified by Hummel's drawings. In *How Picturebooks Work*, Maria Nikolajeva and Carole Scott discuss the various relationships that can exist between the words and images in picture books, including congruency (where the images mirror the text), enhancement (where the images augment the text), and counterpoint (where the images contradict or compete with the text) (6–19). Hummel's illustrations clearly fall into the category of enhancement. Throughout the book, Hummel tacitly includes politically charged decorations in Tommy and Lou's house. Coupled with the previously mentioned portrait of "the Gipper," he depicts a holy cross and a picture of the Statue of Liberty adorning the bedroom that the boys share. Hummel has even more fun drawing the various liberals. Mayor Leach, the Ted Kennedy look-alike, for example, is not only grotesquely rotund, but carrying a briefcase that has "I ♥ Tax" written across the side (18). Later, when he unbuttons his suit jacket, the mayor reveals a button that reads "I Love to Tax" and is nearly as big as Lou's head (DeBrecht 20).

Undoubtedly the most powerful example of the way in which Hummel's illustrations augment the politically charged focus of DeBrecht's text is when Tommy and Lou have their nightmarish dream about Liberaland. Hummel's rendering of this "very strange place" (DeBrecht 9) features a cartoonishly long stretch limo snaking its way down the main street. Flanking each side of the automobile is an array of offices, stores, and government buildings, each one with its own parodic name: "Spendbucks Coffee," "K-Marx," "Duey, Taxem, and Howe, LLP," the "Flynt Library," "It Takes a Village Daycare," and "Dean's Cream" (DeBrecht 10). The one locale that does not possess a satiric name apparently doesn't need it: the Ninth Circuit courthouse, presumably, is humorous enough on its own. A hillside billboard mimicking the Hollywood sign in Los Angeles overlooks this whole scene. Foreshadowing the focus of a future book by DeBrecht, it reads "Haughtywood" (10). Completing the heavy-handed nature of this image, a pair of lightning bolts emanate from ominous storm clouds gathered in the right corner of the background.

Hummel's rendering of Liberaland transforms DeBrecht's narrative from simply a heavy-handed but relatively harmless story to an overtly political narrative filled with partisan viewpoints. Although DeBrecht and her publisher apparently identified Hummel's illustration as having "*Shrek*-like" appeal, this passage has little, if any, resonance for a child audience. The portrayal of Liberaland raises the question of how the book intends to teach respect for one political viewpoint by promoting disrespectful attitudes toward another. To be sure, Theodor Adorno's imperative about "the importance of compassion in shaping civic imagination" (11) is absent from DeBrecht's book.

Liberaland also prompts readers to wonder how many of Hummel's visual jabs and word puns a child reader would be able to understand. Michelle Cottle has commented about *Liberals:* "What remains less clear is how anyone could imagine that four- to eight-year-olds for whom the book is ostensibly intended would be entertained by a story dependent upon such context-driven humor as Clunkton's assertion: 'It takes a village to get kids to eat their vegetables!'" (par 6). Moreover, some political references in both DeBrecht's written text and Hummel's illustrations are ironically not "family-friendly." In the words of Cottle once again: "Even hard-core liberal-haters might hesitate to explain to kids a main street featuring 'Teddy's Carwash'" (par 7), presumably a reference to the Chappaquiddick Island tragedy.

Hummel's illustration of Liberaland, however, is only the beginning of an array of visual images and written passages that are not only over the top but also likely to go over the heads of the book's imagined child readers. When Tommy and Lou first open their lemonade stand in the dream sequence, for example, a mysterious man sitting on a bench is reading a newspaper, the headline to which announces, "Sneeze and Gas Tax Enacted" (2005: 11). For a child reader who has limited knowledge about taxes in general let alone the satirical meaning of a "Sneeze and Gas Tax" in particular, the parodic humor of this comment is likely lost. The same remark could be made later in the narrative when the mysterious man returns, and this time the front page of his newspaper reveals, "Toe Nail Sculpture Replaces Nativity" (2005: 26). Once again, this dual jab at the National Endowment for the Arts and the separation of church and state is probably lost on young readers.

Both DeBrecht's written description and Hummel's illustration of Mr. Fussman, the lawyer from the "Liberaland Civil Liberties Union," is even worse, for he embodies possible elements of religious prejudice in addition to adult political parody. Carrying a briefcase that reads "I ♥ Judges" and hissing his "s" like a serpent (DeBrecht 28), Fussman is coded as sinister. Even more alarming though, with his large nose and lascivious love for money, the LCLU lawyer resembles an anti-Semitic caricature. As journalist Azi Paybarah has written, Fussman "is wearing an Abraham Lincoln–style hat that doubtless conceals his devilish Jew horns" (par 17).

When Hummel's illustrations do seem aimed at child readers, they appear designed to frighten them. Given Michelle Cottle's apt observation that no conservative book would be complete without "the requisite Hillary-bashing" (Cottle, par. 12), his portrayal of "Congresswoman Clunkton" is as animated as it is violent. In the picture that accompanies her mandate—"for every glass of lemonade you sell, you must, I say, you MUST give two pieces of broccoli with it" (DeBrecht 32)—the congresswoman slams her fist on the boys' lemonade counter so forcefully that cartoon stars shoot out from the point of impact, three lemons launch off the table, and the glass pitcher of lemonade (along with a significant portion of its contents) become airborne. In a final piece of dictatorial cruelty, Tommy and Lou's adorable little dog lurches out of the way of the congresswoman to avoid being kicked by the sharp point of her high-heeled shoes (DeBrecht 33). In these and other passages, DeBrecht undercuts the credibility of her critique with her hyperbolic characterizations and desire to ridicule contemporary politicians.[4]

The hyperbolic messages of *Liberals*, however, are not limited to secular issues like politics. Closely related to DeBrecht's partisan focus is her religious bent, a detail that reflects the prominence of Christian-based groups in the fight to protect so-called traditional family values. The opening page of the book yokes Tommy and Lou's status as "good little boys" with their status as good keepers of the faith: "they ate most of their vegetables, did their chores, tried not to fight over their toys, and they said their prayers at bedtime—sometimes a little fast if they were extra tired" (DeBrecht 1). Later, DeBrecht locates Christianity specifically at the core of middle-class American values and its capitalist economy. When little Tommy and Lou contemplate their various forms of good fortune—citing their loving parents and loyal customers—they realize: "But what they were mostly thankful for was the beautiful lemon tree that God had provided them. So atop their stand, they hung a picture of Jesus" (25). Reflecting the way in which many conservative Christians in the United States feel that their faith is being persecuted by the liberal project of multiculturalism, no sooner have the boys affixed the image of Christ than the lawyer for the Liberaland Civil Liberties Union promptly informs them that they must take it down. The reason that Fussman gives for the removal is farcical. He tells the boys that his client, the allegorically named "Mr. Afflue," found the portrait offensive "while riding [by] in his limousine" (DeBrecht 27). As a replacement image, the lawyer offers the boys a framed picture of a big toe because, as he goes on to add, "we liberals are NOT against free speech" (DeBrecht 27). Before departing for more important things—"like being on TV"—he warns the boys: "No praying here, either!" (DeBrecht 30).

In the conclusion to DeBrecht's book, as Tommy and Lou work "twice as hard with bigger smiles and extra thank-yous" to compensate for Congresswoman Clunkton's growing piles of unwanted broccoli, Mr. Fussman's frightening image of the big toe, and Mayor Leach's oppressive taxes, the terrible trio of liberals emerges from behind the lemon tree (DeBrecht 38). Carrying picket signs proclaiming "More Taxes" and "Halliburton Is Involved," they hold a circus-like television conference—covered by "LNN," the "Liberal News Network"—and assume control of Tommy and Lou's stand (DeBrecht 39–40). Within days, the liberals run the boys' formerly profitable venture into the ground: Hummel's illustration shows a homeless man sleeping behind the stand, the glass jar containing the boys' money raided and empty, and a spider sitting in the lemonade pitcher (DeBrecht 43).

Just when all seems lost, Tommy and Lou awaken from their nightmarish dream about Liberaland. Although the boys are grateful that they do not live in this frightening place, they simultaneously express concern that pesky liberals may interfere with their plan to open a lemonade stand and save for the swing set. Being the good little boys they are, however, Tommy and Lou decide to go ahead with their venture; after all, they remember, " 'Dad always said to work hard and do our best' " (DeBrecht 44). For readers who are saddened by the abrupt departure of Mayor Leach, Mr. Fussman, Congresswoman Clunkton, and Senator Kruckle, DeBrecht offers "profiles of the dastardly Liberals" in an epilogue to the book (49). In keeping with the hyperbolic tone of the text, these biographies include patently ridiculous details, such as "Senator Kruckle . . . is the author of the Greedy Business Law, which requires all Liberaland companies to give their employees eleven months of vacation time every year. Senator Kruckle is well known for demanding that the Girl Scouts only sell cookies made from spinach and onions" (DeBrecht 51).

The final page of *Liberals* shows a large lemon tree, its branches laden with perfect-looking fruit and idyllically illuminated by the sun. DeBrecht's closing caption about little Tommy and Lou reads: "And off they went to start squeezing lemons, like the good little conservatives they were" (46). For adult readers of the book, this concluding phrase should spark consternation, for, during the time when *Liberals* was written as well as released, conservative members of the Republican party controlled both the U.S. Senate and House of Representatives, while another Republican had recently won a second term in the Oval Office. Since taking control in 2000, the GOP had enacted an array of conservative policies, including increasing federal funding for faith-based afterschool programs, cutting social welfare initiatives like Teach for America, and expanding efforts to block the state-level legalization of same-sex marriage. Given these details, DeBrecht's assertion that conservatives have been handed lemons during this era affirms observations by Amy Johnson Frykholm, Seymour Lipset, and Earl Raab about the rhetoric of persecution that often fuels rightist perspectives. Even during times when these groups constitute the ruling class, they cast their position in the oppositional and often hostile terms of being under attack or even siege. As a result, as Amy Johnson Frykholm has written, for both faith-focused and secular-based groups, the movement "draws strength from this active, if antagonistic, relationship with 'the world'" (*Rapture* 27).

From the moment DeBrecht's narrative hit bookstore shelves on September 20, 2005, it ignited intense reactions on both sides of the political aisle. The very next day, in fact, conservative talk radio host Rush Limbaugh praised his undoubtedly complementary copy of the book: " 'Once again we find conservatives able to be totally honest about who liberals are' " (*Special Guests*,

"Rush Limbaugh," par. 5). Ending his segment by announcing, "Our hat is off to Katharine DeBrecht" (qtd on World Ahead 2005), Limbaugh gave *Liberals* his enthusiastic endorsement; this endorsement is, not surprisingly, reprinted on all subsequent editions of the text.[5]

Fellow conservative radio host Melanie Morgan quickly followed suit. In a comment that closely mirrors Jackson's remarks about his publishing imprint in general and DeBrecht's inaugural title in particular, she told her San Francisco–based audience: "This book is the answer to a baseball mom's prayers. . . . Pick it up, read it to your children, and watch good things happen" (qtd on World Ahead 2005).

More left-leaning public figures had markedly different reactions. Alan Colmes, cohost of the Fox News show Hannity & Colmes, called *Liberals* "Brainwashing" (*Special Guests*, "Liberals Claim," par. 2). Similarly, the popular left-leaning website Daily Kos compared *Liberals* to "Nazi propaganda," while the online forum "Democratic Underground" added DeBrecht to their "Top 10 Conservative Idiots" list. Even Hillary Clinton's press secretary, the outspoken Philippe Reines, entered the fray. In the popular congressional newspaper *The Hill*, Reines is quoted as having made the following humorous comment about DeBrecht's book: "Can't wait for the sequel, *Help! Mom! I Can't Read This Book Because Republicans Have Cut Literacy Programs!*" (Rothstein, par. 5).[6]

Such viewpoints have been echoed both by journalists who have reviewed the book for the popular press and by scholars of children's literature who have critiqued it for fellow members of the profession. In *The New Republic* Michelle Cottle questioned the alleged child audience for the narrative as well as its appeal to the parents who purchased it: "DeBrecht's book is tailor-made for the same readers who regard Ann Coulter as one of the great political thinkers of our age" (par. 6). As a result, Cottle discounted the alleged aim of the Kids Ahead imprint: "Forget championing traditional values . . . Jackson is hawking ideological warfare" (par. 4).

Roger Sutton, editor-in-chief of *The Horn Book*, a magazine that provides highly respected reviews of books for children in the United States, has agreed. Discussing his refusal to review DeBrecht's text in the publication, he explained: "'It's the hectoring adult 'liberals are bad, bad, bad' kind of thing. Kids don't think that way'" (par 7). Making no distinction between the book's author and its publisher, he asserted, "They're using the format of a children's book to cheat. . . . You wouldn't get away with anything said in the book except that it looks like a children's book" (par 11).

Of all the critiques of *Liberals*, by far the most numerous as well as arguably passionate have appeared online, in discussions on the blogosphere and customer reviews posted on websites for book outlets such as Amazon and Barnes and Noble. In fact, given the strong sales that *Liberals* enjoyed, coupled with the equally strong public reactions that it sparked, the book earned a place on the *New York Times* list of the top twenty Most Blogged Books of 2005, a distinction that placed the text in the company of *The DaVinci Code, Freakonomics,* and *Harry Potter and the Half-Blood Prince* ("A Selection"). As venues that provide easy audience access and are the product of fewer institutional filters, blogs and online customer reviewers provide an indication—however limited and self-selecting—of the responses that the book has generated among the public. As one customer at Amazon posted about DeBrecht's work, "This is not a children's book. It is an ideological screed" (Davis). A blogger reiterated such sentiments: "Now we can further insulate our children from America's pluralism. Convince them now and forever that anyone with a different opinion is the equivalent of a monster. Absolutely daft" (Konty).

For every strong denunciation of *Liberals* though, there is sincere praise. One conservative parent—and satisfied *Help! Mom!* owner—wrote on the website for Barnes and Noble: "This book puts the silliness of liberalism into a context that children can understand. It has my five year old asking us questions about liberals which we are happy to answer" (Brent). Another customer echoed this viewpoint, praising DeBrecht's book for helping "kids to understand how out of hand liberalism has gotten in this country" (John).

In an interesting detail that says much about current cultural attitudes regarding children in the United States—and, by extension, public perceptions about the purpose of literature for young readers—both the positive and negative reactions to *Liberals* share a common feature: their belief in the highly impressionable nature of children. In denunciations of DeBrecht's book, critics assert that the elementary-school-aged boys and girls, the ostensible primary audience of *Liberals,* are too young to be subjected to such heavy-handed partisan politics. One outraged customer at Barnes and Noble, for example, posted the following caution about DeBrecht's text: "No, it's not an innocent book to be taken lightly, it's propaganda for impressionable minds" (Anonymous, Barnes and Noble, 5 January 2007). Another patron called the book "Bigotry for little people" (Anonymous, Barnes and Noble, 7 October 2005). Similarly, patrons at Amazon.com have tagged *Liberals* with searchable keywords that include "propaganda," "brainwash," and "hatred" as well as "evil," "trash," and even "child abuse" (Amazon 2005).

Conservative praise for *Liberals* pivots around the same argument; proponents make the case that precisely because readers of DeBrecht's book are still young and impressionable they need to be exposed to its ideas. An Amazon.com customer asserted: "It's about time someone wrote this excellent book for kids. Kids need to know from an early age that the greatest threat to their freedoms is liberalism" (Denny, 2 January 2006). Another reviewer was even more emphatic: "This book really gives parents an opportunity to teach their children good moral values while they are at a very impressionable age. I highly recommend this book if you intend to turn your children over to the government school system to be indoctrinated by the loony left" (Brent, Barnes and Noble, 30 November 2006). The review bears the ironic title "Give your kids a *head start!*," which of course evokes the name of a longstanding "liberal" social welfare program for children from low-income families (Brent, Barnes and Noble, 30 November 2006; my italics). In this reviewer's estimation, if young people need educational enrichment, it should embody lessons from the right.

Help! Mom! There Are Sequels!: DeBrecht and the New Genre of Politically Charged Children's Literature

In the wake of all the attention that *Liberals* received as well as the sales that it generated, DeBrecht decided not simply to write a sequel, but to launch an entire series of books with the *Help! Mom!* name. In March 2006, she released *Help! Mom! Hollywood's in My Hamper!*, which spotlighted the often ridiculous celebrity-driven fashion trends to which young children in general and pre-adolescent girls in particular are vulnerable. In November 2006, her *Help! Mom! The 9th Circuit Nabbed the Nativity!* hit bookstores. As its subtitle—"*or, How the Liberals Stole Christmas*"—suggests, *Nativity* examines the left's perceived assault on Christianity through its misguided insistence on the separation of church and state.

Both *Hamper* and *Nativity* take such a similar tack as *Liberals* that they suggest that DeBrecht is not writing a creative literary series but simply repeating a commercially successful formula. As before, the covers—which are drawn by Jim Hummel once again and are crowded with easily recognizable caricatures of various celebrities or political figures—more closely resemble political cartoons than children's books. In addition, the plots to both narratives recycle much of the same premise as *Liberals*. Each book focuses on a pair of child protagonists whose earnest efforts and wholesome desires are stymied by a parade of pesky liberals. In *Hamper*, sisters Janie and Sam take jobs babysitting "after they finished their homework, set the table, and fed their kitty" (DeBrecht 1) to earn money for new bicycles. The girls even keep their combined funds in a glass jar not unlike the one used for a charity project in *Liberals*. Janie and Sam's plan is a tremendous success until a series of Hollywood stars—look-alikes of Britney Spears, Madonna, and Barbra Streisand—begin magically appearing from the hamper in the bedroom that they share. As the celebrities repeat the mantra "I am a STAR—which makes me an EXPERT on everything," the girls are unable to resist spending their money on an array of ridiculous-looking clothes and useless trinkets that the stars are selling. After Janie and Sam have lost the bulk of their babysitting jobs because of their bizarre-looking outfits, they reach an important realization about Hollywood figures: "'Just because they're famous doesn't mean we have to do all of the strange things they do'" (DeBrecht 45). *Hamper* ends with the girls piling all of their celebrity clothes in a trash can and uttering an empowering variation on the recurring line from the book: "'I think we are EXPERTS at being ourselves!'" (DeBrecht 45).

Nativity is much the same. Best friends and all-American boys Johnny and Luke are thrilled to learn that this year's holiday production at George Washington Elementary School, where they are both students in the third grade, will be the Nativity story. But, soon after parts are assigned and rehearsals begin, pesky liberals aided by their equally pesky friends, the justices at the 9th Circuit Court, arrive to stop the production. Significantly, several of these figures—namely caricatures of Hillary Clinton, Ted Kennedy, and John Kerry—figured prominently in *Liberals*.

Although DeBrecht gives Janie and Sam some personal agency in *Hamper*, Johnny and Luke must rely on an adult to save the day. While comforting themselves with a cup of cocoa at a local diner—which, incidentally, looks like it came directly out of *Leave It to Beaver*—Supreme Court Justice Clarence Thomas appears on a closed circuit television. He tells the boys about the U.S. Constitution, a document which "'says the government cannot force anyone to celebrate Christmas. But it also says that we must allow anyone who believes in Christmas to celebrate it open and freely'" (DeBrecht 15). This passage collapses the important difference between preventing children from privately celebrating Christmas and requiring them to participate in a Nativity pageant at their public elementary school. In the closing pages, Justice Thomas appears again with a similar statement, declaring that the Founding Fathers called "for freedom OF religion, not freedom FROM religion" (DeBrecht 27).

As even this brief overview indicates, the basic plot and accompanying lessons of DeBrecht's follow-up narratives are as hyperbolic as those in her first book. In passages so excessive that they undercut the validity of her message, the Hollywood celebrities in *Hamper* entice Janie and Sam to buy such ridiculous items as radish earrings, onion-scented perfume, and a hat that is literally nothing more than a broken flowerpot. In addition, they impart sage wisdom like Spears's firm belief that wrapping a sweaty sock around your head makes you smarter: "'EUREKA!' She brightened as though she had made a huge discovery and exclaimed loudly, 'Milk comes from cows!'" (DeBrecht 11). Ironically in light of these details DeBrecht gave the following reply when asked why she made celebrities the focus of her second *Help! Mom!* book: "There's nothing wrong with them expressing their opinions, they're just so heavy-handed about it" (Kesner 43).

Nativity combines the politically charged satire of DeBrecht's first narrative with the lament for the loss of so-called traditional values from her second one. First, Senator Weary—a John Kerry look-alike—offers the following rationale about why the children must stop their production of the Nativity story: "Christmas may seem like a wonderful celebration to you, but not to us liberals!

To us, it represents a *religion*, with *values* and *morals*. Surely your teachers taught you that values and morals interfere with the way we liberals like to run things" (DeBrecht 7; italics in original). Then, later, a carnivalesque press conference held by the liberals is interrupted when environmentalist Al Snore—a.k.a. Al Gore—sees a squirrel running through the parking lot and runs after it, yelling "Here! Squirrelly! Kissy Kissy!" (DeBrecht 11).

Unfortunately, DeBrecht's sequels include another more unsettling element from her first book: religious bias and even intolerance. When Janie and Sam express concern about wearing their clown-like Rayonna pants to church in *Hamper*, the Madonna look-alike responds: " 'Church? *Hello!!!* Who goes to church nowadays?' She flipped her freshly styled hair. 'I'm into Toenailology. It is *absolutely fascinating* ' " (DeBrecht 21; italics in original). Although the author appears to be lampooning Scientology, the singer's real-life devotion to Kabbalah, a type of Jewish mysticism, causes this passage to possess anti-Semitic overtones. In an even more overt reference, on a following page, Barbara Butter-sand—a.k.a. Barbra Streisand—brags about her successful lobbying efforts to have the Yiddish-sounding language "*Babakaluka* instead of English [taught] in schools" (DeBrecht 35).

A similar thread runs through *Nativity*. The menorah is mentioned at various points throughout DeBrecht's discussion of the nativity story and also figures prominently in many of the book's illustrations. While Mary and Joseph were Jewish and while the seven-branched menorah like the one shown in Hummel's drawings is a symbol for the religion (and was especially so during the time of Christ), the item is nonetheless out of place. The Jewish menorah is unrelated to the Nativity story, and thus it appears as a misguided attempt by DeBrecht to make her story seem more inclusive when it is actually making a case for religious privilege and exclusivity.[7]

If the release of DeBrecht's first book sparked critical controversy, then the addition of these sequels set off a full-fledged cultural conflagration. Michelle Cottle criticized: "the company has no indication of publishing real children's books. Rather, it plans to cash in on the right's enduring paranoia about the liberal assault on its values by churning out partisan tracts awash in humor so simpleminded that they could only succeed in the guise of kiddie picture books" (par 4). Likewise, one blogger wryly noted: "I can't decide whether to laugh or to cry. I'm leaning toward the latter" (Schraub, par. 3). Another online reviewer was even more direct in his denunciation. In a post calling the books "Conservative Manifestoes for Idiots," he said of the *Help! Mom!* series: "But, let's be honest about this. These books aren't actually aimed at children. They can't be. Kids won't read books about the Ninth Circuit. These books are cheap propaganda items aimed at the neanderthal [sic] base of the Republican Party" (Digby, par 5). Given this general attitude, perhaps Cottle put it best when she characterized the *Help! Mom!* series with the following simple yet insightful turn of phrase: "not conservative books for children so much as childish books for conservatives" (par. 4).

DeBrecht's *Help! Mom!* books are far from literary anomalies; the texts instead form some of the more visible examples of a growing trend of heavily partisan and overtly politically themed children's books that have emerged since the divisive 2004 presidential election. Propelled by advancements in self-publishing software, the expanded promotional opportunities made possible by the Internet, and the steadily growing sales of children's books over the past several decades,[8] narratives for young people have become not only increasingly popular but also increasingly specialized. Christopher Dreher has aptly noted, "Picture and story books are appearing to match every stripe in the ideological rainbow, often aimed at kids under 10" (*The Globe and Mail*, 27 August 2005, par. 6).

As a result, while DeBrecht's *Help! Mom!* series may be the most successful and thus most visible example of this new genre of politically charged books for young readers, this group was not the first. That distinction belongs to *No, George, No!: The Re-Parenting of George W. Bush*, written by Kathy Eder and illustrated by Clay Butler. With its obvious play on the popular picture book series *Curious George*, the narrative straddles the line between children's literature and narratives intended for adults. Likewise, given its release date in May 2004—a well-timed six months before the election—and its telling subtitle, "*A Primer for the Patriotic*," *No, George, No!* makes its partisan aim as blatant as the *Help! Mom!* series. Briefly, the book focuses on a young U.S. president named George who is visited by the "Truth Fairy" during a dream. The wise and handsome fairy takes George to places far and wide in an effort to teach him an array of important lessons, including how to respect sovereign nations, how to hold fair elections, and how to treat injured soldiers. A small banner at the bottom of each page gives citation listings where readers can turn for additional information concerning the particular lesson about which George is receiving instruction. For example, on the page in which the fairy instructs the president about fair elections, Eder offers John Dean's essay "The U.S. Supreme Court and The Imperial Presidency" at www.findlaw.com (4).

The following year, in response to the success of DeBrecht's *Liberals*, another politically charged picture book made its debut: *Why Mommy Is a Democrat* (2005), written by Jeremy Zilber and illustrated by Yuliya Firsova. By adopting virtually the same strategy as DeBrecht and inverting the cast of "good" and "bad" characters, Zilber's book spotlights a mother squirrel—who appears to be a single parent—explaining to her two young children the reasons for her political affiliation. During this process, she points to factors like the Democratic party's commitment to fairness, tolerance, peace, diversity, and concern for the well-being of others. Of course, the "other" political party—which, although never named, is symbolically represented by a large careless elephant—is, by implication, completely lacking in these traits. In 2007, Zilber released a sequel to the book, *Why Daddy Is a Democrat*. The following year, he added a third title to his oeuvre, *Mama Voted for Obama!* (2008).

The books by Zilber and Eder have received much the same reception as those by DeBrecht. Journalist Nick Gillespie, in an article humorously titled "Suffer the Little Children," for example, calls them "misguided—and, one hopes, unread—attempts to politicize and indoctrinate tykes, to force future voters to choose between Red and Blue America" (par 5). Likewise, Kathleen Horning, the president-elect of the American Library Association's division of Library Service to Children in 2005 when these books came to the public's attention, agreed. She commented on narratives such as *No, George, No!* and *Mommy Is a Democrat* along with the *Help! Mom!* series: "I can't really imagine anyone sitting down and reading these books to children, and if they tried, I doubt very much that children would pay attention. . . . They are very message-driven, very didactic" (Mapes A1).

Whether individuals loved these partisan books or hated them, they were now receiving national media attention. Together with being the subject of reviews in various high-profile publications, such as *The New Republic* and *Publisher's Weekly*, Jon Stewart's popular current events and news commentary program *The Daily Show* ran a segment on *Why Mommy Is a Democrat* and the *Help! Mom!* series on October 3, 2007. In a moment of titular zeitgeist with this author and apologies to Dr. Seuss, the show dubbed its story "One State, Two State, Red State, Blue State."

The release of *Goodnight Bush*—a parody of Margaret Wise Brown's *Goodnight Moon*—completes the sub-genre to date. Written by Erich Origen and Gan Golan, the picture book was published in late summer 2008. Lest the narrative's political leanings are not clear from its title, the back cover shows an image of Dick Cheney wearing a robe and bunny slippers, sitting in a rocking chair topped with a skull and crossbones, and holding on his lap a xylophone whose rainbow-colored keys are marked "Terror"—presumably after the different levels of national alert. A representative passage from the text reads: "Goodnight ballot box, Goodnight FOX, Goodnight towers, And goodnight balance of powers."

"Oh, the Children! Will Someone Please Think of the Children!": The Propagandistic Purposes of Childhood Innocence and the Politicized Use of Children in the Culture Wars

Although books like *Why Mommy Is a Democrat* and the *Help! Mom!* series have been in the public spotlight during the past few years, political commentaries—emanating from both the left and the right side of the spectrum—are certainly no strangers to children's literature. Almost since the origins of books for young readers, publishers have distributed narratives that engage divisive social issues and include political themes. From the commentary on colonialism permeating Lewis Carroll's *Alice in Wonderland* (1865) to the symbolic arms race depicted in Dr. Seuss's *The Butter Battle Book* (1984), books for boys and girls have historically been didactic and sometimes—as Roger Sutton has commented—even "messagey" (Dreher, par. 26). Given the way in which political issues have formed a consistent—if often overlooked—feature of children's literature, Julia Mickenberg and Philip Nel have remarked:

> To those who would argue that politics have no place in children's literature, we would reply that there is no way to keep politics out. All literary expressions inevitably embody an author's political sensibility. The useful question is not whether children's literature *should* be political, but rather how children's literature should engage with political issues because, after all, children cannot be separated from growing up in the world. (352)

This current crop of partisan picture books, however, adopts a drastically different approach from previous narratives to the question of "how children's literature should engage with political issues." In prior socially minded books for young readers, the political messages were typically coded. The agrarian populism embedded within *The Wonderful Wizard of Oz* (1900), for example, is so subtle that it is commonly overlooked even by adult readers. By contrast, texts like *No, George, No!*, *Why Mommy Is a Democrat*, and the *Help! Mom!* series, take the opposite approach. With their flimsy plots and heavy-handed messages, the political issues presented in these books are—in the words of Christopher Dreher—"about as subtle as a foghorn" (par. 7).

Books by DeBrecht and her cohort differ even from the increasing number of socially minded children's books published during the past few decades. While narratives like *Heather Has Two Mommies* (1989) and *It's Just a Plant* (2004) address topics that are certainly divisive between liberals and conservatives—same-sex parenting and marijuana use, respectively—the books focus on a particular topic instead of advocating for the wholesale adoption of a comprehensive sociopolitical perspective. As Mickenberg and Nel have asserted, "Pushing children to blindly follow a particular doctrine—whatever that doctrine may be—is not liberating" (352). To be sure, while the *Help! Mom!* series and similar titles claim to represent a courageous new literary form, "Truly radical children's literature encourages its readers to question received wisdom, to think independently, and to resist simple solutions to complex problems" (Mickenberg and Nel 352–353).

Whether we read the *Help! Mom!* series, *Why Mommy Is a Democrat* and *No, George, No!* as narratives for adults, for children, or for both, the books participate in a series of literary, cultural, and material transformations to childhood during the past few decades in the United States. If we see these texts as sincerely intended for children—a claim that strikes me as specious despite their authors' repeated protestations to the contrary—then they signal a change in the representation of politics in children's literature and accompanying attitudes about the purpose or function of narratives for young readers. Mitzi Myers, U. C. Knoepflmacher, and Sandra Beckett have demonstrated that cross-writing—or the practice of simultaneously appealing to an adult and child audience—has been a longstanding feature of children's literature. But they would also likely agree that, in this new crop of partisan books, the line separating these supposedly different groups has vanished. Given the similarities in tone as well as content between works like DeBrecht's *Help! Mom! The 9th Circuit's Nabbed the Nativity! (or, How the Liberals Stole Christmas)* and Ann Coulter's *Godless: The Church of Liberalism*, a book cannot be cross-written when it lacks a distinction between the intellectual interests of a child and adult audience. Indeed, as Christopher Dreher has noted, this nonfiction fare for adults (not the children's fiction by Carroll, Baum, or Seuss) forms the literary lineage and narrative counterparts for the work by DeBrecht and her cohort (*Help!* F4). Even when children's books have been most overtly political, as Michelle Cottle has observed, it is difficult to imagine anyone grouping *The Lorax* or *The Butter Battle Book* with titles like Michael Savage's *Liberalism Is a Mental Disorder* (2005) or Michael Moore's *Stupid White Men* (2004) (par 9).

Alternatively, if we consider books such as the *Help! Mom!* series as political satire written in the style of juvenile literature, then the implications are even more radical. First, these texts participate in what Jerry Griswold has termed the "adulteration" of childhood or the various adult uses and misuses of popular print and material items intended for young people. Citing examples such as the rise of pop psychology during the 1970s predicated on nurturing your "inner child," to the fad of businessmen wearing neckties emblazoned with cartoon characters like the Tasmanian Devil during the 1990s, Griswold notes how adults during the second half of the twentieth century have increasingly longed to return to the seemingly carefree days of youth. In a symbolic if not actual attempt to do so, adults have appropriated the language, literature, and culture of children (Griswold 39).

In an even more important implication, works such as the *Help! Mom!* series—along with many other narratives featured in this project—form a further facet to the propagandistic purposes for which beliefs about childhood innocence have been used in the United States, a phenomenon that encompasses the heavily politicized place of children in the current culture wars. As Philippe Ariès, Peter Hunt, and James Kincaid have written, from the era of the Enlightenment onward, childhood has commonly been seen as a time of innocence and purity, a period when young people are blissfully ignorant of seemingly adult concerns like politics.

Work by Henry Giroux, Lawrence Grossberg, and Henry Jenkins has demonstrated, however, that this view of childhood—far from removing children
from the seemingly adult world of politics—actually serves acutely politicized
purposes. First, Giroux has called attention to the racialized nature and also
class biases inherent in this construction. All too often, images of the "innocent
child" are images of white, middle-class, blue-eyed, and blond-haired children.
In the words of Giroux, "When dealing with kids whose lives do not fit the
Ozzie and Harriet family profile, middle-class adults invoke the antithesis of
innocence" (9). With Latino and especially black children often cast as lacking
inherent purity, the rhetoric about childhood innocence is—to borrow a popular
phrase from contemporary critical theory—"always already" politicized.

The *Help! Mom!* books—and many of the other titles profiled in previous
chapters—reflect the racial as well as socioeconomic elements on which
childhood innocence has been historically predicated. Of the six pre-adolescent protagonists that DeBrecht depicts, for instance, all but one—Johnny in
Nativity!—are white. Moreover, with his buck teeth and token status, the young
black boy is as much a stereotyped figure as an anomalous one. An article
posted on the website for the public relations firm which handles DeBrecht's
engagements gives further credence to this reading. In it, DeBrecht speculates
on possible causes for the downfall of Hillary Clinton's character in her next
book, *Help! Mom! There Are Lawyers in My Lunchbox!* One offense that DeBrecht
identifies is riddled with racially-charged overtones: "'perhaps she'll [Clinton]
be sent up the river for trying to snatch gifts from Santa's sleigh for an affirmative action program for naughty kids'" (*Special Guests*, "EBay Auction"). In
spite of DeBrecht's oft-stated concern for children, broadly defined, this remark
indicates how, as Giroux might say, in her conception of innocence "a line is
drawn between those kids worthy of adult protection and those who appear
beyond the pale of adult compassion and concern" (21).

Childhood innocence is likewise predicated on the equally problematic
premise of nostalgia, another politically fraught category because it is usually
historically fraudulent. In the words of Jenkins, "nostalgia is the desire to re-
create something that has never existed before, to return to some place we've
never been, and to reclaim a lost object we never possessed. In short, nostalgia
takes us to never-never land" (Jenkins 4). Adults view children as naive, pure,
and innocent not because they necessarily are, but because it is pleasing to
imagine them in this way. Questions of authenticity as well as those of memory
are perennial ones with regard to children's books; readers and critics wonder
how much an adult author can ever accurately portray the thoughts and actions
of young people as opposed to simply relaying their own personal recollections
or impressions of them. DeBrecht's *Help! Mom!* books root their portrayal of
childhood firmly in the realm of nostalgia. With their settings in some variation
of "a small house, on a small street, in a small neighborhood, in a small city,

in the great USA"—to quote the opening sentence of *Liberals* once again—the three narratives cast their pre-adolescent main characters in an earlier and, ostensibly, more idyllic era. Indeed, in an interesting paradox, given DeBrecht's insistence that *Liberals* is designed for a young audience, both her written text and Hummel's visual images are far more indicative of an adult's romanticized image of children than a realistic portrayal of them. Tommy and Lou's quaint, Norman Rockwell–esque decision to open a lemonade stand (instead of, perhaps, some online venture) and their burning desire for a swing set (as opposed to an MP3 player or video game) are powerful indices of this phenomenon. Likewise, Hummel's repeated inclusion of a backward letter "e" in signs like the one reading "Lemonade 25¢" atop the boys' stand or the one indicating "Open" on their front counter supports reading *Liberals* as a satiric book for adults that is simply written in the style of a picture book for children. Lest Tommy and Lou come across as greedy, self-interested capitalists after the success of their lemonade stand, the duo decides to set aside some of their profits for "kids with no shoes" (15). This unusual phraseology and equally unrealistic classification places DeBrecht's book in dialogue with Gary Cross's work on the origins, history, and uses of children's "cuteness" in the United States. As he asserts, whether genuinely present or artificially fabricated, portrayals of children as charming, endearing, and adorable have been emotionally manipulative and thus culturally powerful forces in the nation's popular culture, print media, and political rhetoric (Cross 43). Analogous comments could be made about the illustrated images of children in William Bennett's *The Book of Virtues* and Lynne Cheney's *America: A Patriotic Primer* and *Our Fifty States: A Family Adventure Across America*.

Finally, longstanding notions about childhood innocence engage with political issues in more direct and particularized ways. Henry Jenkins has written:

> This dominant conception of childhood . . . presumes that children
> exist in a space beyond, above, outside the political; we imagine them
> to be noncombatants whom we protect from the harsh realities of the
> adult world, including the mud spattering of partisan politics. Yet, in
> reality, almost every major political battle of the twentieth century has
> been fought on the backs of our children. (2)

Pointing to examples that include school integration in the 1950s and cross-district bussing in the 1970s, Jenkins demonstrates that beliefs about childhood innocence have not caused young people to exist on the sidelines of adult political debates. On the contrary, such views have consistently placed them at the forefront. Both the political left and the right routinely seek to advance their causes via emotionally manipulative rhetoric about "our innocent children."

As a result, young people are—to quote the title of Lawrence Grossberg's book on the subject—"Caught in the Crossfire." Jenkins describes the exchange: "The myth of childhood innocence . . . 'empties' the child of its own political agency, so that it may more perfectly fulfill the symbolic demands we make upon it" (1). The innocent child, as James Kincaid has discussed, is the vulnerable child whose purity is always in danger of being corrupted by adult influences and is thus in constant need of adult protection. Whether this contamination takes the form of the threat of legalized gay marriage for conservatives or the infiltration of school prayer for liberals, histrionic pleas to "think of the innocent children" are routinely at the center of arguments on both sides of the debate. For these reasons, both Jenkins and Giroux have somewhat provocatively asserted that the belief in child innocence is just that, a belief or myth. This idea is a construction by adults, for adults, to satisfy adult desires, suit adult needs, and further adult causes.

All of the conservative-themed books featured in chapters 1 through 5 participate in this process. As I have discussed, from William Bennett, Terri Birkett, and Tim LaHaye to Lynne Cheney and Bill O'Reilly, these right-leaning authors have written their narratives out of a desire—whether explicitly or implicitly stated—to protect the "innocent" children. Katherine DeBrecht and her *Help! Mom!* series broadens and expands such claims. The books demonstrate that children occupy not the imagined periphery but an actual focal point in the lived reality of the culture wars. The cry "Help! Mom!," the titular element unifying all three books, announces that young people are desperately depending on adults in general and their mothers in particular to protect them. At the same time, DeBrecht makes a case that it is insufficient for children to be used as mere tools or prongs in the culture wars. Both the content of her narratives and her frequent comments about her texts embody not merely a new but a necessary genre; the author feels that the children should be encouraged to take a side in it themselves. As a result, DeBrecht and her cohort push the relationship between children and partisan politics from one of nominal evocation to direct participation and even conscription. With the effort to protect so-called traditional family values often cast as a struggle to prevent the demise of American civilization itself, the politicized uses of children and childhood have only increased.

For generations of pre-adolescent boys and girls in the United States, the terms "left" and "right" have denoted mere directional differences that they must learn to distinguish. However, books such as the *Help! Mom!* series—along with *Truax*, *The O'Reilly Factor for Kids*, and *America: A Patriotic Primer*—clamor to redefine the politicized meaning and culturally loaded use of these terms for young readers. In so doing, they help construct an environment—as Henry Giroux has written—in which "Kids are not allowed to be kids" (11) and thus paradoxically further erode the period of childhood that the authors claim so ardently to be defending. Once framed as a time of relative ignorance about—and even protection from—divisive adult concerns, childhood is being reconstituted in this growing crop of politically charged books as a time of children's thorough education and even indoctrination. As boys and girls in the United States move from being nominal pawns to new partisan participants in arguments over complex sociopolitical issues—from pro-logging environmental policies in *Truax*, school prayer in the Left Behind series, and moral values in *The Book of Virtues*—perhaps DeBrecht had something right after all: "Help! Mom!," indeed.

CONCLUSION

"The Gosh-Darnit, Doggone It, You-Betcha Wink Heard 'Round the World"

The 2008 Presidential Election, the State of the Conservative Movement, and the Future of Rightist Books for Young Readers

After enjoying a reign spanning several decades, the conservative social movement and rightist political clout showed noticeable signs of weakening by late 2008. Perhaps the most obvious indicator of this shift was the dramatic drop in public support for President George W. Bush. By mid-October, only 7 percent of Americans said they were generally satisfied with the way things were going in the country, the lowest such figure ever recorded by the Gallup polling organization (Gallup, "Americans' Satisfaction at New All-Time Low"). Meanwhile, Bush's overall job approval rating had dropped to a paltry 25 percent, a statistic that was only slightly higher than Richard Nixon before his resignation—when only 24 percent of Americans approved of his job performance—and Harry S. Truman, who left office amidst the worst approval rating in U.S. history, at a mere 22 percent (Gallup, "Bush's Job Approval").

These polling numbers were not the only pieces of bad news. Other important indices regarding the strength of conservatism also pointed to a movement in decline. By late 2008 Jay Tolson wrote that the "symptoms of culture-war fatigue were widespread" (40). The ongoing military engagements in Iraq and Afghanistan abroad, coupled with the onset of a massive financial crisis at home, moved so-called values issues from the forefront to the background of U.S. politics. Although Americans were certainly still concerned about subjects like abortion, creationism, and school prayer, they were no longer the only or even primary topics of interest. Instead, after the Dow Jones lost nearly 3,000 points from its pre-July 2008 value,[1] unemployment rates climbed to their highest in more than a decade,[2] and banks foreclosed on homes at a pace not seen since the Great Depression,[3] the national economy, rather than traditional values, was on the minds of individuals living in both Red States and Blue States. Indeed, in a Gallup poll conducted during the first week of October, a full 69 percent of respondents identified the nation's "net economic problems" as the most important problem facing the country today, while a mere 4 percent pointed to "Ethics/Morals/Religious/Family Decline" (Gallup, "Americans' Satisfaction at New All-Time Low").

This shift in priority regarding domestic social issues precipitated even bigger shifts in opinion regarding appropriate approaches to governance. "For the first time in ten years, according to a Pew Research Center poll, a slim majority of Americans, including conservative voters, were saying that they wanted less religion in politics, not more" (qtd in Tolson 40). Even more astounding, many individuals who had been at the forefront of the fight over so-called moral issues agreed with that majority. "Such prominent culture warriors as Pat Buchanan had declared that values issues were more appropriately resolved at the state and local levels than at the national one" (Tolson 40).

The selection of John McCain as the Republican presidential nominee seemed to solidify these changes. Jay Tolson noted: McCain "was notoriously uncomfortable talking about religion, and many conservative Christians were uncomfortable talking about him" (40). During a speech in February 2000 amidst his previous run for president, for instance, McCain not only blasted Jerry Falwell and Pat Robertson as "agents of intolerance," but he also asserted that the Republican party's pandering to the far right was "harming GOP ideals" (*CNN*, "Special Event"). Lest his viewpoint was not clear, McCain ended his speech by affirming, "We are the party of Ronald Reagan, not Pat Robertson. . . . We are the party of Abraham Lincoln, not Bob Jones" (*CNN*, "Special Event"). McCain's comments had not been forgotten: "In a straw poll held at last year's Values Voter Summit, he came in last among the Republican hopefuls. And James Dobson, head of the influential Focus on the Family, let it be known that he wouldn't vote for McCain 'under any circumstances'" (Tolson 40). The fusionism that had brought the conservative movement to power and helped it to remain a sociopolitical force for nearly fifty years was falling apart. Indeed, as George H. Nash observed, as early as 2006, the former unity among libertarians, traditionalists, and anticommunists/antiterrorists was being splintered "by neocons, paleocons, 'theocons' (theological or religious conservatives), and 'Leocons' (disciples of Leo Strauss). Traditionalist conservatives with 'green' sensibilities and countercultural tastes were known as 'crunchy cons.' Conservatives under the age of 25 had been labeled minicons. All this was rather playful and amusing, but it suggested the fissiparous impulses at work" (577).

As a consequence, by the time that the presidential campaign began in earnest in spring 2008, *The New Yorker* magazine published an article that would have seemed absurd just a few years before; it was titled "The Fall of Conservatism." George Packer opened his discussion with the bold assertion that the era of American politics which had begun with the rise of the New Right in the 1960s "has been dying before our eyes" (47). He continued: "The fact that the least conservative, least divisive Republican in the 2008 race is the last one standing—despite being despised by significant voices on the right—shows how little life is left in the movement that Goldwater began, Nixon brought to power, Ronald Reagan gave mass appeal, Newt Gingrich radicalized, Tom DeLay criminalized, and Bush allowed to break into pieces" (Packer 48). Whether viewed from a political or cultural perspective, a paradigm shift seemed to be occurring.

This trend changed on August 29, 2008, when McCain announced his selection for a running mate: Alaska Governor Sarah Palin. Palin had only three years of experience as the governor of a state with a population smaller than many U.S. cities and, prior to that, only six years' experience as the mayor of an even smaller Alaskan town—Wasilla, which contained, at the time, roughly 9,700 people. But McCain did not nominate her for her political prowess. Instead, he chose Palin, as both professional pundits and campaign insiders noted, for her appeal to "the conservative base" of the Republican party. One element that both attracted McCain to Governor Palin and introduced this former political unknown to the American public was her strong view about abortion. In interviews and press releases, Palin proudly asserted that she was "as pro-life as any candidate can be" (qtd in Gorski, par 1). These words were far from mere hyperbole, for Palin opposed abortion under any circumstances, even in cases of rape and incest. Appealing to another strong faction of the Republican Right, Palin was also a born-again evangelical; she had been "baptized as a teenager at the Wasilla Assembly of God Church" (Gorski, par 4). Moreover, she used these beliefs to shape her viewpoint on an array of policy issues, including opposing same-sex marriage rights, advocating for teaching creationism in public schools, and also supporting abstinence-only sex education programs.

Given these viewpoints, from the moment news broke about McCain's choice for vice president, Palin reinvigorated the conservative movement, reenergized evangelical voters, and reignited the culture wars. As Mark Leibovich noted, suddenly Republican rallies throughout the nation were being attended by more church groups, more large families, and more young children "wearing matching clothing (often with abortion-themed messages)" (par 15). In addition, audience members were holding signs with slogans like "Pro God, Pro Life, Pro Gun, Pro Sarah" (Tolson 40). Her nomination immediately reversed previous condemnations of McCain's moderate stance on conservative social issues and his historically uneasy relationship with the evangelical branch of the GOP. Eric Gorski, writing for the Associated Press, noted, "Focus on the Family founder James Dobson, who initially said he could not vote for McCain but has since opened the door to an endorsement, called Palin 'an outstanding choice that should be extremely reassuring to the conservative base' of the GOP" (par 12).

Matthew Staver, the dean of Liberty University's School of Law, echoed these sentiments, calling McCain's selection of Palin "an absolutely brilliant choice" (qtd in Gorski par 13). Meanwhile, Gary Bauer, a prominent evangelical Christian and political advisor, was even more enthusiastic in his support. In a public statement, he gushed that McCain, in his choice of Sarah Palin, had hit "a grand slam home run" (qtd in Gorski, par 1).

Within a few weeks, commentators went from predicting the demise of conservative forces to announcing their rejuvenation. Tolson assessed the shift: "What may be happening is that right-wing politics and the conservative movement is not waning, it is merely changing, transforming and, ultimately, reinventing itself. As one party organizer asserted after the surge of support for the Republican ticket—especially among white women—in the wake of the Palin nomination, 'There is something happening that hasn't happened since Reagan'" (Tolson 42).

Even to many within the Republican party, the thought of comparing relative political newcomer Sarah Palin to venerated two-term president Ronald Reagan was unsettling. But the two figures did have some important traits in common. Like Reagan, Palin cast herself as a populist by asserting in numerous speeches and interviews that she was just a "hockey mom" who was from "outside the Washington Beltway" not only geographically but also ideologically. In addition, echoing Reagan's political mantra to "get government off our backs," she also railed against legislative pork and ballooning government programs. In a comment that appeared in *The New Yorker* and which Palin repeated throughout the campaign, she contended: "I've championed reform to end the abuses of earmark spending by Congress" (qtd in Mayer, par 7). Finally, and in a detail that constitutes her most important connection to Reagan, Palin was a media charmer. With her personal charisma, well-placed eye winks, and folksy colloquialisms—"gosh-darnit," "you betcha," and "doggone it" quickly became signature among them—the former beauty pageant contestant and Miss Congeniality award-winner (see Strange, par 1) knew how to package herself for mass appeal. To be sure, Palin's Reagan-like qualities in this regard were touted by a *New York Post* op-ed piece that was cowritten by prominent political commentator Dick Morris. In the wake of the vice presidential debate, the column announced "Palin Wins Big with a Reagan-Like Flair." Even more significant, the columnists credited her victory as emanating not from her response to the issues but—much like Reagan—from her image. Morris and Eileen McGann noted: "She showed originality, charisma and *sass*" (par 2; italics in original).

Even left-leaning media outlets couldn't help but acknowledge these qualities in Palin. A skit that aired on the popular comedy and satire show *Saturday Night Live* on September 27, 2008, commented on the Alaska governor's charm. Near the end of the mock interview, cast member Amy Poehler, posing as Katie Couric, asks comedian Tina Fey, playing Sarah Palin: "Mrs. Palin, it seems to me that when cornered, you become increasingly adorable" (*Saturday Night Live*). Caitlin Moran, writing for the UK-based *Times Online*, aptly described the candidate's response: "Palin/Fey responds by wrinkling her nose, making a series of silly 'pew, pew, pew!' noises and saying 'I dunno—is it?' in a cute little mouse voice" (par 19). Indeed, even Palin's political missteps—such as her naïve assertion during a television interview with Charles Gibson that Alaska's geographic proximity to Russia gave her foreign policy experience (*ABC World News*)—somehow only enhanced her appeal. Back in the 1980s, the media dubbed Ronald Reagan the "Teflon president" because no matter how damaging a news story, misguided a policy decision, or glaring a personal shortcoming, nothing seemed to "stick" to him; the bad press just "slid right off" the president, and the public still loved him (Kurtz "15 Years" C1). Following in the footsteps of Reagan once again, Palin in many ways could have been deemed the "Teflon candidate."

Whether or not one was an enthusiastic supporter of the Alaska governor, she was the subject of seemingly endless press coverage, political commentary, and water-cooler conversation in Red States and Blue States alike. The *Saturday Night Live* skits, featuring Tina Fey as Sarah Palin, became so hugely popular that, after making their way as viral videos across the Internet, they prompted the show to air a primetime Thursday night version to showcase its election-based skits. On October 18, 2008, Palin herself appeared as a guest on *SNL* to confront her döppelganger. A news report featured on the website of rival network ABC asserted: "Palin's appearance was, no doubt, the most anticipated 'SNL' event of the season" (Marikar and Fisher, par 2). The article revealed that "preliminary numbers show [that the Alaska governor's appearance] boosted the late-night comedy show to its highest ratings in 14 years" (Marikar and Fisher, par 2). By Halloween, a whole series of masks, wigs, and full-body costumes featured Palin's likeness; one of them—a Miss Wasilla costume—was marketed to 'tweens (Belkin, par 7). It was difficult to remember the last time any other political candidate—male or female, local or national—had generated such mass interest, widespread appeal, and popular fascination.

Although Sarah Palin energized evangelical voters, reinvigorated the presidential campaign, and brought new life to the Republican ticket, her inclusion was ultimately not enough to carry the day: Democratic nominee Barack Obama and his running mate Joseph Biden won the 2008 presidential election by a firm margin: the Obama-Biden ticket received 365 electoral votes while McCain and Palin were able to capture less than half that number, earning a total of only 162 electoral votes ("President Map"). The popular vote, while not quite as lopsided, was decisive nonetheless, with more than 66.6 million ballots cast for Obama-Biden compared to the roughly 58.5 million for McCain-Palin ("President Map"). The Republicans also lost in Congress. All 435 seats in the House of Representatives were at play in the election, and the Democrats won 257 of them to expand the majority control that they had attained in 2006 by 24 more seats. Meanwhile, in the Senate, Democrats likewise obtained a firm majority by winning 58 of the 100 seats, plus 2 independents who caucus with the Democrats.

This outcome aside, many predicted that the Democratic victory in 2008 embodied a minor, temporary setback for the GOP. The morning after the election, in fact, an article in the *Wall Street Journal* said it all; the headline flatly stated: "Conservative Isn't Finished" (Frank). Thomas Frank's opinion piece justified this statement by providing a brief overview of the conservative movement since the 1960s, along with its astounding political, economic, and social successes. Frank ended his piece with a statement that offered both promise and threat: "This movement will be back, and the biggest fights are yet to come" (par 12).

Indicating the accuracy of this prediction, conservative-themed books for young readers show no sign of letting up or even slowing down. While 2008 witnessed the fluctuating status of this movement in the nation's adult culture, it was marked by the steady appearance of these narratives for children. In September, for instance, Meghan McCain released *My Dad, John McCain*, a picture-book biography of the Republication presidential nominee. The blurb on the jacket flap sounds as much like a campaign sound bite as it does a plot summary: "Senator McCain has lived an incredible life driven by love of his country and a desire to serve it to the best of his ability" (McCain).

As if not to be outdone, several authors featured in the previous chapters also released new children's books during the 2008 election year. William Bennett published yet another title in his already impressive pantheon of virtues-themed books: *The Book of Virtues for Boys and Girls*. The text, a further variation on his 1993 original, was geared for young people ages twelve and up. The volume spotlights five of the original character traits profiled in Bennett's best-selling *The Book of Virtues*, but these selections collectively span only about two hundred pages. The novelty of the 2008 release was its accompaniment by a Warner Home Video DVD that featured three episodes from the PBS cartoon series based on Bennett's original book—*Adventures in Honesty*, *Adventures in Courage*, and *Adventures in Faith*.

Bennett also expanded his repertoire beyond the *Virtues* franchise to other conservative themes and subjects. As mentioned in the closing pages of chapter 4, in late November 2008, he released *The American Patriot's Almanac: Daily Readings on America*. Coauthored with John T. E. Cribb, the book models its format after Bennett's popular *Book of Virtues* series, and it also markets itself in an analogous way. Bennett tells his young readers in the opening paragraph of the introduction: "Just as it's a virtue to honor your parents, it's a good and admirable thing to honor the land you call home" (vii).

Bennett's heir at the NEH, Lynne Cheney, similarly released a new narrative for children, *We the People: The Story of Our Constitution* (2008). Akin to her previous works, the picture book offers a celebratory view of American history and positive portrayal of patriotism. More specifically, *We the People* details the way in which the framers of the Constitution, as Cheney states in the introduction, accomplished nothing short of "a blessing, creating a new and stronger American union and flying in the face of prevailing wisdom as they did so" (3). She continues: "History might have gone otherwise but for the framers' genius, and we should be grateful for James Madison, George Washington, Benjamin Franklin, and the others who gathered in Philadelphia" (3).

Finally, political pundit Bill O'Reilly also made headlines in 2008 when he signed a massive new contract with the Fox network, extending *The O'Reilly Factor* for another four years at an astounding annual salary of more than ten million dollars (Kurtz "O'Reilly" C1). Ratings for his cable news and talk program had never been stronger. During the final month preceding the presidential election, *The O'Reilly Factor* averaged more than four million viewers each night, a number that various industry insiders deemed "unheard of" (qtd Kurtz "O'Reilly" C1). O'Reilly also released a second edition of his nonfiction advice book, *Kids Are Americans Too*. The text appeared in time for the holiday shopping season and boasted a new jacket design as well as new cover photo of the author. In changes that seemed designed to make *Kids* more appealing to young readers, the word "Americans" in the book's title is written in red, white, and blue school chalk and O'Reilly is pictured against a photographer's backdrop instead of leaning against a television camera as on the previous cover.

As even these few examples indicate, the conservative viewpoint and rightist political perspective were very much alive and thriving commercially in the United States even by late 2008. Given that this subgenre of books for young readers began in the 1990s after the inauguration of a Democratic president, and also given the Right's numerous concerns about President Obama, this phenomenon may be re-energized in the coming years. Libertarians have decried Obama's alleged socialist leanings, the Christian Right has spread rumors that he is really a "closet" Muslim, and the racist Right has exploited cultural anxiety over the loss of white hegemony in the Oval Office. Such sentiments are not limited to small groups on the sociopolitical fringe; for example, in November 2008, Beverly Daniel Tatum wrote, "Twenty-seven percent of the recent Gallup poll respondents said the results of the election 'frightened' them" (par 6). Echoing the antiprogressive and even antimodernist strain of the conservative movement, Tatum provided the following possible explanation for such sentiments: "A shifting paradigm creates anxiety—even psychological threat—for those who feel the basic assumptions of society changing in ways they can no longer predict" (par 6). She notes that conservative traditionalism cannot account for the reactions of all respondents; the same may be true of sentiments in the racist Right. For some portion of the population "the fear may be related to an unvoiced and maybe even unconscious recognition that the racial calculus of our society has been changed by the election, a change that threatens the position of privilege white people have occupied for so long" (Tatum par 6).

In a horrifying portent of this possibility becoming a reality, Jesse Washington of the Associated Press on November 15, 2008, discussed the large number of racially fueled threats, crimes, and acts of violence that had transpired since the election: "Cross burnings. Schoolchildren chanting 'Assassinate Obama.' Black figures hung from nooses. Racial epithets scrawled on homes and cars" (par 1). Washington offers a more specific example of such hateful sentiments: "One was in Snellville, Ga., where Denene Millner said a boy on the school bus told her 9-year-old daughter the day after the election: 'I hope Obama gets assassinated.' That night, someone trashed her sister-in-law's front lawn, mangled the Obama lawn signs, and left two pizza boxes filled with human feces outside the front door, Millner said" (par 5).

This incident was far from isolated or atypical. "From California to Maine, police have documented a range of alleged crimes, from vandalism and vague threats to at least one physical attack. Insults and taunts have been delivered by adults, college students and second-graders" (Washington, par 3). Washington continues, "There have been 'hundreds' of incidents since the election, many more than usual, said Mark Potok, director of the Intelligence Project at the Southern Poverty Law Center, which monitors hate crimes" (par 4). As a matter of fact, Obama received more death threats than any other president-elect in history (Sullivan "Obama" par 1). Potok's explanation for this phenomenon reveals how racist Right groups like Aryan Nation and the Ku Klux Klan, whose message had previously seemed extreme to many American whites, may, in the wake of Obama's election, become more appealing: "there is 'a large subset of white people in this country who feel that they are losing everything they know, that the country their forefathers built has somehow been stolen from them'" (qtd in Washington, par 8).

Within the first hundred days of Obama's presidency, such private sentiments were being translated into public action. On April 7, 2009, the Department of Homeland Security issued a ten-page report bearing the ill-omened title *Right-Wing Extremism: Current Economic and Political Climate Fueling Resurgence in Radicalization and Recruitment.* The document explained that the rising rate of home foreclosures, increasing pace of unemployment, and mounting hardships from the recession—coupled with the election of the first black U.S. president and growing cadre of disgruntled military veterans and their families—were creating a "fertile recruiting environment" for radical groups like white supremacists, antigovernment extremists, and citizen militias (2). Exploiting fears that the Obama administration will expand immigration, impose restrictions on gun ownership,[4] increase social welfare programs, and weaken the sovereignty of the United States, these organizations have been "focusing their efforts to recruit new members, mobilize existing members, and broaden their scope and appeal through propaganda" (United States, Dept. of Homeland 2). Although the report did not identify any specific groups by name and asserted that such threats still remained "largely rhetorical" (2), it cautioned that "drivers for rightwing radicalization and recruitment" are "likely to accelerate if the economy is perceived to worsen" (2, 3). By accelerating, the movement will expand not simply in size but also in scope. The Department of Homeland Security explained, for instance, that one right-wing faction attributes the economic crisis "to a deliberate conspiracy conducted by a cabal of Jewish 'financial elites'" (3). Meanwhile, other organizations are gaining momentum from various "antigovernment conspiracies"—including "theories involving declarations of martial law, impending civil strife or racial conflict, suspension of the U.S. Constitution, and the creation of citizen detention camps"—as well as, echoing the focus of the popular Left Behind novels for kids, "end-times prophecies" and arguments advocating for Christian nationalism (4). The Department of Homeland Security concluded its report with the rather ominous proclamation: "To the extent that these [social, political and economic] factors persist, right wing extremism is likely to grow in strength" (8).

Although officials at the Republican party may be appalled to learn of these events, GOP candidates in general and vice presidential nominee Sarah Palin in particular tapped into such fears during the 2008 campaign. Palin's frequent accusations that Obama was "palling around with terrorists" because of his former acquaintance with Weather Underground organization cofounder William Ayers, her repeated attacks on Obama's patriotism, and—perhaps most shocking—her failure to say or do anything when crowd members at her rallies in Florida began shouting "kill him" after she mentioned the Democratic presidential nominee[5] demonstrated how—in a history that stretches from George Wallace to the Willie Horton campaign ads—the GOP still appeals to the racist Right. Palin's fear-mongering tactics during the campaign and the post-election rise in racially motivated violence may not be entirely unrelated. As the *London Telegraph* reported, "The Secret Service warned the Obama family in mid October that they had seen a dramatic increase in the number of threats against the Democratic candidate, coinciding with Mrs Palin's attacks" (Shipman, par 4).

Signs showing the resurgence or, at least, continued existence of the conservative movement are not limited to the extreme faction of the racist Right. Political commentators at venues ranging from Fox News to *Newsweek* asserted in the weeks following the election that in spite of the sweeping Democratic victory on November 4, the United States is still a "center-right nation."[6] Whether or not one agrees with this observation, the fact remains that, while conservatives may have lost control of both the Oval Office and Congress, they enjoyed victories on an array of so-called morals-based ballot issues. All four states that had measures on the ballot either prohibiting same-sex marriage or expanding the language of existing prohibitions passed the measures on November 4, 2008. Most notable among them was California, where the victory of Proposition 8 was a landmark for social and religious conservatives. Not only did it repeal the existing right of same-sex couples to marry—the first time that any such right has been successfully rolled back—but it did so in a state that is largely seen as one of the most left-leaning in the nation.[7]

Such results have cheered social conservatives, evangelical Christians, and the political right; they have also highlighted a possible path for the resurgence of the movement and its ultimate return to power. At events like the Republican governors' conference held in Miami two weeks after the election, GOP members discussed both current problems within the party and its future opportunities. Such post-mortems have alighted on several key issues about which the leadership agrees action is needed. If the GOP is going return to power either at the midterm elections in 2010 or during the presidential race in 2012, Republicans argue that the party first needs to return to its conservative social, political, and especially economic roots. Political consultant Greg Mueller observed an interesting paradox regarding the 2008 election results, "It is very unpopular to be a Republican right now, but it is very popular to be a conservative. The conservative brand is the most popular brand in the country" (qtd in Simon par 12). Thus, he offered a prediction about the future of the Republican party: "the next chairman of the party must be an 'ideological conservative.' We need full-throttle conservatism" (qtd in Simon, par 11). Reflecting the Right's longstanding libertarian strain, Mueller felt that the GOP needed a return to fiscal conservatism. Mueller reflected, "We went to Washington to be fiscal conservatives and we became profligate spenders and big-government bureaucrats" (qtd in Simon, par 12). The wars in Iraq and Afghanistan have not only been long and expensive, but they also caused the size of the federal government to balloon; such programs took Republicans far afield from their long-standing commitment to small government and decreased federal spending.

The Republican party's renewed connection with conservatism, however, cannot simply be limited to economic policy. Texas Governor Rick Perry, for example, observed that the GOP needs to remain focused on issues related to values, morals, and the family. According to an article that appeared in the *New York Times* in the days following the election, the governor "pointed to the success of ballot measures opposing same-sex marriage to show the continued potency of such issues" (Cooper A17). In a speech shortly thereafter Perry elaborated: "'The defense-of-marriage initiative that voters supported in California, Arizona and here in Florida ought to be proof enough that conservative values still matter to the American people and are worthy of our party's attention'" (qtd in Cooper A17). To be sure, while measures concerning so-called values issues like same-sex marriage were on ballots in four states, that number was a fraction of the eleven states that considered them in 2004 (see Campbell and Monson 126).

A second strategy that many political analysts identify as a key component to the future success of the Republican party—and the one that is most germane to the concerns of this book—is the need to attract young voters. The *Washington Post* reported that an astounding "sixty-six percent of 18–29 year olds voted for President-elect Obama" (Griffith, par 4). More than any other single factor, the Associated Press identified this as "the most dire indicator of the [Republican] party's future prospects" (Associated Press, "GOP Faces Future" par 1). It continued: "Republicans have lost that generation at a time when young people are forming the political beliefs and associations they will likely carry for the rest of their lives" ("GOP Faces Future," par 5). Unless this trend changes dramatically over the next few years, the AP concluded: "The Grand Old Party is increasingly becoming the bastion of its middle name. And without cultivating a young generation of stalwarts to continue the tradition, it will have difficulty remaining grand" (Associated Press, "GOP Faces Future," par 3).

A number of leading GOP strategists agree. David Frum, a conservative political columnist and resident fellow at the American Enterprise Institute, has noted: "since 1990, the GOP has lost its connection to the young, and the problem gets worse with every passing election. Today's twenty-somethings are the most anti-Republican age group in the electorate" (par 3). For these reasons, in an article that was posted on the AEI website and appeared simultaneously as an opinion piece in *USA Today*, Frum outlined his vision about how to remake the Republican party; his plan specifically spotlighted the need for a special focus on bringing in young people. In a series of step-by-step action points, Frum argued that by addressing issues like the environment, working to fix Social Security and reaching out to minorities, the GOP can return to a time, not so long ago during the Reagan era, when "Republicans owned the youth vote" (Frum, par 1). If this is truly the case, then the American public can surely count on an increase in the number of kids' books with conservative themes and right-leaning political messages. After all, today's generation of young children forms tomorrow's bloc of young voters.

It is interesting that returning to a strong conservative stance on so-called family, moral, and values issues—a main tactic for reviving the GOP—is at odds in many ways with the goal of attracting young voters. Various pundits have commented, "Social conservatism doesn't appeal to the majority of young Americans" (Associated Press, "GOP Faces Future," par 14). Raised during a different era with different views about social liberties and civil equality, many members of what is commonly known as the Millennial Generation hold more left-leaning attitudes on issues like immigration, abortion, same-sex marriage, global warming, and health care. Rather than arguing over values, one journalist noted, "young voters want to talk about health care, jobs, and student loans" (Associated Press, "GOP Faces Future," par 15). Moreover, they are also far more racially, ethnically, and culturally diverse; that is, they have grown up with ideas of multiculturalism. In the *San Francisco Chronicle*, a political pollster noted that young voters "see the Republican Party as profoundly different on tolerance and identity" (qtd in Marinucci, par 24). Meanwhile, John Weaver, who worked for the McCain campaign until summer 2007, was even blunter. Long before the primaries, he "warned that given the demographic changes sweeping the country, the Republicans could no longer afford to be seen as what he called an 'angry white men's party'" (qtd in Cooper A17). The GOP's selection in late January 2009 of Michael Steele as the first African American chairman of the Republican National Committee was consequently seen by many not as a sincere sign of ideological change, but as a mere cosmetic gesture designed to retool the party's image as well as distance itself from former associations with the racist Right (see Adesioye, pars 1–3). One thing is clear: the GOP needs to appeal to young voters, and the party needs new strategies, approaches, and messages to do it. Journalist Sam Tanenhaus has every confidence that Republicans will find a way to accomplish this task. As he observed two days after the sweeping Democratic victories: "Movements are conditioned to absorb setbacks. Tuesday's election is the latest, and probably not the last. It has given the Republican Party a fresh challenge—one it has not shied from in the past" (Tanenhaus P1).

By all accounts, Republicans seem to be meeting this challenge. Within six months after the election, the conservative movement and political right were already showing signs of rejuvenation. Somewhat appropriately, one of the first areas to indicate this renewed energy was right-wing radio. By March 2009, ratings for Rush Limbaugh—who made a very well received and much publicized speech at the Conservative Political Action Committee (CPAC) during February—had nearly doubled since the Democrats took office (Imponeni, par 3; see also Kurtz "Healthy," par 22). Meanwhile, other conservative media figures, most notably radio personality turned television host Glenn Beck, found almost immediate success with the launch of conservative cable news and social commentary programs. As the *New York Observer* reported, "in [the] few short months since joining Fox news, [Beck] has turned the 5 P.M. hour into the third most popular show in cable news" (Gillette, par 11).

Indications of the steady revival of the conservative movement in 2009 were not merely limited to the realm of mainstream media; they also permeated facets of the nation's sociopolitical culture. Most notable among these were the conservative-led "Tea Party" protests, which were held on April 15, 2009, and attracted more than one-quarter million participants nationwide (Harshaw, par 3). Staged on Tax Day, they were focused—echoing the libertarian tenet of conservatism—on criticizing the economic policies of Obama administration in general and its multibillion bank and corporate bailout bills in particular.

At locales throughout the nation, Tea Party participants, some of whom were dressed in three-cornered hats and colonial-era garb, marched, rallied, and held signs with slogans like "No Taxation without Deliberation," "Stop Generational Theft," and "You Can't Put Lipstick on Socialism" ("Nationwide," pars 1, 2, 18). Some protestors even reimagined the word "tea" as an acronym, standing for "Taxed Enough Already!" (see Hertzberg, par 1). Although many Democrats, including Speaker of the House Nancy Pelosi, dismissed the events as faux populism staged by the right's public-relations machine and not by the grassroots efforts of concerned citizens (see Harshaw, par 6), they generated lots of public interest and media attention.

So, too, has Sarah Palin. She has remained in the media spotlight almost continuously since the 2008 election: giving speeches, attending GOP functions, and appearing at fundraisers both in her home state and in the "Lower 48." Affirming her status as the "Teflon candidate," Palin weathered a seemingly endless barrage of accusations concerning financial misconduct, abuses of power, and ethics violations in the months following the GOP defeat. Indicating the sheer number of these grievances, she spent a half million dollars of her own money defending herself from various legal attacks, while the state of Alaska spent several million dollars ("Ann Coulter").

Even Palin's surprise resignation as the Alaska governor in early July 2009 seemed neither to damage her public reputation nor hamper her presidential aspirations in 2012. In an article posted on the website for Fox News, Peter Ferrara, a staff member at the White House Office of Policy Development under Reagan, called the decision a "brilliant liberating move for her career, and a potential turning point for the national conservative movement" (par 1). Ferrara continued, in even more laudatory language, that by freeing herself from public duty in a state that is geographically far removed from the rest of the nation, "She could pick up the mantle for social conservatism for the late Paul Weyrich in Washington, reinvigorating the pro-life cause and defense of traditional values" (par 4). Ann Coulter agreed. During a television appearance on a segment of *Geraldo at Large* just days after Palin's announcement, the prominent political commentator deemed the resignation "brilliant" ("Ann Counter: Sarah"). Amidst Republican presidential hopefuls like South Carolina Governor Mark Sanford and Nevada Senator John Ensign falling to sex scandals, Palin emerged as a frontrunner for the 2012 election. Indeed, later during that same television interview, Coulter referred to Palin as "a huge, huge star" who "is too big for the position" of a mere governor ("Ann Coulter: Sarah").

More radical elements of the conservative movement and political right have also been on the upswing. In late February 2009, a new social advocacy group aimed at college students made its debut at the annual Conservative Political Action Conference (CPAC): Youth for Western Civilization (YWC). As

Jack Stripling has written, YWC is founded on platform of "stated opposition to 'radical multiculturalism, political correctness, racial preferences, mass immigration, and socialism'" (par 2). From campus administrators and fellow students to various watchdog organizations and the Southern Poverty Law Center, "the group has drawn early critics who view its members as intolerant at best, and are linked to white supremacists at worst" (Stripling, par 2). Less than two months after the debut of Youth for Western Civilization, eight more chapters of the organization had cropped up on campuses around the United States (Stripling, par 2).

These indicators aside, even if 2008 did mark an unlikely close to the more than half-century reign of the conservative movement, it has had a powerful influence and lasting legacy. Charles Noble has noted that Reagan's election marked the commencement of a conservative era; "conservatives argue[d] that the triumph of New Right ideas (and the inevitable triumph of New Right policies) reflect[ed] a large shift to the right in American public opinion" (Noble 118). Such predictions were not wrong. In *What's the Matter with Kansas?*, Thomas Frank discussed the twentieth-century conservative social movement and its attendant political agenda, which has turned even former hotbeds of liberal progressivism, like the American Midwest in general and Kansas in particular, into right-wing strongholds. The plains states, which endorsed a number of progressive social initiatives and legislative reforms from the antebellum era through the New Deal, succumbed to the conservative rhetoric and value-laden arguments of the later twentieth and early twenty-first centuries. In the words of Frank, locales like Kansas were now little more than "a burned over district of conservatism" that provided a home base for right-wing efforts like Operation Rescue, various survivalist splinter groups, and the evangelical preacher who marshals the 'God Hates Fags' movement" (*What's* 31–35).

NINETEENTH-CENTURY AMERICAN MINISTER AND AUTHOR James Freeman Clarke wrote: "A politician thinks of the next election. A statesman, of the next generation." While most of the authors featured in the previous six chapters cannot comfortably be called statesmen, they do put Clarke's theory into practice. Texts such as *The Book of Virtues*, *The O'Reilly Factor for Kids*, and *Help! Mom!* series demonstrate the growing belief that success in the new millennium for social movements and political viewpoints depends upon reaching across not only the political aisle but also the age demographic. Echoing this observation, on August 11, 2008, *Publisher's Weekly* printed a review of Meghan McCain's picture book about her father. The main title for the piece suggested the next great sociopolitical objective represented by these narratives: conservatives seek to bring the soapbox to the sandbox.

In the final analysis, the political influence and social impact of these books ultimately remains to be told. Only future elections will reveal the comparative success or relative failure of messages contained in the texts like *Truax*, *A is for America*, and the Left Behind series for kids on the next generation of U.S. citizens, voters, and policy-makers. For now, these volumes offer a powerful example of the increasingly imbricated nature of youth culture, commercial print media, and sociopolitical movements in the United States.

In the mid-1960s, after the crushing defeat of conservative Republican presidential candidate Barry Goldwater, Benjamin A. Rogge, writing for the conservative journal *New Individualist Review*, reflected: "The lesson would seem to be that the real function of conservatism in America is not to try to win elections but to try to win converts. The real battle is, as always, a battle of ideas" (29). The conservative social movement and Republican New Right was founded with these ideals and—if the children's books profiled in the previous chapters demonstrate anything—they are still operating by them more than fifty years later. The one significant difference is the age of the intended converts.

NOTES

INTRODUCTION "IN ADAM'S FALL, WE SINNED ALL"

1. In 1951, Buckley published *God and Man at Yale*, which sociologist Sara Diamond has aptly described as "a scathing critique of left-liberalism and secularism within the academy" (*Roads* 30). Exactly fifty-five years later, David Horowitz released *The Professors: The 101 Most Dangerous Academics in America* (2006). The book not only argued that college and university campuses in the United States are populated overwhelmingly by liberals but also identified by name professors who, he claimed, seek to indoctrinate their students to this viewpoint or, failing that, to stifle the free exchange of ideas.

2. Congressional Republicans were not the only figures commenting on the important role that right-leaning radio programs played in the outcome of 1994 midterm elections. So, too, did political analysts. In "Dial-In Democracy: Talk Radio and the 1994 Election," for example, Louis Bolce, Gerald De Maio, and Douglas Muzzio examine the bloc of individuals "who voted in 1994 the way they did because talk radio so amplified their interest and concerns that they turned out to vote where they would not have otherwise. And there were undoubtedly still other voters who were converted or persuaded in some way to change their vote because of their talk radio listening" (477).

3. Interestingly, Coulter began her career publishing politically charged books with conservative themes in the late 1990s, with *High Crimes and Misdemeanors: The Case Against Bill Clinton* (1998).

4. To be fair, Russert would likely object to this classification. Many of the values that his book espouses—including family, tradition, and faith—are neither overtly political nor are they the exclusive purview of the right. They have, however, been coopted by this movement.

5. The conservative wing of Simon & Schuster is Threshold Editions. The division is headed by nationally known political strategist Mary Matalin. Most recently, Matalin has served as chief of staff for the Republication National Committee, counselor to Vice President Dick Cheney, and assistant to the president for George W. Bush. Meanwhile, the conservative branch of Random House is Crown Publishing and that of Penguin Group is Sentinel. Both have enjoyed immediate commercial success: the former imprint was the home of Ann Coulter's books, while the latter one has released much-discussed nonfiction titles like John Gibson's *The War on Christmas: How the Liberal Plot to Ban the Sacred Christian Holiday Is Worse than You Thought* (2005) and Mark Krikorian's *The New Case Against Immigration* (2008).

6. The same is not true for the versions of their books that are intended for adults. In a powerful demonstration of the ongoing neglect of books for young readers, the

Left Behind series for an older audience has been the subject of more than a dozen books, essays, and articles from a variety of disciplines.

7. See Donald Haase's "German Fairy Tales and America's Culture Wars: From Grimms' Kinder- und Hausmärchen to William Bennett's *Book of Virtues*," in *German Politics and Society* 13.3 (Fall 1995): 17–25, and Anastasia Ulanowicz's "Preemptive Education: Lynne Cheney's *America: A Patriotic Primer* and the Ends of History," in *Children's Literature Quarterly* 33:4 (Winter 2008): 341–370.

8. To be fair, Goldwater himself did not subscribe to Wallace's prosegregationist views. On the contrary, in *The Conscience of a Conservative*, Goldwater argued that the integration of public schools was both "wise and just" (37). Moreover, as George Nash has written, "Conservatives pointed out that Goldwater had helped to integrate the Arizona Air National Guard and the Phoenix Sky Harbor Airport" (435–436).

9. Indeed, when Duke left the Klan in 1980, he revived the National Association for the Advancement of White People (Swain 224).

10. Buckley's *Treasury of Children's Classics* was not his first tome for young readers. Almost twenty years earlier, Buckley penned a picture book, *The Temptation of Wilfred Malachey*. Published in 1985—around the midpoint of the Reagan era—the book tells the story of the eponymous character who is a type of prep school Robin Hood. The blurb on the inside jacket of the book provides the following plot summary: "Wilfred Malachey, possibly the poorest boy at the elite Brookfield Academy, is in the habit of improving his own finances by secretly removing funds from the wealthier students." This seemingly straightforward reworking of a classic folk hero contains many classic or quintessential Buckley-esque passages, including the following one from the text's opening paragraph: "The Malacheys had been forced to sell the family automobile when his father's most recent manuscript was rejected. The publishers, Hartfield & Hartfield, had told him it wouldn't sell, because 'Nobody wants to read about the Vietnam war'" (9).

CHAPTER I   "GIVE ME SOME OF THAT OLD-TIME READING"

1. The specific remark that Bennett often quoted is one from Jefferson's report of the commissioners for the University of Virginia. Together with highlighting the importance of teaching history, geography, mathematics, and philosophy, the third president of the United States also underscored the need "to instruct the mass of our citizens in these, their rights, interests and duties, as men and citizens" (qtd in Bennett *De-Valuing* 56).

2. In July 2004, Empower America merged with Citizens for a Sound Economy to form FreedomWorks, a conservative nonprofit group based in Washington, D.C. The goals of FreedomWorks include reducing the size of the federal government, lowering taxes, and encouraging political leaders to protect American freedom by maintaining a strong militaristic stance in the war on terror (FreedomWorks).

3. In a speech delivered at the Center for Arizona Policy in May 1999, for example, Bennett asserted that the event "provides us with a window onto our times, our moral order . . . virtue and vice . . . sexual morality and standards of personal conduct" (qtd in Holthouse, par 38).

4. Bennett declared both on television and in print, "The best available research suggests that the average life span of male homosexuals is around 43 years of age. Forty-three." Walter Olson contends, however, that there is "no satisfactory

measure of actual life expectancy among gay men" (par 11). For more information on both Bennett's source of this statistic and its lack of scientific validity, see Walter Olson's "William Bennett, Gays, and the Truth: Mr. Virtue Dabbles in Phony Statistics." *Independent Gay Forum*. 18 December 1997. *http://www.indegayforum.org/show/26857.html.*

5. Bennett makes no attempt to obfuscate the connection between promoting values in his 1993 anthology for children and advocating for them in his many previous writings for adults. Several passages from his introduction to *The Book of Virtues* overlap almost exactly with those from his nonfiction work *The De-Valuing of America* published the previous year. During a discussion about where parents and teachers can turn for sources of "values education" for children, for instance, Bennett argues: "I believe our literature and our history are a rich quarry of moral literacy. We should mine that quarry" (*De-Valuing* 59). He makes almost the exact same statement in his introduction to *The Book of Virtues*: "The quarry of wonderful literature from our culture and others is deep, and I have barely scratched the surface" (13).

6. During an appearance on *The MacNeil/Lehrer NewsHour*, on March 29, 1994, Bennett went one step further, asserting the ten virtues spotlighted in his book: "these describe people's values unless you're a criminal. I mean, unless you're pathological or criminal, these are values you ought to agree with" ("Conversation—American's Values")

7. An analogous phenomenon occurs with the two other passages that Bennett includes about African American history, experience and events. The passage profiling Rosa Parks (489–492) is not told in her own words or even those of a black historian. Instead, Bennett uses an excerpt from a book about Parks that was written by Kai Friese, a journalist from New Delhi. Likewise, the selection about the courageous actions of Harriet Tubman is not taken from her well-known autobiography (501–504); instead, Bennett presents Tubman's work on the Underground Railroad via an account written by white British author Sarah Bradford.

8. Although each of the ten sections in *The Book of Virtues* suffers from this lack of diversity, the final one on Faith is, perhaps not surprisingly, the most limited in range and scope. Bennett draws on an array of readings that fall outside of his own Roman Catholic tradition, but he selects very few that fall outside Judeo-Christian theology. Bennett baldy announces this focus in the first sentence to his explanatory headnote for the section: "Faith, Hope, and Love are formally regarded as 'theological' virtues in traditional Christian doctrine" (741). Accordingly, most selections are taken directly from the Bible, are "retold" from the Bible, or are heavily influenced by the Old and New Testaments.

A few selections are drawn from other major world religions or, at least, modes of spiritual thought: "The Path of Virtue," from the Buddhist *Dhammapada* (810); "Man's Nature Is Good" (812), by the Confucian thinker Mencius; and "The Way to Tao," by the Taoist philosopher Chuang-tzu (815). In an omission that seems especially conspicuous today and would have been noticeable even during the 1990s, Bennett does not include any selections from Islam, Hinduism, or American Indian spirituality. Had Bennett included more materials drawn from non-Western cultures and non-Judeo-Christian traditions, he might have changed not only his spotlighted virtues but also his whole conception of what constituted admirable moral traits. Some foundational traits of Jainism, for instance, include a commitment to nonviolence and a reverence for all living things. Likewise, many central teachings in Hinduism emphasize altruism and the care as well as protection of others.

9. Many other examples of this phenomenon permeate *The Book of Virtues*. Bennett's version of the fairy tale "Jack and the Beanstalk," which is retold by Andrew Lang, forms a powerful example: "In every account of Jack in the Beanstalk that I have ever read, Jack is a lazy scamp, who steals the giant's gold and magic hen and harp. As is typical in folk tales, we root for him because he's clever (and because the giant is hideous)" (Schulman par 17). However, Lang transforms the eponymous character into a brave and heroic figure who, as Bennett claims in prefatory comments, teaches us that "Courage leaps upward, and sooner or later we must all climb our own beanstalks" (450).

10. A similar phenomenon occurs in the two passages by Thomas Jefferson, featured in the section on Friendship and the one on Faith. Bennett, of course, does not mention that the man who wrote the line "All men are created equal" also owned slaves, an admission that would allow his young readers to ponder this powerful moral paradox.

11. Another illuminating, although admittedly less pressing, issue is the amount of space that Bennett devotes to each of the ten virtues spotlighted in his book. Although he ostensibly presents the moral qualities that he features as equally important, they are not given equal space. The traits of Work, Self-Discipline, and Courage occupy the longest end of the scale—where Work is allotted ninety-four pages, and Self-Discipline and Courage are each assigned eighty-six pages. Meanwhile, the traits of Honesty and Loyalty are at the shortest end of the spectrum, at sixty-six pages each—almost a third less than the longest section on Work.

12. Even selections from the nineteenth and early twentieth centuries that do not contain problematic messages about gender and race are not always entirely suitable for a contemporary, post-Freudian audience. The opening lines to the short story "Please" by Alicia Aspinwall, found in the opening section devoted to the virtue of self-discipline, form an emblematic example. The story tells the tale of the word "Please," which "lived in the mouth of a boy named Dick" (24). For many parents and also possibly for some older children, these lines, especially when read aloud, are blush-worthy.

13. Bennett's book also inspired one unauthorized parody, Tony Hendra's *The Book of Bad Virtues* (1994). Encouraging readers to "give their consciences a break," the book spotlights the qualities of Cynicism, Disobedience, Greed, Blasphemy, Self-Indulgence, Egotism, Cold Hard-Heartedness, Slacking, and Sex. Moreover, it contains selections drawn from Greco-Roman mythology, the Old and New Testaments, fairy and folk tales, and the Founding Fathers to illustrate these vices.

14. Many found this event surprising and even slightly hypocritical given Bennett's previous vocal criticisms of television and—as chairman of the NEH—his distaste of what he felt were left-leaning media platforms like PBS. Bennett defended his decision to turn *The Book of Virtues* into an animated television series by asserting that instead of simply "cursing the darkness" he wanted to "light a candle" (qtd in Bash 3D).

15. Exacerbating the situation, the conservative political lobbying group Empower America, which Bennett had cofounded and codirected, had campaigned only a few years before against the state expansion of gambling in general and casinos in particular. The group released a report that revealed "5.5 million American adults as 'problem' or 'pathological gamblers'"; the document also detailed the

way in which heavy gambling leads "to divorce, bankruptcy, domestic abuse, and other family problems" (qtd in Green, par 16). Bennett wrote the introduction to this document and—in a powerful irony—he also listed the address of Empower America as his own residence on the customer profile that he provided to at least one casino (Green, par 6).

16. Bennett countered by saying that his gambling was simply a hobby and not a habit for him. Nonetheless, he vowed to quit, announcing in a public statement: "I have done too much gambling, and this is not an example I wish to set. Therefore, my gambling days are over" (qtd in "GOP Moralist," par 8). This promise was short-lived. After staying out of the public eye for a few months, Bennett reemerged, appearing on Sean Hannity's right-wing radio program in July 2003. During the broadcast, he clarified that when he said that his "gambling days were over," he only meant "the excessive gambling is over" (qtd in Benen, par 7). When Bennett was pressed further on the issue of gambling and especially high-stakes gambling (the kind in which he had engaged), he gave the following brusque response: "I view it as drinking. If you can't handle it, don't do it" (qtd in Green, par 18).

CHAPTER 2   "I SPEAK FOR THE NATIONAL OAK FLOORING MANUFACTURERS ASSOCIATION"

1. Nathalie op de Beeck has explored this issue in a 2005 journal article. As she observes, "In *The Lorax*—and in children's publishing and print media generally—there is a telling disconnect between a commonsense save-the-forest narrative and the material actualities of mass production and everyday shopping. Random House USA, part of the international corporate entity that publishes Dr. Seuss' books, prints children's picture books on high-quality, chlorine-bleached white paper made from cut trees rather than recycled pulp" (266).

2. Early editions of the book also indicate that *Truax* was cosponsored by the Hard-wood Forests Foundation. Despite its name, the HFF is not an environmental group. Tax returns reveal that it and the National Hardwood Lumber Association are closely related, if not in fact the same entity: the two organizations share many of the same offices, donors, and even employees. Acknowledgment about the Hard-wood Forests Foundation's involvement in *Truax*, however, is omitted from later versions of the book.

3. *Truax* does not contain page numbers; neither does Dr. Seuss's *The Lorax*. Although critics sometimes assign pagination for convenience and ease of reference, I have decided to maintain fidelity to the source material and refrain from doing so. Both books are relatively brief and finding the passages quoted in my discussion should be unproblematic.

4. See, for example, Richard Monastersky's "Releaf for Greenhouse? Don't Cut Old Forests," in *Science News* 137, no. 6 (10 February 1990): 85. Akin to the article by Harmon, Ferrell, and Franklin, this report and the information that it contains was available during the time that Birkett was writing *Truax*.

5. Seuss's interest in fighting overdevelopment did not cease with the publication of *The Lorax*. In 1972, one year after the release of his children's book, he drew an environmentally themed cover illustration for *San Diego Magazine*. As Philip Nel describes, the image is overtly political: "A bird in flight approaches a weary bird, perched atop a pole that looks out over buildings as far as the eye can see. The first bird asks, 'Pardon me, sir . . . but which way to the nearest park?' Further text

adds, 'This is what you and your Birds and your Kids will be facing unless you Vote YES on Propositions A and B.'" (*Icon* 203n7). Appropriately titled "Leave Something Green," Seuss's illustration "was used (with his permission) by Citizens to Save Open Space, a group trying to curb overdevelopment" (Nel *Icon* 59).

6. Seuss's motivation for writing *The Lorax* may have also had an emotional or personal component. The children's author-illustrator first made a name for himself by conceiving the 1928 advertising campaign, "Quick, Henry, the Flit!" The product was a DDT-based pesticide that was manufactured by the corporate giant Standard Oil. Of course, Seuss's involvement in the ad campaign for Flit predated both the environmental movement and widespread knowledge about the personal as well as environmental hazards of DDT. However, the publication of Rachel Carson's book *Silent Spring* in 1962 brought this information into the public eye and, in the wake of the widespread attention and alarm, helped to launch the green movement.

7. For more on deep ecology and its viewpoints, see Frederick L. Bender's *The Culture of Extinction: Toward a Philosophy of Deep Ecology* (Prometheus Books, 2003). Early in the book, he offers the following observation about a premise for this environmental philosophy: "The key lies in reframing human identity as inextricably part of nature, i.e., as fully embedded in the ecosphere" (19).

8. The website for the American Forest & Paper Association (AF&PA) identifies their mission as "to influence successfully public policy to benefit the U.S. paper and forest products industry" ("About," par 1). In addition, the section directly below that discusses the organization's group vision and primary tasks, the first two bullet points assert that the AF&PA "sustains and enhances the interests of the U.S. forest products industry" and "sets the agenda for national industry issues" ("About AF&PA" par 2). Not surprisingly, the AF&PA website contains a direct link to their lobbying efforts on Capitol Hill. The page provides information on "politics and important issues for the forest products industry, offers suggestions on how to "take action," and also registers new voters, an effort that is called "Grow the Vote," a somewhat ironic title, given the AF&PA's representation of an industry whose products are made from cutting down trees ("Welcome to Grow the Vote").

CHAPTER 3   NOT JUST CHRISTIANITY, BUT THE CHRISTIAN RIGHT

1. In *Rapture Culture*, Amy Johnson Frykholm explains the emergence of this concept, which religious historians commonly trace back to John Nelson Darby during the nineteenth century: "Darby's use of the word *rapture* was derived from the Latin Vulgate translation of the Greek text of 1 Thessalonians 4:16–17: 'For the Lord Himself will descend from heaven with a shout, with the voice of the archangel, and with the trumpet of God; and the dead in Christ shall rise first. Then we who are alive and remain shall be caught up together with them in the clouds to meet the Lord in the air, and thus we shall always be with the Lord.' In the Vulgate translation, 'caught up' was translated *rapiemur*, from the Latin verb *rapio*. In medieval Latin, *rapio* became a noun, *raptura*, which then became in English 'rapture'" (Frykholm 16; emphasis in original). Critics of the concept of Rapture in general and the Left Behind books in particular note that this term does not actually appear anywhere in the Bible.

2. In *Rapture Ready!*, Daniel Radosh discusses yet another spin-off product based on the novels: "a videotape of instructions for the unraptured, so they can become true Christians. . . . [R]eaders can buy copies of this exact tape [that was made by

character Pastor Billings] from LeftBehind.com to leave in a conspicuous place for their unsaved loved ones to find after the real Rapture. Alternatively, readers can use a web site like RaptureLetter.com to send an automated post-Rapture e-mail" (78). Unfortunately, I was unable to find any sales figures or subscriber statistics for these services.

3. The content of the book can be gleaned from its title. In *The Unhappy Gays*, LaHaye lists sixteen pernicious traits that all homosexuals allegedly share. These qualities include loneliness, guilt, selfishness, depression, deceit, self-hatred, "incredible promiscuity," and "vulnerability to sadism-masochism." Not surprisingly, given the openly homophobic attitudes expressed in *The Unhappy Gays*, it is currently out of print. In an interesting detail, the 1978 treatise was published by Tyndale, the same press that later released LaHaye and Jenkins's Left Behind series for kids.

4. Giving further credence to this assertion, Jerry B. Jenkins, prior to working on the Left Behind novels, had a long history of both ghost writing—assisting Billy Graham with his autobiography, *Just as I Am* (1997)—and what might be called "biographical dictation": writing multiple "as-told-to" biographies of sports figures such as Hank Aaron, Orel Hershiser, and Nolan Ryan. As Bruce David Forbes and Jeanne Halgren Kilde note, Jenkins routinely skirts questions regarding the specific theology and even overall content of the Left Behind books, telling journalists and interviewers that he defers to LaHaye on these matters.

5. This detail denotes a powerful irony in the books. During the same time that Jenkins and LaHaye are emphasizing God's reverence for the lives of unborn children, they are simultaneously presenting mass human carnage. Millions die in the numerous plane crashes, car wrecks, and fires that break out in the wake of the initial disappearances. Then, as the characters discuss in book five, *Nicolae High*, a full three-quarters of the world's population perishes in the numerous biblically related earthquakes, plagues, and disasters that take place during the seven years leading up to the second "soul harvest" before the Apocalypse.

6. The incident occurred at a middle school in Willis, Texas. According to an article that appeared in the *Houston Chronicle*, "a teacher at Lynn Lucas Middle School pulled two sisters from class after discovering that they were carrying Bibles and threatened to have them picked up by child-welfare authorities. Another teacher told a pupil he was not allowed to read the Bible during free reading time and forced him to put it away, the lawsuit alleges. The boy also was required to remove a Ten Commandments book cover from another book, the lawsuit states" (Rice, par 2–3). A federal lawsuit was filed on behalf of the families by the Liberty Counsel legal defense, based in Orlando, Florida, and was settled out of court.

7. Such sentiments are mirrored by a few teachers. Mrs. Waltonen, a physical education instructor, muses about the gag order surrounding religion in the wake of the disappearances: "I don't know. Seems nothing should be off-limits now. We have the freedom to talk about everything under the sun, including stuff I never thought I'd hear in public, but not God. No way" (*Nicolae* 94–95).

8. Jefferson's exact language is as follows: "Believing with you that religion is a matter which lies solely between man and his God, that he owes account to none other for his faith or his worship, that the legislative powers of government reach actions only, and not opinions, I contemplate with sovereign reverence that act of the whole American people which declared that their legislature should 'make no law respecting an establishment of religion, or prohibiting the free exercise thereof,' thus building a wall of separation between church and State" (par. 2).

9. As the Left Behind books for kids progress, misrepresentations of *Engel, Abington,* and the First Amendment—as well as the accompanying presentation of evangelical Christians as persecuted by the "secular humanist" philosophy of public schools—become even more pronounced. While arguing with a teacher in *Nicolae High,* Vicki conflates the establishment clause with the free exercise clause while discussing the separation of church and state: "You said it was designed to keep the government out of the church. Now it's used to keep the church out of the government" (101). The First Amendment was actually designed for both purposes. The free exercise clause was created to keep the government out of the church. Conversely, the establishment clause was designed to keep the church out of the government. A "wall of separation" does both.

10. Even more preposterously, when the fourteen-year-old girl is caught in the detention facility with a Bible—an item that is considered contraband—she is placed in solitary confinement.

CHAPTER 4   PATRIOT ACTS

1. One almost needs to see the row after row, shelf upon shelf of titles by celebrity authors to comprehend the sheer magnitude of this phenomenon. Since the 1990s, for instance, narratives have been released by well-known singers LeAnn Rimes, Sting, Queen Latifah, Naomi Judd, Kylie Minogue, Paul McCartney, Britney Spears, Bob Dylan, and Woody Guthrie. Likewise, notable actors from both the silver and the small screen have published children's books; these authors include Will Smith, Jason Alexander, Spike Lee, John Travolta, and Julianne Moore. In a similar vein, an array of professional sport figures, including Tiki Barber, Jorge Posada, Mia Hamm, John Madden, Keith Hernandez, and Shaquille O'Neal have also released picture books. Not to be outdone, stage performers like Mikhail Baryshnikov, Bernadette Peters, Julie Andrews, Debbie Allen, and Harvey Fierstein have penned titles. In what constitutes perhaps the most unlikely category, various political figures, including Ed Koch, Desmond Tutu, Prince Charles, Sarah Ferguson, and Jesse Ventura, have written books for children. So, too, have media personalities Katie Couric, Larry King, Carson Kressley, and Brooke Shields. For some reason comedians seem especially drawn to this genre, as Jerry Seinfeld, Jay Leno, Bill Cosby, Jeff Foxworthy, Whoopi Goldberg, Billy Crystal, and Ray Romano have all added children's book authorship to their list of professional credits. While most celebrities have penned one solitary title for children, others have released multiple texts. To date, Maria Shriver, Jamie Lee Curtis, Jon Lithgow, and Madonna have each already exceeded the half-dozen mark.

2. And, in a clear corollary to the aims of this manuscript, also in 1995, Cheney founded the American Council of Trustees and Alumni (ACTA), a conservative lobbying group that seeks to "to alert alumni to actions it deems politically intolerant and that threaten academic freedom on campuses, such as speech codes and erosion of the Western civilization–oriented curriculum" (Stefancic and Delgado 127). ACTA then encourages alumni to write letters, withhold financial gifts, and/ or get involved in university governance in response to the events happening on campus. "As Chairperson Lynne Cheney puts it, 'It comes down to the question of who owns the university'" (Stefancic and Delgado 128).

3. In large part because of Cheney's opposition to the national standards in United States History—and the publicity that it generated—they were scrapped, vetoed in a

Senate vote of 99 to 1. Because the project had actually begun under Cheney's direction when she was chair of the NEH, many saw her opposition as disingenuous; as arising from a partisan-fueled dislike for the new Democrat-appointed NEH chair. The future second lady, however, claimed that the architects of the proposed Standards—the National Center for History in the Schools at UCLA—had strayed far afield from the proposal that she had approved when she headed the organization. As Cheney wrote in her *New York Times* op-ed piece, the group had "promised to adhere to traditional scholarly precepts of balance and evenhandedness"—a promise which she felt they had broken ("Mocking" A29).

4. Later in the acknowledgments, Cheney singles out three coworkers in particular for their support and assistance with the book: "Walter Berns for the inspiration he has provided on the subject of patriotism; Robert Goldwin for his profound knowledge, so willingly shared, of the founding period; and Chris DeMuth, president of the American Enterprise Institute, for his constant encouragement." Even a cursory examination of the careers of each of these men reveals their staunchly conservative political views and often reactionary social attitudes. One book by Walter Berns, an expert in constitutional law, for example, "'decries the pious sentiment' of those who maintain that criminals need to be rehabilitated," according to its own jacket blurb. Berns concludes, in a comment that stands in marked contrast to so-called "compassionate conservatism," that "justice demands the death penalty." Meanwhile, Robert Goldwin, has published, among other works, a book with the revealing title, *Why Blacks, Women, and Jews Are Not Mentioned in the Constitution and Other Unorthodox Views*.

5. For an example from the popular press, see Michiko Kakutani's "To Stars, Writing Books Looks Like Child's Play," in the *New York Times*, (23 October 2003): E1. Meanwhile, for an example from literary criticism, see Anastasia Ulanowicz's "Preemptive Education: Lynne Cheney's *America: A Patriotic Primer* and the Ends of History," in *Children's Literature Association Quarterly* 33.4 (Winter 2008):341–370.

6. Indeed, celebrity-authored picture books are as profitable as they are prolific. In the words of Robert D. Hale, the current phenomenon is a publishing "pot of gold" (239). Through a combination of capitalizing on name recognition, piquing audience curiosity, and exploiting an area of literature about which many adults feel unknowledgeable, many books achieve best-seller status. Ed Pilkington noted in an article in *The Guardian* in November 2006, "Over the past two months, the top five slots in the *New York Times* bestseller list for children's picture books have featured no fewer than three works by people famous in other fields: *Is There Really a Human Race?*, by the film star Jamie Lee Curtis; *Noelle's Treasure Tale*, by the singer-songwriter Gloria Estefan; and the *Big Book of Manners*, by the comedian and actor Whoopi Goldberg" (par 4).

7. The one notable exception to this trend occurred in the 1960s when AEI supported the presidential campaign of conservative Republican Barry Goldwater. As former AEI research fellow Howard J. Wiarda noted, the organization's president "rallied to the support of the 1964 Goldwater campaign. For this overtly politicized role, and technically . . . violating the structures against tax-exempt organizations engaging in political activities, AEI incurred the wrath of Johnson who had the IRS go after AEI" (5).

8. Theresa Pennefather, manager of publishing services and publications at the Heritage Foundation, confirmed this information. In an email exchange with Joan Ruelle, the Hollins University librarian, she asserted: "Heritage had no involvement

with the production or publication of *Book of Virtues*. It was a personal project of William Bennett" (Pennefather "A research question").

CHAPTER 5   PUNDIT KNOWS BEST

1. *The O'Reilly Factor* reached #1 on November 12, 2000; *The No Spin Zone* attained this status on November 11, 2001; *Who's Looking Out for You?* became a *New York Times* #1 best-seller on October 13, 2003; and finally, *Culture Warrior* did so on October 16, 2006. For more information on the sales and rankings of O'Reilly's books, see the Performance Statistics analysis available through *Publisher's Weekly*: http://www. publishersweekly.com/

2. A segment of his show called "Pinheads and Patriots" takes this insult one step further. As the dichotomy of its title suggests, the individuals discussed in these stories are not simply stupid but un-American or even anti-American. "Pinheads and Patriots" debuted on *The O'Reilly Factor* on September 11, 2007.

3. After a series of exchanges in which O'Reilly had interrupted or talked over Glick, the young man accused the host of exploiting 9/11 "to rationalize everything from domestic plunder to imperialistic aggression worldwide" (*O'Reilly Factor*, 4 February 2003). O'Reilly became angry and shot back: "That's a bunch of crap. I've done more for the 9/11 families by their own admission—I've done more for them than you will ever hope to do" (*O'Reilly Factor*, 4 February 2003). The two began to argue and a few moments later, O'Reilly told Glick to "shut up" twice in quick succession. Incredulous, Glick responded by telling his host, "Oh, please don't tell me to shut up" and continued to argue his points. At this point, O'Reilly ordered his producers, "Cut his mic. I'm not going to dress you down anymore, out of respect for your father. We will be back in a moment with more of *The Factor*" (*O'Reilly Factor*, 4 February 2003). Glick inquired while still on the air, "That means we're done?" to which the host responded with finality, "We're done" (*O'Reilly Factor*, 4 February 2003). Glick later told *Rolling Stone* magazine that during the commercial break O'Reilly said to him: "Get out of my studio before I tear you to fucking pieces" (Colapinto, par 24).

4. Here is a transcript of O'Reilly's exact remarks: "I don't even want to talk about the far left. Barney Frank—disgusting—pointing fingers. It's you, you big fat toad! You, Frank—you! Dodd, sitting there, 'Uh, we have to'—it's you, Dodd, you! You knew! I swear to God, if they were in this room right now, I would hit them. Dodd and Frank—the House Finance and Senate Finance. They knew. Don't point a finger at anybody, I'll break that finger off!" (*Radio Factor*, 25 September 2008).

5. About six months later, when fellow senator Evan Bayh appeared, O'Reilly returned to this sentiment by asking his guest for the following favor: "If you see [Sen. Tom Daschle] for me, Senator, tell him to shut up. For me. You can be nice" (*O'Reilly Factor*, 17 March 2003).

6. Less than six months later, O'Reilly reprised such themes on his radio show, saying in response to a caller who questioned the patriotism of the wife of the Democratic presidential nominee, "I don't want to go on a lynching party against Michelle Obama unless there's evidence" (*Radio Factor*, 19 February 2008). When his remarks were widely criticized, he offered a conditional apology, saying on the February 21, 2008, broadcast of his cable show: "I'm sorry if my statement offended anybody" (*O'Reilly Factor*, 21 February 2008).

7. *The O'Reilly Factor for Kids* first appeared on the *New York Times* hardcover advice list on October 17, 2004. Meanwhile, it charted the paperback list on the following dates: October 23, 2004; November 6, 2004; November 27, 2004; December 4, 2005; December 11, 2005; December 18, 2005; and December 25, 2005.

8. Thanks to Rhonda Brock-Servais for pointing out this final connection.

9. O'Reilly's comments about homosexuality on his cable and radio programs, however, have not been this supportive. As Peter Hart has documented, during his cable news show on July 2, 2002, O'Reilly made the following comment about gay pride parades: "People who see that have a right not to like homosexuals the way they're being portrayed in the parade. . . . They have an absolute right to condemn that behavior, to say it's corrupting to my children, I don't want them to see it, and if this is what the gay pride thing is all about, then *blank* them" (qtd in Hart 44; italics in original). Less than two weeks later, O'Reilly, returning to the subject of the LGBTQ movement, described it not as the efforts of an oppressed minority to obtain civil rights but as a malevolent special interest group: "I believe that there is a lobby, and it's based around the gay lobby too, that wants to mainstream homosexuality and AIDS, because AIDS is obviously an offshoot of homosexual conduct in many instances" (qtd in Hart 43). The following year, on June 21, 2003, *The O'Reilly Factor* ran a now-infamous story about the epidemic of so-called "teenage lesbian gangs" who carry pink pistols and roam the streets in various cities throughout the United States, attacking men, raping women, and indoctrinating young girls into homosexuality by forcing them to perform sex acts. Both the Southern Poverty Law Center and the Gay and Lesbian Alliance Against Defamation found the story completely baseless (see Yelsey as well as Buchanan and Holthouse). Finally, Jack Shafer has catalogued a number of other instances in which O'Reilly has urged LGBTQ people on the air to "shut up" about their sexual orientation (pars 25–32).

10. O'Reilly's attitude about "harder" drugs, like narcotics or hallucinogens, is much more firm. In the paragraphs following his discussion of marijuana, he informs his readers: "If you're using Ecstasy—especially the 'designer brands' sold around schools today—you're really crazy . . . it is a drug that presents great danger to your mind and body, particularly to your central nervous system. It's a time bomb and you would be wise to stay away from it no matter what kind of physical pleasure it promises" (68).

11. Of course, these comments took a hypocritical turn when the scandal involving O'Reilly's alleged extramarital affair with Andrea Mackris broke the same month that *The O'Reilly Factor for Kids* was published. In the wake of reports about O'Reilly's numerous sexually explicit phone calls and repeated erotic overtures to his former producer, lines from his self-help book like "And guys, if you exploit a girl, it will come back to get you. That's called 'karma'" (75) acquired a new ironic significance.

CHAPTER 6   "ONE STATE, TWO STATE, RED STATE, BLUE STATE"

1. DeBrecht has been heavily criticized for not using her real name, with detractors calling her adoption of a pseudonym personally cowardly and also—if her actual partisan viewpoints do not match those of her fictional profile—even politically disingenuous. In keeping with her image as a sincere suburban wife and mother,

the author has maintained that she adopted the pen name to safeguard herself and her loved ones. In an interview soon after the release of *Liberals*, she remarked "there are some real liberal nuts out there, and I wanted to protect my family" (Sirano).

2. As the professional biography for Jim Hummel on the website for the National Cartoonists' Society indicates, he is a regular contributor to the *San Jose Mercury-News*. Prior to that, he had a long career as a cartoonist in the Navy. During the war in Vietnam, Hummel drew for military publications distributed at bases throughout Southeast Asia as well as for the *Saigon Post* and the *Bangkok Post*. Then, after the war ended, he served as art director for *Stars and Stripes* in Tokyo and then as promotional director of the Associated Press in New York (National Cartoonists Society 2005). Ironically, one endeavor that the National Cartoonists Society biography for Hummel conspicuously omits is his work on DeBrecht's book.

3. DeBrecht's book has also received some international coverage, in newspapers such as London's *Guardian*, Melbourne's *The Age*, and the *Calcutta Telegraph* ("Hillary Unhinged," Special Guests, 4 November 2005).

4. In an added example of this phenomenon, Mayor Leach, the Ted Kennedy look-alike, offers the following sardonic explanation about the meaning and purpose of taxes: "'That is where you give the government half of your money so that we can spend it better'" (DeBrecht 19). When Tommy and Lou object by explaining how hard they have worked to make their lemonade stand a success, he is unmoved: "'[W]hy work hard when you can have the government provide for you?'" (DeBrecht 19). Then, in a passage that completes the comparison of the Kennedy-doppel-gänger to a figure who is stealing candy from babies, "Mayor Leach grabbed the bag of cash with half the boys' money" (DeBrecht 21). Later that night, while Tommy and Lou are dutifully squeezing lemons, they learn what the intrusive liberal has done with their hard-earned money. At a television press conference, the mayor announces: "'We liberals know how to take care of children with no shoes . . . That is why I want to announce today that I have purchased three million, yes, THREE MILLION, dustpans for our shoeless children'" (DeBrecht 23).

5. As one might imagine, DeBrecht was flattered by the on-air attention. In an article posted on the website for the public relations firm who handles her appearances, she is quoted as saying: "'I am honored by Rush Limbaugh's praise of the book. I've always dreamed of being named an associate professor at the University for the Limbaugh Institute for Advanced Conservative Studies'" (*Special Guests*, 21 September 2005, par. 7).

6. DeBrecht offered a retort to Reines's comment in an article posted on the website of the public relations firm which handles her press and public appearances. With characteristic wit, she asserted, "'Who needs parents when you've got bureaucrats in the Department of Education taking care of our kids? Evidently Hillary thinks it takes a village to teach a child to read!'" ("Rush Limbaugh," Special Guests 2006). Meanwhile, she has dismissed the comments made by other left-leaning media figures as classic "liberal whining" ("Rush Limbaugh," Special Guests 2006).

7. Giving further credence to this reading, the spinsterish librarian at Johnny and Luke's school has never heard of the Constitution, but she does brag about her newly created section of books on "Toenailology." Apparently, DeBrecht found this pun so clever that she felt compelled to include it in all of her narratives. Even

more troublesome, however, is this derogatory reference to Scientology—which, despite its often poor public image as recognized by the U.S. government for tax-exempt purposes as a formal organized religion—appears in a book that is, ironically, about freedom of worship.

8. As Jerry Griswold has noted about the booming market for children's books during the past few decades, sales figures quadrupled during the period between 1982 and 1990 alone (1997: 37). Moreover, as Laurie Langbauer has written, these numbers have only risen in the new millennium amid the Harry Potter and Lemony Snicket crazes. Rowling's books have sold more than 400 million copies to date; meanwhile, in March 2004, "Handler's books held seven out of ten spots on the *New York Times* children's chapter-book best-seller list. . . . By then, the series had already spent a combined six hundred weeks on the list; by book 13, it had sold fifty-one million copies" (Langbauer 2007: 506). The resulting spike in profits has been so strong that "some publishers have said that their children's departments have kept their firms afloat during economic hard times" (Griswold 1997: 37).

CONCLUSION   "THE GOSH-DARNIT, DOGGONE IT, YOU-BETCHA WINK HEARD 'ROUND THE WORLD"

1. As a table compiled by the New York Stock Exchange reveals, the Dow Jones Industrial Average on July 4, 2008 was 11,288.54; by October 24, 2008, it had dropped to 8,378.95.

2. According to the Bureau of Labor Statistics, the unemployment rate reached 6.5 percent in October 2008, the highest since March 1994 ("Labor Force Statistics").

3. As David C. Wheelock noted in the closing section of his article, "Changing the Rules: State Mortgage Foreclosure Moratoria during the Great Depression": "In 2008, residential real estate foreclosure rates are at their highest levels since the Great Depression" (581).

4. Journalist Schuyler Kropf, in an article that appeared on April 1, 2009, in the Charleston, South Carolina, *Post and Courier*, said of this phenomenon, "One yardstick [in the increase of gun sales since election day] has been the FBI's background-check figures showing that the bureau made more than 4.2 million checks from November to January, a 31 percent increase over [the] 3.2 million done the year prior, according to published reports" (A1). Sales of ammunition have likewise spiked. As one gun-store owner interviewed for Kropf's article reported, "I've had people come up from Florida and buy 15,000 to 20,000 rounds" (A1). Ben Neary, writing for the Associated Press, has detailed that analogous accounts have been reported in states throughout the nation, (pars 3–8). In some areas of the South and the West, sales of semiautomatic rifles or pistols have been so brisk that they have led to a shortage, which caused at least one store—in Lynne Cheney's home state of Wyoming—to begin rationing sales (Neary, par 7).

5. For an overview of these incidents, which took place in early October 2008, as well as a video of the outburst at the rally in Jacksonville, see Rachel Weiner's "Obama Hatred at McCain-Palin Rally: 'Terrorist!" 'Kill Him!'" on October 6, 2008 in *The Huffington Post*.

6. For an overview of the various individuals who made this remark in the days and weeks following the election, as well as the venues in which they made it, see Tod

Lindberg's "The Center-Right Nation Exits Stage Left" in the *Washington Post* (16 November 2008): B1.

7. The measures related to gay marriage or at least the rights of same-sex families that passed in the three other states—Arizona, Arkansas, and Florida—were just as notable. The Arizona ballot initiative barring same-sex couples from marrying passed after being previously rejected by the state's voters. Meanwhile, the measures in Arkansas and Florida built on existing bans and were thus even more sweeping and draconian. Voters in Arkansas approved a ballot initiative that barred any unmarried individual from adopting or becoming a foster parent ("Equality's" A2). While the measure targeted unwed heterosexuals, it was, as the *New York Times* reported, "intended to bar gay men and lesbians from adopting children" (McKinley and Goodstein A1). Finally, voters in Florida expanded the state's antipathy toward non-nuclear family configurations, as they "approved a more sweeping amendment intended to bar marriage, civil unions, and other family protections" ("Equality's" A2).

WORKS CITED

2004 Election Results. Federal Elections Commission Popular and Electoral Vote Summary. <http://www.fec.gov/pubrec/fe2004/tables.pdf> 16 December 2008.

Abate, Michelle Ann. *Tomboys: A Literary and Cultural History*. Philadelphia: Temple UP, 2008.

ABC World News. With Charles Gibson. American Broadcasting Company. Transcript. 11 September 2008. LexisNexis. Hollins University. 17 December 2008.

Abelson, Donald E. *Do Think Tanks Matter?: Assessing the Impact of Public Policy Institutes*. Montreal: McGill-Queen's UP, 2002.

"About AF&PA." American Forest & Paper Association (AF&PA). Posted 2002. <http://www.afandpa.org/Content/NavigationMenu/About_AFandPA/Mission/Mission.htm> 10 August 2008.

Adesioye, Lola. "Lipstick on a Pig." *The Guardian* (London). Online. 2 February 2009 <http://www.guardian.co.uk/commentisfree/cifamerica/2009/feb/02/michael-steele—republicans-race> 18 April 2009.

Adler, Jonathan. "Little Green Lies: The Environmental Miseducation of America's Children." *Policy Review* 61 (Summer 1992): 18–26.

Adorno, Theodor. "Education after Auschwitz." *Critical Models: Interventions and Catchwords*. New York: Columbia UP, 1998.

Ahrens, Frank. "FCC Indecency Fines, 1970–2004." *Washington Post*. 2005.

Albom, Mitch. *The Five People You Meet in Heaven*. New York: Hyperion, 2003.

Alcott, Louisa May. *Little Women*. 1868. Ed. Elaine Showalter. New York: Penguin, 1989.

——. *The Selected Letters of Louisa May Alcott*. Ed. Joel Myerson and Daniel Shealy. Boston: Little, Brown and Company. 1987.

Allen, Brooke. "Book Review—*The Age of American Unreason*." Barnes and Noble Review. 20 May 2008. http://www.barnesandnoble.com/bn-review/note.asp?note=16828706 11 April 2009.

Allen, Mike. "For Lynne Cheney, the Children's Hour." *Washington Post*. 18 September 2002. A7.

Allen, Scott. "Truth or Scare?: Environmental Teaching Under Fire." *Boston Globe*. 15 June 1997: A1.

American Conservatism: An Encyclopedia. Ed. Bruce Frohnen, Jeremy Beer, and Jeffrey O. Nelson. Wilmington, DE: ISI Books, 2006.

American Enterprise Institute. "AEI's Organization and Purpose." 8 December 2005. <http://www.aei.org/about/filter.all/default.asp> 3 January 2008.

Americans United for the Separation of Church and State. "Prayer and the Public Schools: Religion, Education and Your Rights." <http://www.au.org/site/PageServer?pagename=resources_brochure_schoolprayer> 20 July 2008.

Amy. "Really Aimed at Kids?," customer review of *No, George, No!* 24 October 2005. <www.amazon.com> 31 May 2007.

"Ann Coulter on Palin's Resignation." *Hannity*. FoxNews. Fox. 7 July 2009. Transcript. <http://www.foxnews.com/story/0,2933,530433,00.html> 6 August 2009

"Ann Coulter: Sarah Palin Is Too 'Big' To Be Alaska's Governor." *Geraldo at Large*. FoxNews. Fox. 5 July 2009. Streaming video clip of segment available at <http://www.youtube.com/watch?v=46vH8kFt9Sc> 6 August 2009.

Anonymous. "Bigotry for little people," customer review of *Help! Mom! There Are Liberals Under My Bed*. 7 October 2005. <www.bn.com> 5 July 2007.

Anonymous. "Horrible," customer review of *No, George, No!*. 2 November 2005. <www.amazon.com> .31 May 2007.

Apol, Laura. "Shooting Bears, Saving Butterflies: Ideology of the Environment in Gibson's 'Herm and I' (1894) and Klass's *California Blue* (1994)." *Children's Literature* 31 (2003): 90–115.

Ariel, Yaakov. "How are the Jews and Israel Portrayed in the Left Behind Series?: A Historical Discussion of Jewish-Christian Relations." *Rapture, Revelation, and the End Times: Exploring the Left Behind Series*. Ed. Bruce David Forbes and Jeanne Halgren Kilde. New York: Palgrave, 2004. 131–166.

Ariès, Philippe. *Centuries of Childhood: A Social History of Family Life*. New York: Vintage, 1962.

Aronowitz, Stanley. "Considerations on the Origins of Neoconservatism." *Confronting the New Conservatism: The Rise of the Right in America*. Ed. Michael J. Thompson. New York: NYU P, 2007. 56–70.

Askehave, Inger. "If Language is a Game—These Are the Rules: A Search into the Rhetoric of the Spiritual Self-Help Book *If Life is a Game—These Are the Rules*." *Discourse & Society* 15 (2004): 5–31.

Associated Press. "GOP Faces Future without Youth Vote." *Boston Herald*. 17 November 2008. <http://www.bostonherald.com/news/us_politics/view/2008_11_17_GOP_faces_future_without_youth_vote/srvc=home&position=recent> 20 November 2008.

Baker, James A. III, and Lee H. Hamilton. *The Iraq Study Group Report: The Way Forward—A New Approach*. New York: Vintage, 2006.

Barone, Michael. "The New Politics of Virtue." *U.S. News and World Report*. 18 April 1994: 50.

Bash, Alan. "Bennett Uses 'Toons To Teach His 'Virtues.'" *USA Today*. 7 December 1995: 3D.

Beavis and Butt-Head. MTV. 1993–1997.

Beckett, Sandra, ed. *Transcending Boundaries: Writing for a Dual Audience of Children and Adult*. New York: Taylor and Francis, 1999.

Beder, Sharon. *Global Spin: The Corporate Assault on Environmentalism*. White River Junction, VT: Chelsea Green, 2002.

Beeck, Nathalie op de. "Speaking for the Trees: Environmental Ethics in the Rhetoric and Production of Picture Books." *Children's Literature Association Quarterly* 30.3 (Fall 2005): 265–287.

Belkin, Lisa. "Girls' Costumes Gone Wild." *New York Times*. 29 October 2008. <http://parenting.blogs.nytimes.com/2008/10/29/girls-costumes-gone-wild/> 17 December 2008.

Bellant, Russ. *The Coors Connection: How Coors Family Philanthropy Undermines Democratic Pluralism*. 1988. Boston: South End Press, 1991.

Bender, Frederick L. *The Culture of Extinction: Toward a Philosophy of Deep Ecology.* Amherst, NY: Prometheus Books, 2003.

Berlet, Chip. "The Write Stuff: U.S. Serial Print Culture from Conservatives to Neo-Nazis." *Library Trends* 56.3 (Winter 2008): 570–600.

"Biography." *Bennett Mornings.* <http://www.bennettmornings.com> 28 August 2008.

"Bill Bennett Edits Inspirational 'Book of Virtues.'" *CNN.* 23 January 1994. News, Domestic, 0:21 AM. Transcript. LexisNexis. Hollins University. 10 November 2008.

"Bill O'Reilly's Bio." *Fox News: The O'Reilly Factor.* 29 April 2004. <http://www.foxnews.com/story/0,2933,155,00.html> 23 October 2008.

Birkett, Terri. *Truax.* Illus. Orrin Lundgren. Memphis, TN: National Oak Flooring Manufacturers Association, 1995.

Belasco, Amy. "The Cost of Iraq, Afghanistan, and Other Global War on Terror Operations Since 9/11." Congressional Research Service. 15 October 2008. http://fpc.state.gov/documents/organization/112047.pdf 13 April 2009.

Benen, Steve. "Are Bill Bennett's Gambling Days Over or Not?" *The Carpetbagger Report.* 1 August 2003. <http://www.thecarpetbaggerreport.com/archives/474.html> 24 September 2008.

Bennett, William J. "Answer the Question." *Wall Street Journal.* 23 August 1999: A14.

——. *Body Count: Moral Poverty . . . and How to Win America's War Against Crime and Drugs.* New York: Simon & Schuster, 1996.

——. *The Book of Virtues: A Treasury of Great Moral Stories.* New York: Simon & Schuster, 1993.

——. *The Book of Virtues for Girls and Boys: A Treasury of Great Moral Stories.* New York: Simon & Schuster, 2008.

——. *The Book of Virtues for Young People: A Treasury of Great Moral Stories.* New York: Simon & Schuster, 1997.

——. *The Broken Hearth: Reversing the Moral Collapse of the American Family.* New York: Broadway, 2001

——. *The Children's Book of America.* Illus. Michael Hague. New York: Simon & Schuster, 1998.

——. *The Children's Book of Faith.* Illus. Michael Hague. New York: Simon & Schuster, 2000.

——. *The Children's Book of Heroes.* Illus. Michael Hague. New York: Simon & Schuster, 1997.

——. *The Children's Book of Home and Family.* Illus. Michael Hague. New York: Simon and Schuster, 2002.

——. *The Children's Book of Virtues.* Illus. Michael Hague. New York: Simon & Schuster, 1995.

——. *The Children's Treasury of Virtues.* Illus. Michael Hague. New York: Simon & Schuster, 2000.

——. *The Death of Outrage: Bill Clinton and the Assault on American Ideals.* Mankato, MN: The Free Press, 1999.

——. *The De-Valuing of America: The Fight for Our Culture and Our Children.* New York: Summit, 1992.

——. *The Index of Leading Cultural Indicators: Facts and Figures on the State of American Society.* New York: Simon & Schuster, 1994.

——. "A Lifetime of Lies." *Wall Street Journal.* 11 October 2000: A26.

——. *The Moral Compass: Stories for a Life's Journey.* New York: Simon & Schuster, 1995.

——. *To Reclaim a Legacy: A Report on the Humanities in Higher Education.* Washington, D.C.: National Endowment for the Humanities, 1984.

——. *Why We Fight: Moral Clarity and the War on Terrorism*. Washington, D.C.: Regnery, 2003.

Bennett, William J., and John T. E. Cribb. *The American Patriot's Almanac: Daily Readings on America*. Nashville, TN: Thomas Nelson, 2008.

Berlet, Chip. "The New Political Right in the United States: Reaction, Rollback, and Resentment." *Confronting the New Conservatism: The Rise of the Right in America*. Ed. Michael J. Thompson. New York: NYUP, 2007. 71–106.

Berns, Walter. *For Capital Punishment: Crime and the Morality of the Death Penalty*. New York: University P of America, 1991.

Bettelheim, Bruno. *The Uses of Enchantment: The Meaning and Importance of Fairy Tales*. New York: Vintage, 1975.

Blumenthal, Max. "The Pentagon Sends Messengers of Apocalypse to Convert Soldiers in Iraq." *The Nation*. 8 August 2008. <www.thenation.com> 20 June 2008.

Blumenthal, Sidney. *The Rise of the Counter-Establishment: The Conservative Ascent to Political Power*. New York: Sterling Publishing, 2008.

——. *The Strange Death of Republican America: Chronicles of a Collapsing Party*. New York: Union Square Press, 2008.

Bodmer, George. "The Post-Modern Alphabet: Extending the Limits of the Contemporary Alphabet Book, from Seuss to Gorey." *Children's Literature Association Quarterly* 14.3 (Fall 1989): 115–117.

Boland, M. "ABC for Martin." *Tales for Little Rebels: A Collection of Radical Children's Literature*. Ed. Julia Mickenberg and Philip Nel. New York: NYU P: 19–21.

"Book Review: *Truax*." Posted by Mary Wirth. National Oak Flooring Manufacturing Association. <www.nofma.org> 5 May 2008.

Bolce, Louis, Gerald De Maio, and Douglas Muzzio. "Dial-In Democracy: Talk Radio and the 1994 Election." *Political Science Quarterly* 111.3 (Autumn 1996): 457–481.

Bowman, James. "The Leader of the Opposition, Political Commentator Rush Limbaugh." *National Review*. 6 September 1993. <http://findarticles.com/p/articles/mi_m1282/is_n17_v45/ai_14293009> 10 November 2008.

Boylan, Anne M. *Sunday School: The Formation of an American Institution, 1790–1880*. New Haven: Yale UP, 1998.

Boyles, Deron. "Would You Like Values With That? Chick-Fil-A and Character Education." *Journal of Curriculum Theorizing* 21.2 (Summer 2005): 43–60.

Bradford, Clare. "The Sky Is Falling: Children as Environmental Subjects in Contemporary Picture Books." *Children's Literature and the Fin de Siècle*. Ed. Roderick McGillis. Westport, CT: Praeger, 2003. 11–20.

——. *Unsettling Narratives: Postcolonial Readings of Children's Literature*. Waterloo, Ontario (Canada): Wilfred Laurier U, 2007.

Brent. "Give Your Kids a Head Start!" Customer review of *Help! Mom! There Are Liberals under My Bed!* posted at Barnes and Noble. 30 November 2006. <www.bn.com> 30 December 2006.

Briggs, Rosland. "Toys That Teach Family Values are a Success." *London Free Press* (Ontario, Canada). 26 April 1999: 13.

Bridges, Tyler. *The Rise of David Duke*. Jackson: UP of Mississippi, 1995.

Brink, Carol Ryrie. *Caddie Woodlawn*. 1935. New York: Collier Books, 1970.

British Plastics Federation. *The World of Plastics*. London: British Plastics Federation in Corporation with the Plastics Industry of the United Kingdom, 1986.

Buchanan, Patrick. "PJB: 1992 Republican National Convention Speech." 17 August 1992.

<http://buchanan.org/blog/1992/08/1992-republican-national-convention-speech/>
18 December 2008.

Buchanan, Susy, and David Holthouse. "The Oh-Really Factor: Fox News' Bill O'Reilly Offers Up an 'Expert' to Claim that Pink Pistol-Packing Lesbian Gangs Are Terrorizing the Nation." *Southern Poverty Law Center*. 3 July 2007. <http://www.splcenter.org/intel/news/item.jsp?aid=274&site_area=1>22 October 2008.

Buckley, William F. Jr. Introduction. *Treasury of Children's Classics*. Wilmington, DE: ISI Books, 2003. xii–xv.

——. "Publisher's Statement." *National Review* 1 (19 November 1955): 5.

——. *The Temptation of Wilfred Malachey*. New York: Ariel Books/Workman Publishing, 1985.

Bureau of Labor Statistics. U.S. Department of Labor. "Labor Force Statistics from the Current Population Survey." Databases, Tables and Calculators by Subject. Web. <http://data.bls.gov/PDQ/servlet/SurveyOutputServlet?data_tool=latest_numbers&series_id=LNS14000000> 17 December 2008

Burroughs, Edgar Rice. *Tarzan of the Apes*. 1914. New York: Ballantine, 1963.

"Bush Slammed over 'God's War' on Iraq." *Evening Times* (Glasgow). 7 October 2005: 8.

Butler, Judith. *Gender Trouble: Feminism and the Subversion of Identity*. New York: Routledge, 1990.

Butt, Sheila. *Does God Love Michael's Two Daddies?* Illus. Ken Perkins. Montgomery, AL: Apologetics Press, 2006.

California Licensed Foresters Association. "Planting Trees in the Forest." <http://www.clfa.org/planting_trees_in_the_forest.htm> 20 August 2008.

Campbell, David E., and J. Quin Monson. "The Case of Bush's Re-election : Did Gay Marriage Do It?" *A Matter of Faith: Religion in the 2004 Presidential Election*. Ed. David E. Campbell. Washington, D.C.: Brookings Institution Press, 2007. 120–141.

Campbell, James E. "Book Review—*Midterm: The Elections of 1994 in Context*." *Political Science Quarterly* 112.4 (Winter 1997/1998): 698–700.

Carlson, Margaret. "Public Eye." *Time*. 24 June 2001. <http://205.188.238.109/time/magazine/article/0,9171,163548,00.html> 9 November 2008.

Carton, Evan, and Gerald Graff. "Politics and American Criticism." *The Cambridge History of American Literature*. Vol. 8: *Poetry and Criticism, 1940–1995*. Cambridge: Cambridge UP, 1996. 265–280.

Cashburn, Steve. "Lynne Cheney and the Culture Wars." MA Thesis: Ohio State U, 1996. <www.io.com/~casburn/pers/acad/osu/cheney.pdf> 12 July 2008.

Chait, Jonathan. "Lynne Cheney, Policy Assassin." *The American Prospect*. 30 November 2002. <http://www.prospect.org/cs/articles?article=lynne_cheney_policy_assassin> 7 February 2009.

Cheap, Elizabeth. *My Station and Its Duties: A Narrative for Girls Going to Service*. New York: T. Mason & G. Lane, for the Sunday School Union of the Methodist Episcopal Church, at the Conference Office, 200 Mulberry-street, J. Collord, printer, 1810.

"Cheney: There's Just Something Somewhat Funny About This." *The Hotline*. 23 February 2005. Lexis Nexis. Hollins University. 7 February 2009.

Cheney, Lynne V. *A Is for Abigail: An Almanac of Amazing American Women*. Illus. Robin Preiss Glasser. New York: Simon & Schuster, 2003.

——. *America: A Patriotic Primer*. Illus. Robin Preiss Glasser. New York: Simon & Schuster, 2002.

——. "The End of History." *Wall Street Journal*. 20 October 1994: A22.

——. *Humanities in America: A Report to the President, the Congress, and the American People.* Washington, D.C.: NEH, 1988.

——. "Mocking America at U.S. Expense." *New York Times.* 10 March 1995: A29.

——. "Mrs. Cheney's Remarks on 'Teaching for Freedom' at Princeton University." 29 November 2001. Office of Lynne Cheney. The White House. <http://www.whitehouse. gov/mrscheney/news/20011130.html> 22 June 2007.

——. "Multiculturalism Done Right." *The Essence of Living in a Free Society.* Ed. E. Lawson Taitte. Dallas: U of Texas at Dallas P, 1997.

——. *Our 50 States: A Family Adventure Across America.* Illus. Robin Preiss Glasser. New York: Simon & Schuster, 2006.

——. *Telling the Truth.* Washington, D.C.: NEH, 1992.

——. *Telling the Truth: Why Our Culture and Our Country Have Stopped Making Sense—and What We Can Do About It.* New York: Touchstone, 1995.

——. *Tyrannical Machines: A Report on Educational Practices Gone Wrong and Our Best Hopes for Setting Them Right.* Washington, D.C.: NEH, 1990.

——. *We the People: The Story of Our Constitution.* Illus. Greg Harlin. New York: Simon & Schuster, 2008.

——. *When Washington Crossed the Delaware: A Wintertime Story for Young Patriots.* Illus. Peter Fiore. New York: Simon & Schuster, 2004.

CNN. "Special Event: Sen. John McCain Attacks Pat Robertson, Jerry Falwell, Republican Establishment as Harming GOP Ideals." *Cable News Network.* 28 February 2000. Transcript. http://transcripts.cnn.com/TRANSCRIPTS/0002/28/se.01.html 3 November 2008.

Code, Lorraine. "Taking Subjectivity into Account." *Women, Knowledge and Reality: Explorations in Feminist Philosophy.* 2nd ed. Ed. Ann Garry and Marilyn Pearsall. New York: Taylor and Francis, 1996. 191–221.

Colapinto, John. "Mad Dog." *Rolling Stone.* 11 August 2004. <http://www.rollingstone.com/ politics/story/6417561/mad_dog/> 20 October 2008.

Collum, Mark. "Bill Bennett Strikes a Blow for Virtue." *Birmingham News.* 7 November 1993: 601.

"Conservative." *The Oxford English Dictionary.* vol. 3. 2nd ed. 1989: 765.

Constitution of the United States. U.S. National Archives and Records Administration. <http://www.archives.gov/exhibits/charters/constitution.html> 10 December 2008.

"Conversation—America's Values." Interview with William Bennett by Charlayne Hunter-Gault. *MacNeil/Lehrer NewsHour.* PBS. 29 March 1994. Transcript. LexisNexis. Hollins University. 6 March 2009.

Cooper, Michael. "Among Republicans, a Debate Over the Party's Road Map Back to Power." *New York Times.* 17 November 2008: A17.

Cordesman, Anthony H. *The Uncertain Cost of the Iraq War.* Center for Strategic and International Studies (CSIS). Burke Chair in Strategy. 9 May 2006. <http://www.csis. org/index.php?option=com_csis_pubs&task=view&id=3235> 11 April 2009.

Cottle, Michelle. "Nitwit Lit: The Right's Bedtime Monster." *The New Republic* Online. 3 July 2006. <www.tnr.com> 31 May 2007.

Coulter, Ann. *Godless: The Church of Liberalism.* New York: Random House, 2006.

——. *High Crimes and Misdemeanors: The Case Against Bill Clinton.* Washington, D.C.: Regnery, 1998.

——. *How to Talk to a Liberal (If You Must): The World According to Ann Coulter.* New York: Random House, 2004.

———. *If Democrats Had Any Brains, They'd Be Republicans.* New York: Random House, 2007.

———. *Slander: Liberal Lies about the American Right.* New York: Random House, 2002.

———. *Treason: Liberal Treachery from the Cold War to the War on Terrorism.* New York: Random House, 2003.

Covington, Sally. *Moving a Public Policy Agenda: The Strategic Philanthropy of Conservative Foundations.* Washington, D.C.: National Committee for Responsive Philanthropy, 1997.

Coyle, Wanda. "Disintegrating Family a Real National Crisis, Bennett Says." *Fresno Bee.* 25 February 1994: A17.

Crampton, Gertrude. *Scuffy the Tugboat.* Illus. Tibor Gergely. New York: Golden Books, 1946.

———. *Tootle.* Illus. Tibor Gergely. New York: Golden Books, 1945.

Cross, Gary. *The Cute and the Cool: Wondrous Innocence and Modern American Children's Culture.* Oxford: Oxford UP, 2004.

Crupi, Alexander. "MSNBC Closing Gap on CNN." *Mediaweek.* 28 November 2007. <http://www.mediaweek.com/mw/news/recent_display.jsp?vnu_content_id=1003678708&imw=Y> 16 October 1008.

Daniel, Clifton, ed. *America's Century: Year by Year from 1900 to 2000.* New York: Dorling Kindersley, 2000.

David, Laurie, and Cambria Gordon. *The Down-to-Earth Guide to Global Warming.* London: Orchard Books, 2007.

Davis, N. A. "Profoundly Inappropriate." Customer review of *Help! Mom! There Are Liberals under My Bed!* 2 June 2007. <www.amazon.com> 22 June 2007.

DeBrecht, Katharine. *Help! Mom! There Are Liberals Under My Bed!* Longwood, FL: Xulon Press, 2004.

———. *Help! Mom! There Are Liberals Under My Bed!* Los Angeles: Kids Ahead, 2005.

———. *Help! Mom! Hollywood's in My Hamper!* Los Angeles: Kids Ahead, 2006.

———. *Help! Mom! The 9th Circuit Nabbed the Nativity (or, How the Liberals Stole Christmas).* Los Angeles: Kids Ahead, 2006.

"Democrats Retake Congress." America Votes 2006. *CNN.* 8 November 2006. <http://www.cnn.com/ELECTION/2006/> 3 April 2009.

Denny. Untitled customer review of *Help! Mom! There Are Liberals under My Bed!* 2 January 2006. <www.amazon.com> 22 June 2007.

Diamond, Sara. *Roads to Dominion: Right-Wing Movements and Political Power in the United States.* New York: The Guilford Press, 1995.

Digby. "Conservative Manifestos for Idiots." 28 June 2006. <http://digbysblog.blogspot.com/2006_06_01_archive.html> 5 June 2007.

Dreher, Christopher. "Help! Mom! There Are Politics in My Children's Books!" *The Globe and Mail* (Canada). 27 August 2005: F4.

———. "Red and Blue in Black and White." *The Globe and Mail* (Canada). 8 January 2005: F8.

Drew, Elizabeth. "Power Grab." *New York Review of Books* 53.11. 22 June 2006. <http://www.nybooks.com/articles/19092> 3 April 2009.

Dreyfuss, Richard. "Reverend Doomsday." *Rolling Stone.* 28 January 2004. <http://www.rollingtones.com/politics/story/5939999/reverend_doomsday/> 1 July 2008.

Duin, Julia. "Project Grounds Children in Virtues: Group Raises Consciousness of Consciences." *Washington Times.* 5 March 1996: A2.

Duffy, Michael, and Karen Tumulty. "The Democrats Savor Their Victory." *Time.* 8 November 2009. <http://www.time.com/time/nation/article/0,8599,1556335,00.html?cnn=yes> 4 April 2009.

Dwyer, Janet Ingraham. "Fool's Paradise: The Unreal World of Pop Psychology/*Self-Help, Inc.: Makeover Culture in American Life*." *Library Journal* 130.13 (15 August 2005): 106–107.

Eastland, Terry, ed. *Religious Liberty in the Supreme Court*. Washington, D.C.: Ethics and Public Policy Center, 1993.

Edelman, Rob. "Pulp Fiction." *Bowling, Beatniks and Bell-Bottoms: Pop Culture of the 20th Century*. Vol. 5: *1980s–1990s*. Ed. Sara Pendergast and Tom Pendergast. Detroit: Thompson Gale, 2002. 1244–1245.

Empower America. www.empower.org. [cached] 28 August 2008.

"Enter, Truax; Exit, Dr. Seuss." *TimberLine Magazine*. Industrial Reporting, Inc. 1 November 1999. <http://www/timerlinemag.com/articledatabase/view.asp?articleID=116> 6 August 2008.

Entous, Adam. "Bush to Ease U.S. Logging Rules, Citing Fie Danger." Reuters News Service. 23 August 2002. http://www.reuters.com/ Also accessible at <http://www.planetark. com.dailynewsstory.cfm/newsid/17408/newsDate/23-Aug-2002/story.htm> 19 August 2008.

"Equality's Winding Path." *New York Times*. Opinion Page. 5 November 2008: A28.

Ewan, Stuart. Book Jacket. *Self-Help, Inc.: Makeover Culture in American Life*. By Micki McGee. Oxford: Oxford UP, 2005.

Falling Buzzard, Karen S. "The Coca-Cola of Self-Help: The Branding of John Gray's *Men Are from Mars, Women Are from Venus*." *Journal of Popular Culture* 35.4 (Spring 2002): 89–102.

Falwell, Jerry. *America Can Be Saved*. Murfreesboro, TN: Sword of the Lord Publishers, 1979.

Farhi, Paul. "The Life of O'Reilly." *Washington Post*. 13 December 2000: C1.

Fellman, Anita Clair. *Little House, Long Shadow: Laura Ingalls Wilder's Impact on American Culture*. Columbia: U of Missouri P, 2008.

Ferrara, Peter. "Sarah Palin Outsmarts the Left." FoxForum. FoxNews.com. 4 July 2009. <http://www.foxnews.com/opinion/2009/07/04/sarah-palin-outsmarts-left/> 6 August 2009.

Fink, Mitchell. With Emily Guest. "Virtues of Change." *New York Daily News*. 12 May 1999. <http://www.nydailynews.com/archives/gossip/1999/05/02/1999–05–02_virtues_ of_change.html> 6 March 2009.

Foege, Alec. *Right of the Dial: The Rise of Clear Channel and the Fall of Commercial Radio*. New York: Faber and Faber, 2008.

Forbes, Bruce David, and Jeanne Halgren Kilde. Introduction. *Rapture, Revelation and the End Times: Exploring the Left Behind Series*. Ed. Bruce David Forbes and Jeanne Halgren Kilde. New York: Palgrave, 2004. 1–32.

Ford, Marcia. "Finding Help on the Shelves." *Publisher's Weekly*. 23 May 2005: 2–4. Foundation Center. 990 Finder. American Enterprise Institute. Years 2002–2006. <http://dynamodata.fdncenter.org/990s/990search/esearch.php> 30 January 2009.

Frank, Thomas. "Conservatism Isn't Finished." *Wall Street Journal*. 5 November 2008. <http://online.wsj.com/article/SB122584338026799165.html> 6 November 2008.

——. *What's the Matter with Kansas?: How Conservatives Won the Heart of America*. New York: Harcourt College, 2004.

Franken, Al. *Lies and the Lying Liars Who Tell Them: A Fair and Balanced Look at the Right*. New York: Dutton, 2003.

FreedomWorks. <http://www.freedomworks.org/> 28 August 2008.

Fretwell, Holly. *The Sky's Not Falling!: Why It's OK to Chill about Global Warming*. Los Angeles: World Ahead/Kids Ahead, 2007.

"From Soapbox to Sandbox: Politics in Picture Books." *Publisher's Weekly*. Children's Book Reviews. 11 August 2008. <http://www.publishersweekly.com/article/CA6585441. html> 28 November 2008.

Frum, David. "Why the GOP Lost the Youth Vote." *USA Today*. 9 April 2008. <http://blogs. usatoday.com/oped/2008/04/why-the-gop-1 -1.html> 18 December 2008. (Also posted on the website for the American Enterprise Institute. See: Short Publications. 9 April 2008. <http://www.aei.org/publications/pubID.27777,filter.all/pub_detail.asp>)

Frykholm, Amy Johnson. *Rapture Culture: Left Behind in Evangelical America*. Oxford: Oxford UP, 2004.

Gallup, Inc. "Americans' Satisfaction at New All-Time Low of 7%." 15 October 2008. <http://www.gallup.com/poll/111169/Americans-Satisfaction-New-AllTime-Low. aspx> 18 November 2008.

——. "Bush's Job Approval at 25%, His Lowest Yet." 6 October 2008. <http://www.gallup. com/poll/110980/Bush-Job-Approval-25-Lowest-Yet.aspx> 18 November 2008.

Gandhi, Mahatma. *Mahatma Gandhi: Essential Writings*. 3rd ed. Ed. John Dear. Maryknoll, NY: Orbis Books, 2004.

Garner, James Finn. *Politically Correct Bedtime Stories: Modern Tales for Our Life and Times*. New York: Macmillan, 1994.

Garofoli, Joe. "Local Leaders Unleash Vitriol at O'Reilly." *San Francisco Chronicle*. *12 November 2005*. <http://www.sfgate.com/cgibin/article.cgi?f=/c/a/2005/11/12/COIT. TMP> 20 October 2008.

Garrity, Brian. "$400 Million-Mouth: Clear Channel Gives Limbaugh Record-Setting Deal." *New York Post*. 3 July 2008. <http://www.nypost.com/seven/07032008/busi-ness/400_million_mouth_118341.htm> 9 November 2008.

Gay, Jason. "Fox News Superstar Bill O'Reilly Wants to Oppose Hillary in 2006!" *New York Observer*. 9 April 2006. <http://www.observer.com/node/52060> 20 October 2008.

Gerth, Jeff, and Don Van Natta Jr. "In Tough Times, a Company Finds Profits in Terror War." *New York Times*. 13 July 2002. <http://query.nytimes.com/gst/fullpage.html ?res=9A03E1D91E30F930A25754C0A9649C8B63&sec=&spon=&pagewanted=1> 12 February 2009.

Gillespie, Nick. "Suffer the Little Children." *Reason* 38.1 (2006): 64–65.

Gillette, Felix. "The Crying Game: I'm Sad as Hell and I'm Not Going to Take This Anymore!" *New York Observer*. 7 April 2009. <http://www.observer.com/2009/media/ crying-game-i%E2%80%99m-sad-hell-and-i%E2%80%99m-not-going-take-anymore> 19 April 2009.

Gillin, Beth. "Lynne Cheney: Upbeat Historian." *Philadelphia Inquirer*. 16 September 2003: D1.

Giroux, Henry A. "From *Manchild* to *Baby Boy*: Race and the Politics of Self-Help." *JAC* 22.3 (2002): 527–560.

——. *Stealing Innocence: Corporate Culture's War on Children*. New York: Palgrave, 2000.

Goldberg, Michelle. "Fundamentally Unsound." *Salon.com*. 29 July 2002.

Goldwater, Barry. *The Conscience of a Conservative*. Shepherdsville, KY: Victor Publishing Co., 1960.

Goldwin, Robert A. *Why Blacks, Women, and Jews Are Not Mentioned in the Constitution and Other Unorthodox Views*. Washington, D.C.: American Enterprise Institute, 1990.

Goode, Stephen. "Moral Makeover." *Insight on the News*. 15 May 1995: 6.

"GOP Moralist Bennett Gives Up Gambling." 5 May 2003. CNN.com. <http://www.cnn. com/2003/ALLPOLITICS/05/05/bennett.gambling/index.html>. 25 August 2008.

Gopnik, Adam. "Freeing the Elephants." *The New Yorker.* 22 September 2008. <http:// www.newyorker.com/reporting/2008/09/22/080922fa_fact_gopnik?printable=true 26 February 2009.

Gorey, Edward. *The Gashlycrumb Diaries; or, After the Outing.* New York: Houghton Mifflin, 1963.

Gorski, Eric. "Evangelicals Energized by McCain-Palin Ticket." Associated Press. 30 August 2008. Full-text also available at: http://www.politicalbase.com/news/evangelicals-energized-by-mccain-palin-ticket/122341/ 16 November 2008.

Gramsci, Antonio. *Prison Notebooks.* Ed. Joseph A. Buttigieg. New York: Columbia UP, 1991.

Green, Joshua. "The Bookie of Virtue." *Washington Monthly.* June 2003. <http://www.washingtonmonthly.com/features/2003/0306.green.html> 25 August 2008.

Griffith, Alicia. "Democrats, Beware: GOP Can Still Woo Youth Vote in Future Elections." *Washington Post.* Youth Vote '08: Next-Gen Election Coverage. Web. Politics: Opinion. 14 November 2008. <http://youthbvote.washingtonpost.com/2008/11/14/winning_over_the_youth_vote_this_election> 17 November 2008.

Grimm Brothers. "Little Red Cap." *The Classic Fairy Tales.* Ed. Maria Tatar. New York: W. W. Norton, 1999. 13–16.

Griswold, Jerry. "The Disappearance of Children's Literature (or Children's Literature as Nostalgia) in the United States in the Late Twentieth Century." *Reflections of Change: Children's Literature Since 1945.* Ed. Sandra Beckett. Westport, CT: Greenwood, 1997. 35–41.

Grossberg, Lawrence. *Caught in the Crossfire: Kids, Politics, and America's Future.* Boulder: Paradigm, 2005.

Gusfield, Joseph. *Symbolic Crusade: Status Politics and the American Temperance Movement.* Champaign-Urbana: U of Illinois P, 1986.

Haase, Donald. "German Fairy Tales and American Culture Wars: From Grimm's *Kinder- und Hausmärchen* to William Bennett's *Book of Virtues.*" *German Politics and Society* 13.3 (Fall 1995): 17–25.

Hade, Daniel. "Storyselling: Are Publishers Changing the Way Children Read?" *The Horn Book Magazine* (September/October 2002): 509–517.

Hale, Robert H. "Musings." *The Horn Book Magazine.* 69.2 (March/April 1993): 239.

Hannity, Sean. *Deliver Us From Evil: Defeating Terrorism, Despotism and Liberalism.* New York: Reagan Books, 2004.

Hannity and Colmes. "What Do Election Results Indicate?" By Sean Hannity and Alan Colmes. Guest Bill Bennett. Fox News Network. 4 November 2003. Transcript. Lexis-Nexis. Hollins University. 21 February 2009.

Harmon, Mark E., William K. Ferrell, and Jerry F. Franklin. "Effects on Carbon Storage of Conversion of Old-Growth Forests to Young Forests." *Science* 247.4943 (9 February 1990): 699–703.

Harshaw, Tobin. "Weekend Opinionator: Tea Parties, to the Extreme." *New York Times.* 17 April 2009. <http://opinionator.blogs.nytimes.com/2009/04/17/weekend-opinionator-tea-parties-to-the-extreme/> 18 April 2009.

Hart, Peter. With Fairness and Accuracy in Reporting (FAIR). *The Oh Really? Factor: Unspinning Fox News Channel's Bill O'Reilly.* New York: Seven Stories, 2003.

Hawkins, John. "In Defense of the Drug War." *Human Events Online.* 25 January 2007. Lexis-Nexis. Hollins University. 6 March 2009.

"Heavy Hundred." *Talkers Magazine*. June 2008. <http://talkers.com/main/index. php?option=com_content&task=view&id=19&Itemid=44> 3 October 2008.

Heilbrunn, Jacob. *They Knew They Were Right: The Rise of the Neocons*. New York: Bantam, 2008.

Helmore, Edward. "U.S. Schools Told Green Means Ugly." *The Observer* 9 June 1996: 24.

Helvarg, David. *The War Against the Greens: The 'Wise-Use' Movement, the New Right, and Anti-Environmental Violence*. San Francisco: Sierra Club, 1994.

Henderson, Bob, Merle Kennedy, and Chuck Chamberlin. "Playing Seriously with Dr. Seuss: A Pedagogical Response to *The Lorax*." *Wild Things: Children's Culture and Ecocriticism*. Ed. Sidney I. Dobrin and Kenneth B. Kidd. Detroit: Wayne State UP, 2004. 128–148.

Hendra, Tony. *The Book of Bad Virtues: A Treasury of Immorality*. New York: Pocket Books, 1994.

Henneberger, Melinda. "This Second Lady Is Keeping Her Day Job." *New York Times*. 6 February 2001: A1.

Hertzberg, Hendrik. "Talk of the Town: So Long, Pardner." *The New Yorker*. 4 May 2009: 17–18.

Heyman, Michael. "The Performative Letter, from Medieval to Modern." *Children's Literature Association Quarterly* 30.1 (Spring 2005): 100–107.

Higonnet, Anne. *Pictures of Innocence: The History and Crisis of Ideal Childhood*. New York: Thames and Hudson, 1998.

Himmelstein, Jerome L. *To the Right: The Transformation of American Conservatism*. Berkeley: U of California P, 1992.

Hine, Robert. *The American West: An Interpretive History*. Boston: Little, Brown, 1973.

Hixson, William B. Jr. *Search for the American Right Wing: An Analysis of the Social Science Record, 1955–1987*. Princeton, NJ: Princeton UP, 1992.

Hochschild, Arlie Russell. Book Jacket. *Self-Help, Inc.: Makeover Culture in American Life*. By Micki McGee. Oxford: Oxford UP, 2005.

Holthouse, David. "Culture War Heroes: William Bennett and the Right Make Might at a Scottsdale Resort." *Phoenix New Times* (Arizona). 27 May 1999. Lexis Nexis. Hollins University. 20 October 2008.

"Horton Hears a Chainsaw." *Harper's Magazine*. July 2001: 26–28.

Hunt, Peter. *Children's Literature: An Illustrated History*. New York: Oxford UP, 1995.

Ice-T. "Cop Killer." *Body Count*. Sire/Warner Brothers, 1992.

Imponeni, Mark. "Democrat's Strategy Backfires as Limbaugh's Ratings Double." 7 March 2009. <http://news.aol.com/political-machine/2009/03/07/democrats-strategy-backfires-as-limbaughs-ratings-double/> 18 April 2009.

An Inconvenient Truth. Dir. Davis Guggenheim. Perfs. Al Gore, Billy West. Paramount, 2006.

Jacoby, Susan. *The Age of American Unreason*. New York: Knopf, 2008.

Jefferson, Thomas. Letter to Danbury Baptist Association (Connecticut). 1 January 1802. <http://www.usconstitution.net/jeffwall.html> 2 July 2008.

Jenkins, Henry. *The Children's Culture Reader*. New York: NYU P, 1998.

Jenkins, Jerry B., and Tim LaHaye. *Left Behind: The Kids*. Vol. 1. *The Vanishings*. Wheaton, IL: Tyndale, 1998.

——. *Left Behind: The Kids*. Vol. 2. *Second Chance*. Wheaton, IL: Tyndale, 1998.

——. *Left Behind: The Kids*. Vol. 6. *The Underground*. Wheaton, IL: Tyndale, 1999.

——. *Left Behind: The Kids*. Vol. 11. *Into the Storm*. Wheaton, IL: Tyndale, 2000.

——. *Left Behind: The Kids*. Vol. 12. *Earthquake!* Wheaton, IL: Tyndale, 2000.

——. *Left Behind: The Kids*. Vol. 13. *The Showdown*. Wheaton, IL: Tyndale, 2001.

——. *Left Behind: The Kids*. Vol. 15. *Battling the Commander*. Wheaton, IL: Tyndale, 2001.

——. *Left Behind: The Kids*. Vol. 16. *Fire from Heaven*. Wheaton, IL: Tyndale, 2001.

——. *Left Behind: The Kids*. Vol. 17. *Terror in the Stadium*. Wheaton, IL: Tyndale, 2001.

——. *Left Behind: The Kids*. Vol. 18. *Darkening Skies*. Wheaton, IL: Tyndale, 2001.

——. *Left Behind: The Kids*. Vol. 23. *Horsemen of Terror*. Wheaton, IL: Tyndale, 2002.

——. *Left Behind: The Kids*. Vol. 24. *Uplink from the Underground*. Wheaton, IL: Tyndale, 2002.

The Jerry Springer Show. NBC. 1991–present.

John. "A Great Lesson for Kids." Customer review of *Help! Mom! There Are Liberals under My Bed!* 30 October 2005. <www.bn.com> 22 June 2007.

John, Judith Gero. "I Have Been Dying to Tell You: Early Advice Books for Children." *The Lion and the Unicorn* 29 (2005): 52–64.

Josephson Institute of Ethics. "The Ethics of American Youth: 2002 Report Card." 26 October 2002. <http://charactercounts.org/programs/reportcard/2002/index. html> 17 February 2009.

——. "The Ethics of American Youth: 2004 Report Card." October 2004. <http://character-counts.org/programs/reportcard/2004/index.html> 17 February 2009.

Judd, Diana M. "Tearing Down the Wall: Conservative Use and Abuse of Religion in Politics." *Confronting the New Conservatism: The Rise of the Right in America*. Ed. Michael J. Thompson. New York: NYU P, 2007. 125–143.

Kahn, Peter H. Jr., and Ashley Weld. "Environmental Education: Toward an Intimacy with Nature." *Isle: Interdisciplinary Studies in Literature and Environment* 3.2 (Fall 1996): 165–168.

Kakutani, Michiko. "To Stars, Writing Books Looks Like Child's Play." *New York Times*. 23 October 2003. E1.

Kelly, Keith J. "It's OK! And Out for Ivens." 26 September 2008. <http://www.nypost. com/seven/09262008/business/its_ok__and_out_for_ivens_130802.htm?page=0> 20 February 2009.

Kesner, Julian. "Take That, H'Wood!: Parody Book for Kids Tries to 'Hamper' Filmdom's Style." *New York Daily News*. 9 March 2006: 43.

Keynes, Edward, with Randall K. Miller. *The Court vs. Congress: Prayer, Busing, and Abortion*. Durham: Duke UP, 1989.

Kincaid, James. *Child-Loving: The Erotic Child and Victorian Culture*. New York: Routledge, 1994.

Kirk, Russell. *The Conservative Mind: From Burke to Eliot*. Chicago: Regnery, 1953.

Kirkus Reviews. "Book Review: *The New Case Against Immigration: Both Legal and Illegal*." *Kirkus Reviews* 76.10 (15 May 2008): 99.

Knight, Rebecca. "Hey Bill Bennett! You Are the Outrage!" 13 May 2003. <http://www. buzzflash.com/southern/03/05/13.html> 30 October 2008.

Konty. "Whither Pluralism?" 20 September 2005. <http://right-mind.us/blogs/blog_0/ archive/2005/09/20/36639.aspx> 22 June 2007.

Krieger, Doug. "Why the Dems Can't Stand Tom DeLay and Tim LaHaye." 19 June 2005. <http://www.buzzle.com/editorials/6–18–2005–71780.asp> 20 June 2008.

Krikorian, Mark. *The New Case Against Immigration: Both Legal and Illegal*. New York: Sentinel, 2008.

Kropf, Schuyler. "Ammo Flying Off Shelves: Fears of Crackdown Prompt Sales Boost." *The Post and Courier* (Charleston, SC). 1 April 2009: A1.

Kurtz, Howard. "15 Years Later, the Remaking of a President." *Washington Post*. 7 June 2004: C1.

——. "Bill O'Reilly, Producer Settle Harassment Suit." *Washington Post.* 29 October 2004: C1.

——. "Healthy Debate." *Washington Post.* 6 March 2009. Lexis Nexis. Hollins University. 19 April 2009.

——. "O'Reilly: You'll Still Have Me to Kick Around." *Washington Post.* 22 October 2008: C1.

LaHaye, Tim. *The Battle for the Family.* Old Tappan, NJ: Fleming H. Revell, 1982.

——. *The Battle for the Mind: A Subtle Warfare.* Old Tappan, NJ: Revell, 1980.

——. *The Hidden Censors.* Old Tappan, NJ: Fleming H. Revell, 1984.

——. "The Prophetic Significance of Sept. 11, 2001." *Pre-Trib Perspectives* 6.7 (2001): 1–4. Available via cached version of <http://www.timlahaye.com/about_ministry/pdf/lahaye_sept11.pdf>

——. *The Race for the 21st Century.* Nashville: Thomas Nelson, 1986.

——. "Tim's Pre-Trib Perspective." *Pre-Trib Perspectives.* 6.10 (2002): 1–3.

——. *The Unhappy Gays: What Everyone Should Know About Homosexuality.* Wheaton, IL: Tyndale House, 1978.

Langbauer, Laurie. "The Ethics and Practice of Lemony Snicket: Adolescence and Generation X." *PMLA* 122. 2 (2007): 502–521.

LaRosa, John. "Self-Improvement Market in U.S. Worth $9.6 Billion." *PRWeb: Press Release Newswire.* PRWeb. 21 September 2006. Web. <http://www.prwebdirect.com/releases/2006/9/prweb440011.php> 16 February 2009.

Larrick, Nancy. "The All-White World of Children's Books." *Saturday Review* 48 (11 September 1965): 63–65, 84–85.

The Late Show with David Letterman. CBS. 13 November 2002. Transcript. Posted by Michael Z. McIntee. 14 November 2002 <http://lateshow.cbs.com/latenight/lateshow/wahoo/index/php/20021113.phtml> 16 February 2009.

Lauter, Paul. "History and the Canon." *Social Text* 12 (August 1985): 94–101.

Lears, T. J. Jackson. *No Place of Grace: Antimodernism and the Transformation of American Culture, 1880–1920.* Chicago: U of Chicago P, 1981.

Lebduska, Lisa. "Rethinking Human Need: Seuss's *The Lorax.*" *Children's Literature Association Quarterly* 19.4 (Winter 1994–1995): 170–176.

Leibovich, Mark. "At Rallies of Faithful, Contrasts in Red and Blue." *New York Times.* 30 October 2008. <http://www.nytimes.com/2008/10/30/us/politics/30trail.html> 22 February 2009.

Left Behind Games. "The Games FAQ." February 2007. <www.leftbehindgames.com.> 27 June 2008.

Lesnik-Oberstein, Karin. "Children's Literature and the Environment." *Writing the Environment: Ecocriticism and Literature.* Ed. Richard Kerridge and Neil Sammells. London: Zed, 1998. 208–217.

"Lesson Plan and Student Worksheet: *Truax.*" National Oak Flooring Manufacturers Association. <www.nofma.org> 5 May 2008.

Lincoln, Abraham (and Stephen A. Douglas). *The Complete Lincoln-Douglas Debates of 1858.* Ed. Paul M. Angle. Chicago: U of Chicago P, 1991.

Lindberg, Tod. "The Center-Right Nation Exits Stage Left." *Washington Post.* 16 November 2008: B1.

Lindenpütz, Dagmar. "Children's Literature as a Medium of Environmental Education." *The Culture of German Environmentalism: Anxieties, Visions, Realities.* Ed. Axel Goodbody. New York: Berghahn, 2002. 187–201.

Lipset, Seymour Martin, and Earl Raab. *The Politics of Unreason: Right-Wing Extremism in America, 1790–1977.* Chicago: U of Chicago P, 1978.

Lisberg, Adam. "Judge is In Immig Groups' Bad Books." *New York Daily News*. 27 November 2006. Factiva / ProQuest. 6 November 2008.

The Littlest Groom. Hosted by Dani Behr. Fox. 2004.

Lowry, Tom. "The "O'Reilly Factory: The Conservative Commentator Has Spawned a $60 Million-a-Year Empire." *BusinessWeek*. 8 March 2004. <http://www.businessweek. com/magazine/content/04_10/b3873092_mz016.htm.> 22 December 2008.

"Lynne Cheney Returning to American Enterprise Institute." AEI Press Release. American Enterprise Institute. 5 January 2001. <http://www.aei.org/publications/ pubID.15392,filter.all/pub_detail.asp> 12 February 2009.

MacDonald, Ruth. *Dr. Seuss*. New York: Twayne, 1988.

MacLeod, Anne Scott. *American Childhood: Essays on Children's Literature of the Nineteenth and Twentieth Centuries*. Athens: U of Georgia P, 1994.

MacPherson, Karen. "Patriotic Page Turners Sparkle for July 4." *Pittsburgh Post-Gazette*. 2 July 2002: D4.

Mahoney, Michelle. "The Values Debate: Common Ground is Elusive." *Denver Post*. 27 November 1995: F01.

Mandate for Leadership: Policy Management in a Conservative Administration. Ed. Charles Heatherly. Washington, D.C.: The Heritage Foundation, 1981.

Mapes, Jeff. "Look! See Dick Cut Benefits! See Jane Tax and Spend!" *The Oregonian*. 21 December 2005: A1.

Marikar, Sheila, and Luchina Fisher. "Did Palin's 'SNL' Stunt Make Any Difference?" 20 October 2008. <http://abcnews.go.com/entertainment/story?id=6068388& page=1> 16 November 2008.

Marinucci, Carla. "Poll: Young Voters Disenchanted with Republican Party." 27 August 2007. *San Francisco Chronicle*. <http://www.sfgate.com/cgi-bin/article.cgi?f=/c/ a/2007/08/27/MNMIRNDUK.DTL> 19 November 2008.

Marshall, Ian S. "The Lorax and the Ecopolice." *ISLE: Interdisciplinary Studies in Literature and Environment* 2.2 (Winter 1996): 85–92.

Maughan, Shannon. "Moving On Up: A Look Behind Some Current Bestsellers." *Publishers Weekly*. 29 July 2002: 26.

Mayer, Jane. "The Insiders: How John McCain Came to Pick Sarah Palin." *The New Yorker*. 27 October 2008. <http://www.newyorker.com/reporting/2008/10/27/081027fa_fact_ mayer?currentPage=1　16 November 2008.

McCain, Meghan. *My Dad, John McCain*. New York: Simon & Schuster, 2008.

McEvoy, Dermot. "Something New, Something Old." *Publisher's Weekly*. 27 March 2006. <http://www.publishersweekly.com/article/CA6318931.html?q=%220%27reilly+fact or+for+kids%22+sales> 16 February 2009.

McGann, James G. *The Competition for Dollars, Scholars and Influence in The Public Policy Research Industry*. Lanham, MD: University Press of America, 1995.

McGann, James G., with Erik K. Johnson. *Comparative Think Tanks, Politics and Public Policy*. Cheltenham, UK: Edward Elgar, 2005.

McGee, Micki. *Self-Help, Inc.: Makeover Culture in American Life*. New York: Oxford UP, 2005.

McKinley, Jesse, and Laurie Goodstein. "Bans in 3 States on Gay Marriage." *New York Times*. 6 November 2008: A1.

McQuade, Molly, and Sybil S. Steinberg. "Untitled." *Publishers Weekly* 240.26 (28 June 1993): 74.

Meadows, Donella. "Loggers' Seuss Takeoff Is a Caricature." *Charleston Gazette*. 19 October 1998: A4.

"Media Matters Exposes Bennett: '[Y]ou Could Abort Every Black Baby in This Country, and Your Crime Rate Would Go Down.'" 28 September 2005. <http://mediamatters.org/items/200509280006> 28 October 2008.

Media Transparency. "American Enterprise Institute for Public Policy Research." <http://www.mediatransparency.org/recipientprofile.php?recipientID=19> 12 February 2009.

Mickenberg, Julia. *Learning from the Left: Children's Literature, the Cold War, and Radical Politics in the United States*. Oxford: Oxford UP, 2006.

Mickenberg, Julia, and Philip Nel. "Introduction: What's Left?" *Children's Literature Association Quarterly* 30. 4. (Winter 2005): 349–353.

Micklethwait, John, and Adrian Woodbridge. *The Right Nation: Conservative Power in America*. New York: Penguin, 2005.

Mieville, China. "Trick Business for Young Ecologists. *TES Magazine*. 13 April 2007. <http://www.tes.co.uk/article.aspx?storycode=2369614> 15 February 2009.

Miller, Toby, and Alec McHoul. "Helping the Self." *Social Text* 16.4 (Winter 1998): 127–155.

Moje, Elizabeth B., and Woan-Ru Shyu. "Oh, the Places You've Taken Us: *RT*'s Tribute to Dr. Seuss." *The Reading Teacher* 45.9 (May 1992): 670–676.

Mondale, Sarah, and Sarah B. Patton, eds. *School: The Story of American Public Education*. Boston: Beacon, 2001.

Moniz, Dave. "Monthly Costs of Iraq, Afghan Wars Approach That of Vietnam." *USA Today*. 7 September 2003. <http://www.usatoday.com/news/world/iraq/2003–09–07-cover-costs_x.htm> 11 April 2009.

Moore, Scott. "William Bennett Takes His 'Virtues' to Hollywood." *Palm Beach Post*. 29 August 1996: 5E.

Moran, Caitlin. "Tina Fey and Sarah Silverman: The New Queens of Comedy." *Times Online* (UK). 3 October 2008. <http://entertainment.timesonline.co.uk/tol/arts_and_entertainment/stage/comedy/article4869771.ece> 16 November 2008.

Moran, Chris. "Education or Indoctrination?: Motives Questioned for Some Lessons Kids Taught on Environment." *San Diego Union-Tribune*. 13 May 2002: A1.

Morgan, Judith, and Neil Morgan. *Dr. Seuss and Mr. Geisel: A Biography*. New York: Da Capo Press, 1995.

Morley, Thomas. *Discipline Through Virtue: A Discipline Approach That Assists Teachers and Parents in the Effective Use of "The Book of Virtues."* Sugar City, Idaho: ThoMax, 1995. *Morning in America*. Host William Bennett. Audio recording. Originally broadcast on 28 September 2005. <http://mediamatters.org/items/200509280006> 2 October 2007.

Morris, Dick, and Eileen McGann. "Palin Wins Big with Reagan-Like Flair." *New York Post*. 3 October 2008. <http://www.nypost.com/seven/10032008/postopinion/opedcolumnists/palin_wins_big_with_a_reagan_like_flair_131936.htm> 16 November 2008.

Muir, Patirica S. "What Is Happening to the Global Area of Forests?" 18 November 2002. <http://oregonstate.edu/~muirp/fortrends.htm> 20 August 2008.

Murray, William James. *The Right-Wing Press in the French Revolution: 1789–92*. London: Boydell Press for the Royal Historical Society, 1986.

Myers, Mitzi, and U. C. Knoepflmacher. "From the Editors: 'Cross-Writing' and the Reconceptualization of Children's Literary Studies." *Children's Literature* 25 (1997): vii–xvii.

Nash, George H. *The Conservative Intellectual Movement in America, Since 1945*. 30th anniv ed. Wilmington, DE: Intercollegiate Studies Institute, 2006.

National Park Service. "Designation of National Park System Units." 28 March 2000. <http://www.nps.gov/legacy/nomenclature.html> 19 August 2008.

National Public Radio. *Talk of the Nation.* Host Steve Inskeep. Guest Philip Nel. 10 February 2004. Transcript. LexisNexis. Hollins University. 20 August 2008.

"Nationwide 'Tea Party' Protests Blast Spending." CNN. Online. 15 April 2009. <http://www.cnn.com/2009/POLITICS/04/15/tea.parties/index.html> 18 April 2009.

Neal, Steve, and Lynn Sweet. "GOP Hasn't Looked So Good in Years. *Chicago Sun-Times.* 6 August 2000: 22.

Neary, Ben. "Few of New Regs Drive Gun, Ammo Shortage." Associated Press. 29 May 2009. Lexis Nexis. Hollins University. 17 April 2009.

Nel, Philip. *Dr. Seuss: American Icon.* New York: Continuum, 2004.

——. "Is There a Text in This Advertising Campaign?: Literature, Marketing and Harry Potter." *The Lion and the Unicorn* 29 (2005): 236–267.

The New England Primer: Improved for the More Easy Attaining the True Reading of English: To Which Is Added the Assembly of Divines, and Mr. Cotton's Catechism. 1777. Springfield: G. and C. Merriam, 1844.

"Newsmakers: Second Lady Penning a Primer." *Houston Chronicle.* 12 October 2001: A2.

NewsMax. "Hilary Clinton Irked by Children's Book," 18 November 2005. <www.newsmax.com> 31 May 2007.

"Newspaper Column List." <http://www.billoreilly.com/pg/jsp/general/newspapercolumn.jsp> 27 October 2008.

New York Stock Exchange. "Dow Jones Industrial Average (DIJA) History." Web. <http://www.nyse.tv/dow-jones-industrial-average-history-djia.htm> 17 December 2008.

Nikolajeva, Maria, and Carole Scott. *How Picturebooks Work.* New York: Garland, 2001.

Nissbaum, Martha. "Divided We Stand." *The New Republic.* 10 January 1994: 38.

Noble, Charles. "From Neoconservative to New Right: American Conservatives and the Welfare State." *Confronting the New Conservatism: The Rise of the Right in America.* Ed. Michael J. Thompson. New York: NYU P, 2007. 109–124.

O'Conner, Colleen. "'Left Behind' Co-Creator Transcends Religious Realm to Mass Market." *Denver Post.* 10 April 2005. *LexisNexis.* Hollins University. 16 June 2008. <http://lexis-nexis.com/>

Oldenburg, Don. "Kids and Morals in a Me-First World." *Washington Post.* 25 March 1988: D5.

Olson, Walter. "William Bennett, Gays, and the Truth: Mr. Virtue Dabbles in Phony Statistics." Independent Gay Forum. 18 December 1997. <http://www.indegayforum.org/show/26857.html> 28 August 2008.

"One State, Two State, Red State, Blue State." *The Daily Show.* With Jon Stewart. Comedy Central. 3 October 2007.

O'Reilly, Bill. *A Bold Fresh Piece of Humanity: A Memoir.* New York: Broadway, 2008.

——. *Cultural Warrior.* New York: Broadway, 2006.

——. *The No-Spin Zone: Confrontations with the Powerful and Famous in America.* New York: Broadway, 2001.

——. *The O'Reilly Factor: The Good, the Bad, and the Completely Ridiculous in American Life.* New York: Random House, 2000.

——. *Who's Looking Out for You?* New York: Bantam, 2003.

O'Reilly, Bill, and Charles Flowers. *Kids Are Americans Too.* New York: HarperCollins, 2007.

——. *The O'Reilly Factor for Kids: A Survival Guide for America's Families.* New York: Harper-Collins, 2004.

The O'Reilly Factor. Hosted by Bill O'Reilly. Fox News Network. 17 May 2002. Transcript. Lexis Nexis. Hollins University. 25 October 2008.

———. Hosted by Bill O'Reilly. Fox News Network. 4 February 2003. Transcript. Lexis Nexis. Hollins University. 20 October 2008.

———. Hosted by Bill O'Reilly. Fox News Network. 17 March 2003. Transcript. Lexis Nexis. Hollins University. 25 October 2008.

———. Hosted by Bill O'Reilly. Fox News Network. 4 February 2003. Transcript. Lexis Nexis. Hollins University. 16 February 2009.

———. Hosted by Bill O'Reilly. Fox News Network. 5 May 2003. Transcript. Lexis Nexis. Hollins University. 1 November 2008.

———. Hosted by Bill O'Reilly. Fox News Network. 6 June 2005. Transcript. Lexis Nexis. Hollins University. 28 October 2008.

———. Hosted by Bill O'Reilly. Fox News Network. 21 February 2008. Transcript. Lexis Nexis. Hollins University. 20 October 2008.

"*The O'Reilly Factor for Kids*: Winner of the 2005 Juvenile Non-Fiction Bestseller Award Presented by The Book Standard and Nielsen Bookscan." *Business Wire.* 26 September 2005. LexisNexis. Hollins University. 16 February 2009.

"*The O'Reilly Factor for Kids*: Winner of the 2005 Juvenile Non-Fiction Bestseller Award Presented by The Book Standard and Nielsen Bookscan." *Business Wire.* 26 September 2005. LexisNexis. Hollins University. 21 September 2008.

Origen, Erich, and Gan Golan. *Goodnight Bush.* New York: Little, Brown, 2008.

Packer, George. "The Fall of Conservatism." *The New Yorker.* 26 May 2008: 47–55.

Page, Susan. "Lynne Cheney Writing Primer on Patriotism, Letter by Letter." 16 October 2001. *USA Today.* Life section, pg. 1D. 2 May 2008.

Paybarah, Azi. "Under the Covers, Conservative-Style," *New York Press.* 21 September 2005 <http://www.nypress.com/print.cfm?content_id=13767> 31 May 2007.

"PBS Becomes Adventurous and 'Virtuous' in Prime Time." *Selling to Kids* 1.3 (16 October 1996). Lexis Nexis. Hollins University. 17 November 2008.

Peale, Norman Vincent. *The Power of Positive Thinking.* 1952. Greenwich, CT: Fawcett, 1990.

Pellegrom, Daniel. "A Deadly Global Gag Rule." *New York Times.* 27 January 2001. Full text available at: <http://www.jessejacksonjr.org/query/creadpr.cgi?id=2419> 21 April 2009.

Pennefather, Therese. "Re: A Research Question." Email to Joan Ruelle, Hollins University Librarian. 9 February 2009.

Philo, Simon. "Ricki Lake." *Encyclopedia of Popular Culture.* vol. 3. Ed. Tom Pendergast and Sara Pendergast. Detroit: St. James Press, 2000. 78–79.

Pilkington, Ed. "Once Upon a Time." *The Guardian.* 3 November 2006. <http://books.guardian.co.uk/departments/childrenandteens/story/0,,1938506,00.html> 5 May 2008.

Political Economy Research Institute. "Toxic 100: Top Corporate Air Polluters in the United States; Largest Corporations Ranked by Toxic Score, 2002." <http://www.peri.umass.edu/Toxic-100-Table.265.0.html> 12 August 2008.

Porter, Jean. "Book Review: *The Book of Virtues.*" *Christian Century.* 5 October 1994: 896.

Powell, Jim. *FDR's Folly: How Roosevelt and His New Deal Prolonged the Great Depression.* New York: Random House, 2004.

"President Map." Election Results 2008. *New York Times.* 14 November 2008. <http://elections.nytimes.com/2008/results/president/map.html> 16 November 2008.

Provenzo, Eugene Jr. *Religious Fundamentalism and American Education: The Battle for the Public Schools.* Albany: SUNY P, 1990.

Pulp Fiction. Dir. Quentin Tarantino. Perfs. John Travolta, Samuel L. Jackson, Uma Thurman, Bruce Willis, Ving Rhames. Miramax, 1994.

The Radio Factor with Bill O'Reilly. Hosted by Bill O'Reilly. Westwood One. 19 September 2007. Transcript and Sound Clip available via Media Matters: <http://mediamatters. org/items/200709210007>16 February 2009.

——. Hosted by Bill O'Reilly. Westwood One. 19 February 2008. Transcript and sound clip available via Media Matters: <http://mediamatters.org/items/200802200001> 16 February 2009.

——. Hosted by Bill O'Reilly. Westwood One. 25 September 2008. Transcript and sound clip available via Media Matters: <http://mediamatters.org/items/200809250021>. 15 February 2009.

Radosh, Daniel. *Rapture Ready!: Adventures in the Parallel Universe of Christian Pop Culture*. New York: Scribner, 2008.

Ramstad, Evan. "Gangsta Rap Knocked at Time Warner Annual Meeting." Associated Press. 19 May 1995. LexisNexis. Hollins University. 18 November 2008.

Reagan, Ronald. "Address to Members of the British Parliament." Speech delivered 8 June 1982. John T. Woolley and Gerhard Peters, *The American Presidency Project* [online]. Santa Barbara: University of California (hosted), Gerhard Peters (database). Available from World Wide Web: <http://www.presidency.ucsb.edu/ws/?pid=76121>. 15 December 2008.

——. "A Time for Choosing." Speech delivered 27 October 1964. John T. Woolley and Gerhard Peters, *The American Presidency Project* [online]. Santa Barbara: University Of California (hosted), Gerhard Peters (database). Available from World Wide Web: <http://www.presidency.ucsb.edu/ws/?pid=76121>. 15 December 2008.

Republican National Committee. *Contract with America*. 1994. United States House of Representatives. <http://www.house.gov/house/Contract/CONTRACT.html> 17 Dec. 2008.

Reservoir Dogs. Dir. Quentin Tarantino. Perf. Harvey Keitel, Tim Roth, Michael Madsen, Steve Buscemi. Miramax, 1992.

Reynolds, Kimberley. *Radical Children's Literature: Future Visions and Aesthetic Transformations in Juvenile Fiction*. London: Palgrave Macmillan, 2007.

Ricci, David M. *The Transformation of American Politics: The New Washington and the Rise of Think Tanks*. New Haven: Yale UP, 1993.

Rice, Harvey. "Lawsuit Claims Students Not Allowed to Carry Bibles. *Houston Chronicle*. 23 May 2000. <http://www.chron.com/cs/CDA/story.hts/metropolitan/560670> 30 June 2008.

Rich, Andrew. *Think Tanks, Public Policy, and the Politics of Expertise*. Cambridge: Cambridge UP, 2004.

"Right wing." *The Oxford English Dictionary*. vol. 13. 2nd ed. 1989: 937.

"Rightist." *The Oxford English Dictionary*. vol. 13. 2nd ed. 1989: 935.

Rogers, John. "Teaching Children Virtue—A Cartoon Show William Bennett's Way." Associated Press. 11 April 1997. Lexis Nexis. Hollins University. 18 November 2008.

Rogge, Benjamin A. "Note on the Election." *New Individualist Review*. 3.4 (Spring 1965): 28–29.

Romines, Ann. "*The Long Winter*: An Introduction to Western Womanhood." *Great Plains Quarterly* 10 (Winter 1990): 36–47.

Rose, Jacqueline. *The Case of Peter Pan, or The Impossibility of Children's Literature*. Philadelphia: U of Pennsylvania P, 1984.

Ross, Suzanne. "Response to 'The Lorax and the Ecopolice' by Ian Marshall." ISLE: Interdisciplinary Studies in Literature and Environment 2.2 (Winter 1996): 99–104.

Russert, Tim. Big Russ and Me—Father and Lesson: Lessons of Life. New York: Miramax, 2004.

Saloma, John S. III. Ominous Politics: The New Conservative Labyrinth. New York: Hill and Wang, 1986.

Sandler, Lauren. Righteous: Dispatches from the Evangelical Youth Movement. New York: Viking, 2006.

Saturday Night Live. Transcripts. Episode aired 27 September 2008. Skit "CBS Evening News." NBC. <http://snltranscripts.jt.org/08/08cpalin.phtml> 17 December 2008.

Schenck, Theresa. Introduction to "Scarface." Algonquian Spirit: Contemporary Translations of the Algonquian Literatures of North America. Ed. Brian Swann. Lincoln: U of Nebraska P, 2005. 495–500.

Schipper, David. Sellout: The Inside Story of President Clinton's Impeachment. Washington, D.C.: Regnery, 2000.

Schmidt, Susan. "An Outspoken Spouse: Lynne Cheney Not Likely to Fade into the Background." Washington Post. 27 July 2000: A1.

Schmunk, Gail. American Children's Literature and the Construction of Childhood. New York: Twayne, 1998.

Schneider, George A. "Millions of Moral Little Books: Sunday School Books in Their Popular Context." New Dimensions in Popular Culture. Ed. Russel B. Nye. Bowling Green, OH: Bowling Green UP, 1972. 1–30.

"Schools Give Character Another Try; Education Chairman Takes Look at Character Teaching in Schools." Spokesman Review. 13 December 1999: A7.

"Scholarly Editions in Jeopardy." New York Times. Editorial Desk. 21 October 2000: 14.

Schrager, Cynthia D. "Questioning the Promise of Self-Help: A Reading of 'Women Who Love Too Much." Feminist Studies 19.1 (Spring 1993): 177–192.

Schraub, David. "Help Mom!" The Moderate Voice. 28 June 2006. <http://themoderatevoice. com/date/2006/06/page/2/> 31 May 2007.

Schulman, Miriam. "Moral Literacy: The Virtue of The Book of Virtues." The Mark Kula Center for Applied Ethics. Santa Clara University. Posted Online. <http://www.scu. edu/ethics/publications/iie/v7n1/bennett.html> 6 March 2009.

Sedgwick, Eve Kosofsky. Novel Gazing: Queer Readings in Fiction. Durham: Duke UP, 1997.

"A Selection of the Most Blogged-About Books of 2005." New York Times. 18 December 2005, <http://www.nytimes.com/ref/books/blogged-books.html> 26 June 2007.

"Seth Leibsohn." About Us: Fellows and Staff. The Claremont Institute. Web. <http://www. claremont.org/scholars/scholarID.39/scholar.asp> 21 February 2009.

Seuss, Dr. Horton Hears a Who! New York: Random House, 1954.

——. The Lorax. New York: Random House, 1971.

——. The Sneetches. New York: Random House, 1961.

——. Yertle the Turtle and Other Stories. New York: Random House, 1958.

Seymour, Jack L. From Sunday School to Church School. Lanham, MD: UP of America, 1982.

Shafer, Jack. "Bill O'Reilly Wants You to Shut Up." Slate. 28 August 2003. <http://www.slate. com/id/2087706/> 20 October 2008.

Sheff, David. "Bill O'Reilly: A Candid Conversation with TV's Most Pugnacious Newsman, about Gays and Gun Control, His War with George Clooney, Skewering the Red Cross, and that Hilary Clinton Doormat." Playboy. 1 May 2002: 59.

Shipman, Tim. "Sarah Palin Blamed by the U.S. Secret Service over Death Threats Against

Barack Obama." *London Telegraph.* 10 November 2008. <http://www.telegraph.co.uk/news/newstopics/uselection2008/sarahpalin/3405336/Sarah-Palin-blamed-by-the-US-Secret-Service-for-death-threats-against-Barack-Obama.html> 22 February 2009.

Showalter, Elaine. "Lynne Cheney, Feminist Intellectual?" *The Chronicle of Higher Education.* 29 September 2000. <http://chronicle.com/weekly/v47/i05/05b01101.htm> 2 May 2008.

Simon, Roger. "Gingrich Says GOP Is Outmatched." *Politico.* 13 November 2008. <http://www.politico.com/news/stories/1108/15563.html> 18 November 2008.

Simon, Stephanie. "Help Wanted: Left College Seeks Right-Wing Prof." *Wall Street Journal.* 13 May 2008. <http://online.wsj.com/article/SB121062988605186401.html> 3 November 2008.

Siriano, A. M. "An Interview with Katharine DeBrecht." *Intellectual Conservative.* 28 September 2005. <http://www.intellectualconservative.com/artcile4625.html> 31 May 2007.

Smith, Michael R. "Left Behind: Author LaHaye Sues Left Behind Film Producers." *Christianity Today.* 23 April 2001. <http://www.christianitytoday.com/ct/2001/april123/14.20.html> 24 June 2008.

Soper, J. Christopher. "The Politics of Pragmatism: The Christian Right and the 1994 Elections." *Midterm: The 1994 Election in Context.* Ed. Philip A. Klinkner. Boulder, CO: Westview Press, 1996. 115–124.

Special Guests. "Clinton Bans Sugary Drinks!" 3 May 2006. <http://special-guests.com> 31 May 2007.

——. "Is the Democratic Party Imploding?" 31 May 2006. <http://special-guests.com> 31 May 2007.

——. "Ebay Auction Raises $3540 to Send Hillary To Jail!" 31 May 2006. <http://special-guests.com> 31 May 2007.

——. "Hillary Unhinged by 'Liberals under My Bed' Kids' Book." 4 November 2005. <http://special-guests.com> 31 May 2007.

——. "Rush Limbaugh Applauds New Kids' Book." 21 September 2005. <http://special-guests.com> 31 May 2007.

Stanfield, Rochelle L. "The V-Word." *The National Journal* 26.22 (28 May 1994): 1235–38.

Stefancic, Jean, and Richard Delgado. *No Mercy: How Conservative Think Tanks and Foundations Changed America's Social Agenda.* Philadelphia: Temple UP, 1996.

Stille, Alexander. "Children's Books: Of Thee I Sing." *New York Times.* 19 May 2002. Book review section (section 7, column 1): 20.

Strange, Hannah. "Who Is Sarah Palin?" *Times* (London). Online. 29 August 2008. <http://www.timesonline.co.uk/tol/news/world/us_and_americas/article4635147.ece> 19 April 2009.

Stripling, Jack. "Western Expansion." *Inside Higher Ed.* Online. 21 April 2009. <http://www.insidehighered.com/layout/set/print/news/2009/04/21/white> 21 April 2009.

Sullivan, Eileen. "Obama Has More Death Threats Than Any Other Presidents-Elect." Associated Press. 15 November 2009. Full text available at: <http://www.guardian.co.uk/uslatest/story/0,,-8034349,00.html> 19 April 2009.

Sullivan, Jane. "Reading between the Product Lines; Turning Pages." *Sunday Age* (Australia). 2 July 2006: 28.

Sullivan, Kathleen, and Gerald Gunther. *Constitutional Law.* 13th ed. New York: Foundation Press, 1999.

Swain, Carol Miller. *The New White Nationalism in America: Its Challenge to Integration.* Cambridge: Cambridge UP, 2002.

Swinney, Geoffrey N., and Kate Charlesworth. *Fish Facts*. Edinburgh: National Museums of Scotland in Cooperation with the Sea Fish Industry, 1991.

Synopsis of *Help! Mom! There are Liberals Under My Bed!* No date of origin. <www.bn.com> 26 October 2007.

"Talk Radio Audience: 2003 and 2006 [chart]." Pew Research Center. The Project for Excellence in Journalism. Chapter: "Talk Radio." *The State of the News Media 2007: An Annual Report on American Journalism*. <http://www.stateofthe newsmedia.org/2007/narrative_radio_talk_radio.asp?cat=8&media=9 > 16 February 2009.

Tanenhaus, Sam. "A Once-United G.O.P. Emerges, in Identity Crisis." *New York Times*. 6 November 2008: P1.

Tapper, Jake. "The Willie Horton Alumni Association." *Salon.com* 25 August 2000. <http://archive.salon.com/politics/feature/2000/08/25/horton/index.html> 28 February 2009.

Tatum, Beverly Daniel. "Birthing Pains and the Emergence of a New Social Narrative." *Inside Higher Ed*. 13 November 2008. <http://www.insidehighed.com/views/2008/11/13/tatum> 14 November 2008.

Temptation Island. Hosted by Mark L. Walberg. Fox. 2001–2003.

That '70s Show. CBS. 1998–2006.

Thomas, Cal. "Nation Should Ask Santa for Direction and Purpose." *Seattle Post-Intelligencer*. 23 December 1993: A9.

Thompson, Michael J. "Introduction: Confronting the New Conservativism." *Confronting the New Conservatism: The Rise of the Right in America*. Ed. Michael J. Thompson. New York: NYUP, 2007. 1–5.

——. "America's Conservative Landscape: The New Conservatism and the Reorientation of American Democracy." *Confronting the New Conservatism: The Rise of the Right in America*. Ed. Michael J. Thompson. New York: NYU P, 2007. 9–30.

Toohey, Brian. "Whose Side is God On?" *The Sun Herald* (Sydney, Australia). 2 February 2003: 28.

Tolson, Jay. "Culture War Redux." *U.S. News and World Report*. September 29–October 6, 2008: 40–42.

Torgovnick, Marianna. *Gone Primitive: Savage Intellects, Modern Lives*. Chicago: U of Chicago, 1990.

——. *Primitive Passions: Men, Women, and the Quest for Ecstasy*. New York: Knopf, 1997.

Treasury of Children's Classics. Selected by William F. Buckley Jr. Wilmington, DE: ISI Books, 2003.

Trites, Robert Seelinger. *Disturbing the Universe: Power and Repression in Adolescent Literature*. Iowa City: U of Iowa P, 2002.

Truax, R. Hawley. "Unequal Protection: Environmental Justice and Communities of Color." *Environmental Action Magazine* 26.2 (22 June 1994): 12.

"Tween Power: Purchasing Strength of Kids." Video Report. *Business Week*. 12 December 2005. <http://www.businessweek.com/mediacenter/video/bwweekend/2422f1b1427994acc09a849d174d60e620f4d370.html> 20 October 2008.

Ty, Brother, with Christopher Buckley and John Tierney. *God Is My Broker: A Monk-Tycoon Reveals the 7½ Laws of Spiritual and Financial Growth*. New York: Random House, 1998.

Ulanowicz, Anastasia. Preemptive Education: Lynne Cheney's *America: A Patriotic Primer* and the Ends of History." *Children's Literature Association Quarterly* 33.4 (Winter 2008): 341–370.

United Daughters of the Confederacy. *Catechism for Children*. Galveston, TX: United Daughters of the Confederacy, Veuve Jefferson Davis Chapter, 1904.

United States. Cong. Joint Economic Committee. 110th Congress, 2nd Session. *War at Any Cost?: The Total Economic Costs of the War Beyond the Federal Budget*. [Hearing on February 28, 2008 before the Joint Economic Committee]. Washington D.C.: U. S. G.P.O., 2009. GPO Access. 14 April 2009. <http://purl.access.gpo.gov/GPO/LPS109505>

United States. Dept. of Homeland Security. Office of Intelligence and Analysis Assessment. *Right-Wing Extremism: Current Economic and Political Climate Fueling Resurgence in Radicalization and Recruitment*. 7 April 2009. Full text available at http://www.docstoc.com/docs/5410658/DHS-Report-on-Right-Wing-Extremism 17 April 2009.

"Update—Campaign '96." *NewsHour*. With Jim Lehrer. Report by Margaret Warner. PBS. 14 February 1996. Transcript. <http://www.pbs.org/newshour/bb/election/update_2–14.html> 6 March 2009.

Vallone, Lynne. "Children's Literature Within and Without the Profession." *College Literature*. 22 March 1998. LexisNexis. Hollins University. 4 May 2008.

Van Horn, Catherine. "Turning Child Readers into Consumers: Children's Magazines and Advertising, 1900–1920." *Defining Print Culture for Youth: The Cultural Work of Children's Literature*. Ed. By Anne H. Lundin and Wayne Weigand. Westport, CT: Greenwood, 2003. 121–138.

Victoria. "Review: *Help! Mom! There Are Liberals under My Bed!*" 5 February 2006. <http://homeschoolmomtips.blogspot.com/> 5 June 2007.

Wagner, David. "Bill's Dilemma." *National Review*. 19 June 1987. <www.nationalreview.com> 8 September 2008.

Washington, Jesse. "Election Spurs 'Hundreds' of Race Threats, Crimes. Associated Press Wire Story. 15 November 2008. Full Text Available Online via ABC News at: <http://abcnews.go.com/US/wireStory?id=6261962> 22 February 2009.

Weiner, Rachel. "Obama Hatred at McCain-Palin Rally: 'Terrorist!' 'Kill Him!'" *The Huffington Post*. 6 October 2008. <http://www.huffingtonpost.com/2008/10/06/mccain-does-nothing-as-cr_n_132366.html> 18 December 2008.

"Welcome to Grow the Vote: A Guide to Politics and Important Issues for the Forest Products Industry." American Forest & Paper Association (AF&PA). <http://www.bipac.net/page.asp?g=afpa&content=startpage> 10 August 2008.

Westwood One. "The Radio Factor with Bill O'Reilly." Program Profile Page. <http://www.westwoodone.com/program?programID=320&ACTION(viewProgram)=> 19 February 2009.

Wheelock, David C. "Changing the Rules: State Mortgage Foreclosure Moratoria during the Great Depression." *Federal Reserve Bank of St. Louis Review* (November/December 2008): 569–583.

Whitney, Anne. "Writing by the Book: The Emergence of the Journaling Self-Help Book." *Issues in Writing* 15.2 (2005): 188–214.

Who's Your Daddy? Hosted by Finola Hughes. Fox. 2005.

Wiarda, Howard J. *Conservative Brain Trust: The Rise, Fall, and Rise Again of the American Enterprise Institute*. Lanham, MD: Lexington Books, 2009.

Wiener, Jon. "Hard to Muzzle: The Return of Lynne Cheney." *The Nation*. 27 September 2000. <http://www.thenation.com/doc/20001002/wiener/print?rel=nofollow> 7 February 2009.

Wilentz, Amy. "On the Intellectual Ramparts." *Time*. 1 September 1986: 22.

Wilder, Laura Ingalls. *The Long Winter*. 1940. New York: Harper Collins, 1971.

Wilson, John H. *Hot House Flowers.* Illus. by Marina Tsesarskaya. BookSurge Publishing, 2006.

Wilson, Robin. "U of Colorado at Boulder Wants to Hire a 'Professor of Conservative Thought.'" *Chronicle of Higher Education.* 13 May 2008. <http://chronicle.com/news/article/4477/u-of-colo-boulder-wants> 3 November 2008.

Winchester, Elizabeth. "America's Story, from A to Z." *Time for Kids.* 10 May 2002: 7.

Winer, Linda. "Critical Mass / The Other Lynne Cheney." *Newsday.* 6 August 2000: D2.

Winerip, Michael. "In Novels for Girls, Fashion Trumps Romance" 13 July 2008. *New York Times.* <www.nytimes.com> 18 August 2008.

Wolfe, Elizabeth. "Toning Down Role of VP Wife, Lynne Cheney Stays True to Self." The Associated Press. 25 August 2004.

"World Ahead Presses On with 10th Title; Unfazed by Midterms." *Book Publishing Report* 31.31 (14 August 2006): 4.

World Ahead Publishing. (2005) <http://www.worldaheadpublishing.com/> 31 May 2007.

Wyatt, Edward. "Arts, Briefly: Imprint at Simon & Schuster for Conservative Books." *New York Times.* 23 March 2005. <http://query.nytimes.com/gst/fullpage.html?res=9F01E 2DE163FF930A15750C0A9639C8B63> 7 November 2008.

Yelsey, Ross. "Update: Fox News' *The O'Reilly Factor* Offers Unsubstantiated Claims in Lesbian Gang Epidemic Segment." Gay and Lesbian Alliance Against Defamation (GLAAD). 5 July 2007. http://www.glaad.org/action/calls_detail.php?id=4031> 20 October 2008.

Zicht, Jennifer. "In Pursuit of the Lorax: Who's in Charge of the Last Truffula Seed?" *EPA Journal* (September/October 1991): 27–30.

Zilber, Jerry. *Mama Voted for Obama!* Illus. Greg Bonnell. Joplin, MO: Jeremy Zilber, 2008.

——. *Why Daddy is a Democrat.* Illus. Yuliya Firsova. Joplin, MO: Jeremy Zilber, 2007.

——. *Why Mommy is a Democrat.* Illus. Yuliya Firsova. Joplin, MO: Jeremy Zilber, 2005.

Zipes, Jack. *Breaking the Magic Spell: Radical Theories of Folk and Fairy Tales.* Austin: U of Texas P, 1979.

INDEX

ABOUT THE AUTHOR

MICHELLE ANN ABATE is an associate professor of English at Hollins University. She is also the author of the book *Tomboys: A Literary and Cultural History* (2008).